WIN THE
INSIDE
GAME

ALSO BY STEVE MAGNESS

Do Hard Things

The Science of Running

Peak Performance with Brad Stulberg

The Passion Paradox with Brad Stulberg

WIN THE INSIDE GAME

How to Move from Surviving to Thriving, and
FREE YOURSELF UP to PERFORM

STEVE MAGNESS

HarperOne
An Imprint of HarperCollins*Publishers*

HarperCollins books may be purchased for educational, business, or sales promotional use. For information, please email the Special Markets Department at SPsales@harpercollins.com.

FIRST EDITION

Designed by Kyle O'Brien

Library of Congress Cataloging-in-Publication Data has been applied for.

ISBN 978-0-06-333992-7
ISBN 978-0-06-343755-5 (ANZ)

24 25 26 27 28 LBC 5 4 3 2 1

For Haizley, explore widely, be curious, surround yourself with good people, and hold firm to the values you care about the most

CONTENTS

PART THREE | BELONG—CLARITY ON WHERE AND HOW YOU FIT IN

PART FOUR | GETTING UNSTUCK

INTRODUCTION

WHY YOU OFTEN STRUGGLE TO GET BY

CHAPTER 1

WE ARE ALL IN
SURVIVAL MODE

I was frantic. My mind was racing. Overcome by stress and anxiety, I found one thought repeating in my head: *What do I do?* I
left my desk, searching for privacy and solace in the Mia Hamm
building of Nike's world headquarters in Beaverton, Oregon.
Tucked away in the stairwell, I turned to the only people I knew
I could trust. I was twenty-six, supposedly working my dream job
as a coach for the world's premier professional running team, the
Nike Oregon Project, and I called my parents, pleading for advice.
My boss wanted me to fly across the country to Houston to test a
new supplement. Not to pop a pill but to have a liter of an amino
acid called L-carnitine injected straight into my veins. It wasn't
the first time I'd searched for answers, and it wouldn't be the last.

I am a whistleblower. About a year after standing in the stairwell, I reported my experiences to the US Anti-Doping Agency
(USADA). I risked my career and livelihood and ignored advice
from friends, lawyers, and even a prominent judge, who told me,
"It may be the right thing, but whistleblowers seldom come out on

top. You're risking your career before it even gets started." And he was right. I blew the whistle in December 2012. In 2015, I went public with an interview on the BBC. And it wasn't until 2022 that the case was finally over, with my former boss, Alberto Salazar, and the team doctor, Jeffrey Brown, receiving four-year bans from USADA. Salazar further received a lifetime ban by SafeSport for sexual misconduct. I witnessed a lot of crazy and surreal things, from anti-doping violations to gray-area use of supplements and medicines to all sorts of shaming bordering on verbal abuse.

Whistleblowing was miserable. It dragged on, taking over my life and leaving me feeling at times alone, lost, and stuck. When the bans were announced, friends called and congratulated me, told me I was vindicated, and spoke about my courage and willingness to stand up and do the right thing. A win for clean sport, they said, as I got a hearty pat on the back. But I was too drained, exhausted, and numb to feel joy. It was just relief that it was over.

That day in the stairwell wasn't the glorious moment my principles shone through. It wasn't a time when I spoke truth to power. No, that was the moment I was a deeply flawed human being—one who couldn't muster the courage to do the right thing. Instead, I wilted under pressure and went against my values, ethics, and morals.

Days after that phone call, I did the wrong thing and found myself in Houston. I had decided to follow the lead of my physician, who also happened to be the team doctor, and my boss, who, long before he became a coach, was a legend in the sport I loved. He is famous for running to the brink of death to win the Boston Marathon. I sat on a couch in the Houston doctor's office with an IV dripping into my veins. The substance wasn't illegal, but the method of delivery was. I didn't realize this at the time. I was naive and too trusting. Everything was fine, I was assured. But it wasn't. Somehow, I'd been convinced to be the guinea pig to test the procedure before the athletes were put through the routine. I sat in the chair and had a liter of L-carnitine mixed with saline drip into my body.

That wasn't the first moment—and wouldn't be the last—that triggered concern. There was the time I came across official documents from the director of the Nike sports science lab that noted a teenage athlete was "presently on prednisone and testosterone medication." There was the sharing of medications. Inhalers and prescription drugs were shipped to athletes in a cutout of a Clive Cussler novel that seemed like a scene straight from the movie *The Shawshank Redemption.* The overabundance of sketchy-sounding supplements like "testo-boost." And much more. Not all of it broke the rules but much was flat-out strange. Yet, throughout, I rationalized, justified, and kept my position. After all, I was at my "dream job." I was heir apparent to the best-funded professional track team in the country, one with a future Olympic champion and medalists. It was everything I ever wanted professionally. The advice family members kept repeating was, "Can you stick it out through the Olympics?" I was there for a year and a half before I'd had enough.

We like our stories simple. The hero who overcomes adversity. The woman whose values are hard-earned and firmly held who prevails against all odds. We think of ourselves in similar ways—crafting a personal narrative where we are the hero of the story. We even have a psychological immune system, a protective mechanism to thwart negative self-evaluations. We want to think of ourselves as good, moral, decent people. We shove away the messiness. As you read this story, you probably believe you would have done the right thing immediately if thrust into that doctor's seat. Our mind is an expert at convincing ourselves we are always the "good guy."

It's hard to look back on that person who is obviously me and wonder, *What in the world was I thinking?* It's easy to rationalize. To say I was young and naive. To blame it on the pressure or stress. To cite the absurd but true fact that despite my being employed by the largest sportswear company in the world, my pay was mysteriously withheld for six months in the midst of this experiment—all while Salazar offered to loan me money instead of paying me for the job I had signed a contract to do. The simple truth is that I didn't initially do the right thing. That moment would come months later when I finally found the courage to blow the whistle. The Steve who stayed silent and went along and the Steve who spoke up are the same people. But they are also fundamentally different.

For much of my time there, I was living in a delusion. I was stuck chasing success and status—employed as the youngest professional coach in the sport, and working with athletes who would become legends. I wanted to prove I belonged, to make up for my lackluster competitive career. I was in an environment where winning at all costs was the path forward. It was the expectation. Running around in circles faster than all others trumped nearly everything else.

Despite my upbringing and previous beliefs, behaviors, and actions, I could not stand up at that moment. I was stuck. Incapable of seeing things clearly. Incapable of taking action that was both right and necessary. I defaulted to surviving, keeping myself afloat in the job I occupied. In other words: I choked.

LOSING OUR SELF

Manti Te'o was one of the best football players in the country. His accolades speak for themselves: Heisman Trophy runner-up, the Butkus Award for the best linebacker, the Bronko Nagurski Trophy for the best defensive player, the Walter Camp Award for the best college football player, and on and on. On the field, he was known for endless energy and utter fearlessness. Off the field, he was the consummate team captain, balancing humility and confidence. As he was wrapping up his college career, two things were clear: His legendary status was secure. As one writer at the time declared, "He'll live on in Notre Dame lore for as long as the history books are in existence." And football was a game that he'd mastered.

Yet, as Te'o stepped onto the field for the first time as a player in the NFL, his body betrayed him. The natural, fluid, fearless play had eroded, replaced by a numbness, a disconnection between his body and brain that seemed to take his skills with it. As he later reported in a documentary on his life, "Every day was [about] just trying to figure out how to get rid of this anxiety, this numbness, this tingling," It was as if he were occupying someone else's body. Nothing felt or moved right.

The yips, choking, the twisties, whatever name we call it, it's something that every athlete dreads. It's the monster no one wants to mention for fear that it'll somehow wriggle into their mind, unleashing havoc. It's one of those hard-to-explain phenomena that is instantly recognizable. Put simply, you lose the ability to do what once was routine—toss a ball to first base, make a putt from a few feet away, or stand up onstage. How do experts suddenly lose the ability to do the routine?

"The pressure got to him . . ." is the common refrain that well-meaning color commentators use to explain choking. But what does that mean? Pressure elicits a variety of psychological and biological processes. From nervous system activity to different brain areas going on- or offline, to a hormonal response, pressure prepares the body for what's to come. And at first, many of these processes can boost our performance. You aren't going to run as fast when you are alone at the track as when you are in a race. As we move from low to moderate physiological arousal, mostly good things occur, because arousal does several things:

- Enhances memory and cognitive functioning.
- Helps us focus, enhancing the signal-to-noise ratio and allowing us to pick up relevant information.
- Prepares our body for action. Physiological arousal prepares our muscles to work, improving our reaction time and freeing up energy to fuel the task at hand.
- Motivates us. Enhancing the saliency of the reward with a hit of dopamine.

Yet, as we drift from moderate stress or pressure to higher levels, our performance starts heading in the wrong direction. Our cognitive abilities decline, and our memory systems become more flashbulb-like, stuck on the danger in front of us. Our perception systems go a bit haywire. Under high stress levels, our world looks and feels different. Research shows that under these conditions, baseball batters report the ball as shrinking, and golfers estimate the hole to be much smaller than it is. Not only does our perception change, but we also lose our ability to discern relevant from irrelevant information. We can't decipher what matters and what doesn't, often falling prey to paying attention to the wrong feedback, sensations, or thoughts. Or, as an engineer might put it, our signal-to-noise ratio deteriorates. We turn up the volume on the wrong information.

We move from being primed to take action to avoidance. We freeze instead of fight. Play dead instead of run away. When the world seems threatening and chaotic, we can't see the forest for the trees. When it comes to pressure-filled situations, we're left seeing and feeling the game in a completely different way. In a way, we're a bit delusional.

While there's much to uncover still, the latest neuroscience provides a glimpse into why this occurs. As arousal increases, we have an interplay between two areas of the brain, the prefrontal cortex (PFC) and the amygdala. Our PFC is our "mental sketch pad," where executive thinking and planning occur, and the amygdala helps process emotions, filters sensory information, and detects threats. In typical situations, there's a productive interplay between these two systems. Our PFC takes the lead, receiving input from the amygdala and other areas but acting as a brake. It sends the message, "I hear you, but that's not that big of a deal right now, so quiet down." As stress and pressure increase, our PFC goes offline and lets our amygdala start shouting as loud as it wants. We lose our brake and the sensory information we start relying on changes.

In the body, it's much the same. We tend to clump all pressure, stress, or physiological arousal together. But the type of response matters. Our brain and body have different levers to pull. We have a variety of hormones and nervous system activity that push and pull us in different ways. When we see the stressor as more of a challenge, we tend to have a bit more testosterone and adrenaline, nudging us to approach the task at hand. Other times, we have more oxytocin, pushing us toward protecting and comforting friends or family members instead of worrying about ourselves. When we feel threatened, we tend to have more cortisol, which frees up energy but makes us anxious and avoidant. When pressure takes over, we're more likely to:

- avoid instead of approach;
- be selfish instead of selfless;
- get stuck too narrow, unable to see the forest for the trees;
- freeze, faint, or flee; and
- discount future rewards.

Leonard Zaichkowsky, a renowned sports psychologist, explained the process: "When we choke, we feel pressure, cortisol gets released, and our thoughts and attention shift to the negative or irrelevant. We start to analyze our automatic responses. And then it's all over."

We get in our own way. Athletes often experience it as over-thinking about a task that was once ingrained. What they feel and how they act no longer align. It's as if we go back in time. We move from an expert's smooth and automated movements to the segmented approach of a six-year-old learning how to throw a ball. We can feel every step of a once continuous movement. We've regressed. We've lost control. Our brain has locked onto the wrong hypothesis.

PREDICTING DOOM

A twenty-nine-year-old builder hopped down to the ground at a construction site, only to land on a nail—or so reported a small note in the 1995 edition of the *British Medical Journal*. The nail went straight into the builder's boot. Unsurprisingly, he was in a lot of pain! His coworkers rushed him to the emergency room, where doctors provided fentanyl and midazolam to sedate and deal with his immense discomfort. The doctors removed the nail, took off his boot, and saw something astonishing. The nail had penetrated the boot but did so between the toes. The man was uninjured. Yet, the context of seeing a nail through his boot, and his coworkers reacting in horror, all signaled to him that he should be in pain. His brain complied.

Perhaps you've seen the stunning bodycam footage of police officers coming into contact with fentanyl. Officers collapse to the ground, often shaking uncontrollably. We see their partners jump into action, screaming, "Stay with me!" before administering Narcan to treat the accidental overdose. There are numerous cases. They are dramatic and harrowing. The sensations these officers feel are real. There's just one problem. Fentanyl is a serious drug, no doubt, but according to medical experts, it's not physiologically possible for it to poison someone through casual contact. As toxicologist and ER physician Ryan Marino reported, "The dry powder form that's encountered in street drugs is not going to pass through the skin in any meaningful way." If snorted, smoked, or injected, it can have devastating effects. But simply touching it, not a chance. It's not that these officers are weak-minded. It's that their brains are working as they should. There is a fentanyl crisis, after all. Police officers are inundated with media reports and training on its dangers. They make a stop and find the elicit material, which causes a bit of stress and anxiety. It's natural for the brain to predict a bad outcome and for it to make the feelings and sensations align with expectations. In this case, it just guessed wrong.

Our brain is predictive. We subconsciously make a best guess on what we think will happen, what we should feel, and how we should act. This allows us to make sense of ourselves and the world we occupy. We use a combination of expectations and experience to create our hypothesis. Expectations come from top-down sensory processes—our memory, knowledge, and history help create a model for what we think will occur and how we should feel during an event. Experience refers to bottom-up sensory information— what we see, feel, or hear. Most of the time, our expectations and experience match. But sometimes, our reality is more like a fantasy our mind has latched on to.

When choking or the yips occur, it's not too dissimilar from the man with the nail in his boot. Our brain starts making bad predictions. We have two main options when our expectations and experiences don't align. We either update or protect. Updating occurred when the doctors removed the boot, and the man saw no damage. In such a case, new information nudges us to come back to reality. Protection is about keeping the deluded prediction going. We latch on to the wrong information, avoid or ignore anything that contradicts, or even create information to make our expectations and experiences align. Even if it's not accurate. Our brain can push us to act in a way to conform our expectations (i.e., cops falling to the ground) or change what we feel to match predictions (i.e., pain with a nail in the boot). Under pressure, we don't update; we protect. And if we let it linger, it goes from a wrong guess to a cemented reality.

This doesn't just occur in sport or life-threatening situations. Research has found that those who suffer from depression overweigh negative thoughts and self-perceptions and suppress bottom-up signals. Their brains become insensitive to any information that might show us that the world or future isn't hopeless. It's why therapists often describe depression as feeling stuck. As psychologist Lisa Feldman Barrett outlined, "A depressed brain is effectively locked into misery. It's like a brain in chronic pain, ignoring prediction error, but on a much larger scale that shuts you down." It's the same with other mental health disorders. Prediction errors are a hallmark of obsessive compulsive disorder (OCD) and dysphoria's like anorexia. Those who suffer from trauma experience a similar bad predictive rut. Getting stuck responding to a stimulus (sight, sound, smell, etc.) that their brain thinks means they are in real trouble.

Getting stuck, choking, and freezing results from finding yourself in a predictive doom loop. We feel threatened, so we avoid, escape, or shut down. Over time, that loop becomes ingrained, so much so that we stop seeing it as an error but as reality. When we believe we're under threat, we set the stage for poor predictions. We default toward just trying to survive.

For Manti Te'o, that threat had an origin. In 2012, as a senior at

Notre Dame, before playing in the national championship game and taking the next step toward becoming an NFL star, Te'o's world came crashing down. In the relatively early days of social media, just when popular online dating apps like Tinder were launched and before an MTV show popularized the concept, Te'o was dragged through the press for being catfished. The woman he thought he had been dating, Lennay Kekua, didn't exist. Despite hours of phone conversations and conversing with her "relatives," and even listening to her cries for help as she supposedly died of cancer, she wasn't real. She was Ronaiah Tuiasosopo, a person who, at the time, identified as a male.

The media destroyed Te'o. He was accused of being in on the hoax, creating the story, and using his girlfriend's alleged death to curry favor. There were discussions on national television about whether Te'o was using the catfishing as a ruse to cover up that he was gay. It was absurd and a complete circus. The unassuming star from Hawaii was put through the wringer, ridiculed, made fun of, and accused of all sorts of nefariousness. The numbness never left for the first three years of his NFL career. He was being judged, torn apart. His world and sense of self were in complete chaos. The numbness he felt was his brain hitting the escape button, turning off the experience to align with the dread and uncertainty he was stuck under. He was simply trying to survive.

Pressure and stress don't discriminate. It's not just in the performance arena that we experience this disconnect between our perception and action, our desired behavior and actual, who we want to be and who we seem to be. When pressure, uncertainty, and threat overwhelm, we live in survival mode. I experienced it standing in that hallway. You might feel it when simple tasks—responding to an email at work, completing the chores at home—seem overwhelming. Or when you transform into an unrecognizable, anger-filled person when stuck behind a slow driver, all because, in that moment, getting to your office two minutes earlier seems like life or death. Sometimes survival mode looks like anger and rage. Other times burnout, loneliness, procrastination, or anxiety. It's when we find ourselves with a chronic feeling of angst that we aren't good enough, that we don't measure up, that we don't belong. When the world seems uncertain and threatening, our brain tries its best to protect us. And in doing so, it often gets stuck in a bad rut. One that feels just as hard to escape as losing the ability to toss a ball to first base.

We're used to thinking of choking or underperformance as rooted in the sport or activity. We talk about pressure, and as we've seen, it plays a large part. But it's what is underlying that pressure that is the problem, and it isn't a problem isolated to the field or pitch. Our brain predicts doom because it's not just our ability to throw a ball on the line. It's ourselves: our identity, our self-worth, our reputation. Te'o didn't choke because he was weak or couldn't handle the pressure. His brain defaulted to protection because his whole world was in disarray, unmoored from the bearings it had just moments before. He got stuck in a bad predictive rut, where doom pushes us to attach, freeze, or avoid. Often we're not even conscious of the poor prediction lodged in our brains. When our sense of self and our worldview are under threat, is it any wonder why our brain sees doom everywhere and acts in accordance?

Choking is a threat and survival disorder. It's an act of self-preservation, a desperate attempt to shut down, to avoid, to insulate our sense of self, ego, and status from the deluge of attacks it's experiencing. Sometimes that threat is conscious. Other times, it lies deep underneath. It doesn't originate only from physical danger. It doesn't occur only in sports. In a world filled with constant stimulation, comparison, and stress, we all spend a lot of time in survival mode, where protection is the name of the game.

PLAYING "PREVENT DEFENSE"

We're experts at protecting ourselves, and it manifests itself in many different ways. Think back to middle school PE class. Remember the rousing game of dodgeball or basketball you played? Did you try hard during the game? Chances are there was a group huddled in the corner, giving off a distinct vibe of *I'd rather be anywhere but here.* Middle school was a scary time for just about everyone. But there was one thing that the cool kids did to set them apart: They didn't try. Trying was for losers. The cool kids stood on the sidelines, minimizing their effort, even if deep down they wanted to play a sport, read a book, or ace the test. They were protecting their status and image. Giving effort and seeing the nerd or outcast perform better than you wasn't worth the risk. The cool kids convinced others that not caring was the thing to do.

In the classroom, it's much the same. Consider the time-honored tradition in school of giving yourself an out. Instead of spending time studying, students often deliberately self-sabotage before justifying their behavior with, "If I studied, I would have gotten an A. But I just didn't care." We do the same thing in other pursuits; "I didn't really train for this race," or "This job is just to pay the bills." Research has found that depersonalization, where we intentionally detach from aspects of our job, is one of the primary coping mechanisms for workplace burnout. Under preparation is a coping strategy to protect our sense of self. Not giving our all is about shielding our ego from harm. This is the real-world version of choking.

When we feel uncertain, insecure, or under threat, we respond by desperately trying to make ourselves and the world add up. In the aforementioned examples, when we can't hold ourselves up to our or other's ideals, we experience shame, humiliation, or embarrassment. We give ourselves an out, crafting a story that minimizes those negative feelings and keeps alive our view of ourself as competent. The bigger the threat feels, the quicker we try to grasp onto anything that will alleviate the disconnect.

Psychologists have crafted theories around dozens of scenarios and situations, all describing essentially the same phenomenon. There's the group-based control model that explains that when we lose a sense of control, we try to deal with the aversive feelings that arise by further committing to a group. We feel lost or insignificant, so we tie ourselves to our church, political party, or sports team for comfort. There's terror management theory that explains when the realization that we will die someday becomes salient; we desperately reach for ways to buffer that stress. Look no further than the rise of longevity gurus who chase the modern version of the fountain of youth. There's cognitive dissonance theory, the conscious vigilance model, and a half dozen other theories that all state just about the same thing: when we feel threatened, we try to find some way to achieve closure as quickly as possible. In the meaning maintenance model, researchers Steven Heine, Travis Proulx, and Kathleen Vohs summed up dozens of theories with a straightforward paradigm: When our sense of meaning is disrupted, we experience a state researchers' term *disanxiousuncertilibrium*, which then pushes us to restore order and security somehow.

Put another way, when our world, self, or pursuits don't add up, we experience a cacophony of negative sensations, and we do whatever we can to eliminate those feelings and give us some sense of order. We get desperate to make the world, and ourselves, add up to align our expectations and experience—even if it means deluding ourselves. We have a self-preservation system that defaults to the quick fix. This is living in survival mode.

In many ways, we're all the cool kids in gym class. We've made our protective systems hyperresponsive, ready to hit the alarm. Unfortunately, when under a constant sense of threat, we often reach for easy solutions that temporarily help but harm us over the long haul. We can see it with our use of phones. We feel bored standing in line or lonely sitting at home, and we reach for our phone to temporarily quell those feelings, instead of the long-term solution of connecting with people in the real world. In the workplace, we settle for busy distracted work to make us feel like we're making progress, instead of the deep focused work that actually moves the needle. When we're under threat, we focus on eliminating the negative feeling, instead of solving the actual problem. It's why we self-sabotage.

But that's not the only way we defend ourselves. Our protective systems push us to respond by doing one of the following:

1. **Avoid or shut down:** We detach. Tell ourselves that whoever expressed the view is crazy, or ensure we never have to confront that information again.
2. **Fight and defend:** We double down on our position, trying harder to prove that the way we see the world is, in fact, correct. We rationalize and justify.
3. **Narrow and cling:** We shrink our world to the people, groups, things, or stories that confirm our beliefs or worldview. We seek refuge in the places that make us feel secure and valued. We make the world two-dimensional so that we don't have to deal with the messiness of life.
4. **Accept, explore, and update:** We integrate the new information into our mental model—a pathway that emphasizes growth and learning over the long haul instead of simply surviving the immediate threat.

When we live in survival mode, we spend too much time in the former responses. We can see it all around us. Sometimes, we do everything in our power to avoid threats at any cost. Just look at our playgrounds. Slides, monkey bars, and other equipment have been replaced by safer alternatives. Increasingly, research shows that kids don't play outside anymore, with one survey finding a decrease from 80 percent of kids in my parents' generation playing outside to just 27 percent today. Yes, phones and devices, an increase in traffic, and similar factors have an impact. But research also points to another culprit: safetyism. An increase in parents' protectiveness due to fear has led to a decline in unstructured free play. We can see it in adults who need to overengineer everything. Gone are kids playing without adults in the sandlot. Now, the only place sports are played is in adult-led, organized leagues. It's no wonder kids have retreated to video games, the one place where adults can't interfere, control, or critique. The new sandlot is Fortnite.

We can see the instinct to fight and defend all over, from our political tribes to sports teams. But perhaps most depressing is seeing it in the classrooms. During the 2021 school year, a survey of over 15,000 educators found that nearly 30 percent of teachers and 40 percent of administrators had been threatened with violence. No, not from the students, but from parents. Educator Kelly Treleaven saw this trend firsthand, noticing that a surprising number of parents began to see teachers as an enemy. She named them jackhammer parents. They are relentless, loud, destructive, and powered by fear. They are never satisfied and are convinced that the teacher is harming their child's development. They don't just bulldoze obstacles. They act as though the teacher and school are opponents to defeat. Teachers could gain trust with the overprotective helicopter parent. But the jackhammer parent proved nearly impossible to win over.

When you live in threat mode, your world narrows into an us versus them construct. You become defensive and protective, fighting for our side. Or as one longtime educator told me, "Parents used to complain, but it was mostly to be heard. They wanted to know you cared. Now, they want to complain so that the teacher is fired, the curriculum is altered, and any semblance of anything they might not like removed from the building."

If attacking or avoiding aren't your thing, there's another strategy to deal with the gnawing unease: doubling down and hiding behind perfectionism. Instead of being able to be content and step away, we compensate by outworking everyone, all so we can quell our fear that we may not be good enough. We strive for busyness—racking up endless hours at the office—as an antidote to the anxiety. Overworking is another protective mechanism to cope with our insecurity. Instead of dealing with it, we cling to our work to fill the void.

Underperformance in sports, self-sabotaging in the workplace, defaulting to "why try" mode, jackhammer parenting, safetyism, workaholism, seeing enemies everywhere, and losing our minds shouting at trolls and bots on the Internet—these are all variations on the same theme. They are the result of living in a world where we constantly feel as though we are under threat.

And when we are stuck in survival mode, we seldom choose the final path—accept, explore, and update. It's easier to avoid, defend, or narrow—whatever gets us through the moment, forget the long-term consequences. Rigidity provides temporary stability. It's alluring. We reach for the candy that quenches our hunger instead of the vegetables that bring lasting sustenance. We shy away from anything that risks exposing ourselves to the world. We insulate from opposing views. Before we know it, our fear of failing, of being judged, of some exaggerated threat impairs our ability to take action. We shut down. We stop living and experiencing life and instead, see it through a distorted lens that confirms our expectations that nearly everything and everyone is dangerous. So that the next time we face a difficult situation, we default to what we have trained ourselves to do: protect ourselves and our egos from harm.

MOVING FROM SURVIVING TO THRIVING

In 1959, humanistic psychologist Carl Rogers wrote that in order to grow, we need an environment that provides genuineness, acceptance, and empathy. Abraham Maslow, whose eponymous hierarchy of needs has become a bedrock of psychology, found that not only do we need to satisfy our physiological needs but also our psychological ones. Golden State Warriors coach Steve Kerr relayed a similar message: "I want to make sure that my guys feel valued, respected, important, and relevant." In studying meaning in life, existential psychologist Tatjana Schnell simplified to focus on four key components. To have a meaningful life, we need to feel:

1. Coherent: Life adds up. You have a cohesive story. Who you were, are, and will be have a thread that runs through them.
2. Significant: You matter, can make a difference, and can achieve some sort of status in life.
3. Directed: There's purpose to your life and pursuits. You have goals leading you toward something. You can make progress.
4. Belonging: You're part of something bigger than just you—family, friends, and groups. You can weave your story into others' stories.

Whether we like Schnell's, Rogers's, or Kerr's paradigm, all converge on a similar theme: They clarify who we are, what matters, where we're going, and where we belong. They provide clarity on ourselves, our pursuits, and our environment. When we fulfill these needs, we thrive. When we are lacking, we default toward surviving. In short, when our world and our place in it add up, we have hope. We orient ourselves toward growth. We are more likely to feel energized, motivated, and happy. And almost as a by-product, be successful and fulfilled. We approach instead of avoid. We turn down the desire to protect and up the desire to play, create, pursue, and live.

Unfortunately, the modern world has mastered making it damn near impossible to fulfill these needs and experience clarity. It's as if we're competing in a rigged game. Take the aforementioned list. Coherence occurs when we are the writer of our story, and our character has a fleshed-out history that connects current actions and future aspirations. We can see the thread that connects past, present, and future. We may have changed, but we understand how. Sure, there's nuance in there, and sometimes the unexpected occurs, but by and large, our character makes sense.

Yet, we occupy a place where our Instagram self is a carefully crafted beauty, our Twitter self is the right combination of wit and snark, and our TikTok self is outgoing, jubilant, and exquisitely coordinated. Not to mention our real-life self. A century ago, our inner story included a couple dozen friends and family with one or two main locations. Now, it's a complicated, overwhelming mess, and we can't keep track of the characters or their motives. It's much harder to be coherent in a complex, messy world.

Significance used to be easily within our grasp. Among your local community (or, going back centuries, to your tribe) finding a way to be a contributing member of society wasn't too tricky. You could find your place, to hunt or gather, to care for the sick, or tend to newborns. It was easy to find value. We could obtain status somewhere. Being the fastest on the block or the best cook in the family was not difficult to achieve; we were meant to find our place amid a few dozen friends and family members. Comparison helps provide clarity and motivation when the world is small, however. It's much harder when our comparison feels like the entire world.

We now occupy a world that is too big for our minds to handle. We live in a time where every single day we have reminders that we aren't good enough. That we aren't making, providing, or accruing enough status when compared to our peers. Research clearly shows as your status goes up, so does your health. But the status and health connection aren't tied to dollars and cents. It's our perception of our status that impacts our health. We've mastered making everyone feel insignificant, just a cog in the wheel that isn't that good and can easily be replaced.

Direction is about having clarity on your role and purpose. Having a sense that you are making progress toward something meaningful. Unfortunately, many now feel lost and aimless, just wandering through life. This is partly because we've been sold a new religion: workism. As writer Derek Thompson explains, we have many "adherents to a cult of productivity and achievement, wherein anything short of finding one's vocational soulmate amounts to a wasted life. They have found a new kind of religion— one that valorizes work, career, and achievement above all else. And it's making them a little bit crazy." When our work inevitably can't fulfill all of our needs, we're left wondering how we can find something that does.

But what about belonging? We do live in a world that is hyper-connected. You can stay in touch with just about anyone you have ever interacted with. How can we not feel like we belong? The truth is that the modern world has replaced a handful of deep, meaningful connections with the allure of many shallow ones. We forgo the weekend softball team, the in-person book club for a meta world. We value our likes, dislikes, and random comments on social media as much as our best friend's input. We discard what our mentor says about our writing, instead obsessing over the random Amazon review. The distinction between a friend and that random person I follow online gradually disintegrates. After all, you see and hear far more from the current TikTok influencer than from your neighbor down the street. Is it any wonder that we feel more connected to the Instagrammer whose intimate life we watch daily than to our cousin we see a few times a year? We've become intimate strangers, familiar with a lot of people we don't know. Is it any wonder we feel unmoored, lost, or stuck in survival mode? Our environment pushes against our basic psychological needs. And when it does, it starts expecting disaster.

Consider how our predictive brain handles this. If everything around us tells us we are lost, alone, and insignificant, what kind of information do you think our brain latches on to as reliable and vital? We've turned up the volume for threats and turned down the volume on anything that points otherwise. We've created distorted expectations. By not fulfilling our basic needs, by eliminating any sense of security or stability, we've primed our predictive machinery to work against us. To latch on to or value the wrong information. And too often, we solve this uncertainty by falling into a self-fulfilling prophecy. We are like the policeman, stuck in a state of fear over a drug, so we create actions that validate that fear. We avoid instead of approach, disappear instead of exhibit courage, and choke instead of coming through in the clutch. We're setting ourselves up for a bad predictive rut. We default to what we have trained ourselves to do: protect ourselves and our egos from harm. In many ways, we are all choking at something bigger than one important moment. We are choking at life itself.

It's time for a new path to success and fulfillment. One that doesn't leave us feeling lost, threatened, or despondent. The answer lies in how we see and approach ourselves, our work, and our surroundings. To move from surviving to thriving, we need clarity in our inner world. In the rest of this book, I'll introduce a framework for sustainable excellence:

1. Be—Clarity on Who You Are
2. Do—Clarity in Your Pursuits
3. Belong—Clarity on Where and How You Fit In

Clarity doesn't mean aiming or hoping for perfection. It means dealing with the messiness, seeing the imperfections, the tug of war of different motives, the contrasting pull for status and contentment. We need to acknowledge and see all of it; good and bad, hopeful and hopeless, so that we can deal with it. That's winning the inside game.

In part one, "Be," you'll learn why we need to spend less time seeking and chasing and more time exploring. That we need to accept the messiness of who we are and find alignment between our sense of self and our underlying motivation. In part two, "Do," readers will learn why failure seems to eat away at our soul; we've adopted the wrong story. We've let success define us, and what we do is the outlet in which we feed that monster. In order to reach our potential, we need to put space between what we do and who we are, to learn to let go instead of always pressing for gains, and to move our self-worth from something contingent to something meaningful. In part three, "Belong," you'll learn how to create an environment that invites actions that support our work and aligns with who we are and want to be. You'll see why belonging is vital, but far too often we settle for its cheap cousin, fitting in. And when we try to fit in, we essentially hand over our thinking to the group we identify with. True belonging is expansive, allowing us to take on challenges with less fear. Clarity provides us with the security to take risks, potentially fail, but rise again, because our brains aren't locked on doom but on the potential within us. Let's unlock it.

FINDING A WAY OUT

"You're not good enough. You're going to embarrass yourself. Just step aside." Those thoughts were on repeat in Hannah's head. She'd finally made it. She was in college, pursuing her academic dreams and competing on a Division 1 track and field team. But all she could think about was how she didn't deserve it, and her performance followed suit. In her sport of cross-country, she seemed stuck in third gear, incapable of coming anywhere close to what she was capable of. In the classroom, the student who once mastered subjects with ease struggled. She wanted to succeed. Yet, no matter what she tried, it was as if there was an invisible barrier preventing her from fulfilling her potential.

It wasn't always this way. Hannah showed early promise. As a freshman in high school, she'd risen through her team ranks, becoming the third-best runner on a team that barely missed competing in the state championships. She loved competing, seeing it as a challenge. In the classroom, she was curious and driven with a zeal to quench her intellectual thirst. She had dreams of college and professional success.

As Hannah made her way through high school, it all changed. A series of injuries limited her athletic progress. Her relationship with her coaches started to change. One accused her of faking an injury and letting the team down. The pressure mounted to excel academically to make up for it. It didn't work. During final exams, all Hannah thought was, *My parents are helping me get through school. I have to get a perfect score on the test, or I'm not worthy of all the things I have.* Joy and curiosity were replaced with fear and apprehension. The negative voices in her head grew, as she later relayed to me, "I was so used to other people saying negative things to me. Or looking at me as a disappointment, that I started saying it to myself." Fear of failure took over. Hannah was just trying to get by.

She was stuck in survival mode. Her self-worth was on insecure footing. She tried to be who others thought she should be. As she told me, "I spent most of my life taking in what everyone else was telling me. I tried to satisfy others' expectations. My parents wanted me to be this person, so I tried to be that person. My coach wanted me to be this, so I strove to be that. I didn't know how to be my own person until I was in my twenties. I was chasing what I thought others wanted." Years later, Hannah is a licensed social worker and behavioral health specialist at a large hospital in Colorado. When I asked her how she got out of the rut, she replied, "I had to answer the question: Who do I want to be? I had to reframe my view of success, to stop chasing the wrong things. I had to learn how to be me."

To free ourselves up to get back to where we are playing to win, it starts with providing ourselves with the ingredients our modern world so often neglects. Manti Te'o came to the same conclusion Hannah did: "(I had to) figure out ways to reprogram myself. I had to rediscover who I was." His journey started when a therapist asked him if he had forgiven not only Ronaiah, but also himself. His mind jumped back to those who made fun of him, who seemed like supporters one day, but made him the butt of the joke the next. He had to "rise above that," and focus on those who cared and loved him for who he is. To Te'o, that's what he was about: spreading that love to others. "I'll take all this crap. I'll take all the jokes . . . so that I can be an inspiration to the one (person) who needs me to be. That's the whole reason why I'm doing this."

Rediscovering yourself is about getting clarity on what and who matters to develop a robust sense of self that isn't dependent solely on success to make you feel worthy. It's about turning down the threat sensitivity, to realize that every criticism or psychological threat doesn't need to be treated as if it's a lion about to devour us. It's diversifying your sources of status and meaning so that if you blow the presentation, you can move on quickly because you know you are loved and supported by people at home who truly matter. It's creating space between who you are and what you do. It's cultivating genuine connection instead of tying yourself to the transactional or superficial. It's ensuring you pay attention to the right information and that your actions align with your values. It's rewiring your predictions to experience clarity.

The modern world has made it as if we are perpetually living in a middle school lunchroom. Lost, insignificant, feeling left out, and with no clue what we should be doing or who we are. And we are solving the problem the same way we did in middle school: clinging to some group or club just to "fit in." Researchers found that those who score low in self-concept clarity—a measure of how we perceive and think about ourself, our values, and our relationships—resist change. In our work life, lack of role clarity is one of the significant contributors to burnout. In our personal life, low self-concept clarity is linked to materialism and compulsive buying. When we feel uncertain about ourselves, we fill that hole with just about anything to temporarily reduce the negative feelings. We try to compensate for our confusion by reaching for an artificial stability that ultimately hampers growth.

When we have greater self-concept clarity, research finds we have increased levels of well-being and psychological adjustment. We are more trusting in our relationships, cope with stressors better, and are more willing to change when presented with information contradicting our viewpoints. We are more likely to feel in control of our environment and have lower rates of neuroticism, depression, and loneliness.

Survival pushes us to narrow and cope. Thriving requires acceptance, expansion, and growth. Clarity through expansion updates our predictive software, recalibrating our model of who we are, what matters, and how the world works. And with better predictions, our threat alarm turns down. When we explore and experience instead of avoid and rationalize, we grow.

GETTING OUT OF MY OWN WAY

This isn't a book about choking in sports, and it's not about whistleblowing, though both play a central role in explaining a much broader problem. We all get stuck. We don't reach our capabilities. We get in our own way. We feel trapped, like we can't take the action that, deep down, we know we should. This book is about freeing yourself up from whatever is preventing you from going on the journey to realizing your potential. It's allowing yourself to be courageous.

At the beginning of this chapter, I outlined one of the most challenging and shameful experiences of my life, when I was put in a position where I went against everything I believed in. I didn't stand up. I shrunk away. It's easy to imagine that we'd all be bastions of courage in similar situations and blame the person who shies away as lacking intestinal fortitude, ethics, or character. But that's too simple of a story.

The truth is, I wasn't the only person in that situation. After spending ten years of my life in whistleblowing, I watched countless others face the same decision. Do I stand up, or do I self-protect? Most chose the latter. We like to imagine ourselves as righteous and courageous people. We like to blame the individual and assign some character flaw when they "choke," but the reality is much more complex.

The difference between the Steve who stayed silent and the

Steve who found a way to navigate a decade of taking on sporting goliaths wasn't some innate personality trait. It was clarity. It took coming to terms with who I was, what I was pursuing, and where I belonged. It didn't happen overnight. It was a long, arduous journey. I had to stop flattening myself and the world into a good versus evil narrative and stop defining myself and my future by my work and job. I had to get myself out of an environment that held up external success as the defining characteristic of one's self-worth. It took letting go and to stop seeking and chasing outcomes. Clarity gets you out of a bad predictive rut, to see what truly matters—to get out of your own way, so you can do what you already know how to do. For me, the journey started with realizing that everything I'd been taught about success was wrong.

CHAPTER 2

THE AMERICAN DREAM IS TO BLAME

The score was tied with the head referee glancing at his watch, whistle in his mouth, ready to call the end of the game at any moment. Coaches from both sides anxiously paced the sidelines, issuing last-second commands to press forward. The fans were raucous, encouraging their side's star player to come through.

As the clock wound down and fatigue rose, the play on the soccer field became increasingly desperate and chaotic. A tall blond-haired player with speed to burn suddenly broke free with the ball on his feet. With only one man to beat, he cut to his left as the opposing player lunged out for the ball. Their legs intertwined and down to the ground they went. A loud whistle belted out as the referee yelled, "Foul! Free kick."

On the sidelines, boos came roaring out. A nearby man yelled, "That wasn't a foul! He got all ball! Horrible call, ref! You just gave the game away!" As the free kick sailed past the goalie and into the net, a dejected team walked toward the sideline. The game was over. They'd lost. The fans jeered the ref, telling him he should be fired. A few players sank to the ground, others' heads drooped in shame, as if they'd let everyone down. One athlete broke down crying, telling his family and friends as he left the field, "I don't want to play anymore. We should have won."

Others were met by consoling coaches and family. From the sideline, I heard a variety of similar refrains, "Don't worry. It's not your fault. The ref blew it. . . . This never would have happened if we had our best defender in there. . . . You were robbed." It wasn't a happy sideline. I wasn't attending a professional game, an elite club match, or even a high school one. No, I was standing on the sidelines of a youth soccer game. The players were eight years old. The fans on the sidelines were parents.

For far too long we've been told that chasing accolades and achievements will lead us to the promised land. Unfortunately, such an approach often pushes us to behave immaturely, always wanting, never content. The solution isn't to go in the opposite direction, to fully discount achievements. We do need to strive. It's deep wired in us as humans for good reason. But we need to in the right way. To learn how to find a kind of striving that allows us to perform at our best, without losing our mind screaming at a youth soccer game, we need to explore the origin of our incessant need to achieve. Our desire for success, to achieve, starts early. Venture onto the youth sports fields anywhere in America and you'll find a similar scene: parents heavily invested in whether their child's team wins or loses an ultimately meaningless game. One spring morning, I meandered around Burroughs Park in Tomball, Texas, asking, "Should we keep score in youth sports?" Nearly all the answers had the same theme: not keeping score would be sacrilegious. "The entire point of sports is to win. . . . There are always winners and losers. It's a competition. What fun is it if there's no winner. . . . We'd just be making kids soft if we don't keep score."

In America, outcomes matter—a lot. And there's no greater

example than sports. It starts as early as first grade, with tryouts for the illustrious (and expensive) travel teams. As the young athletes develop, private coaches, elite showcases, and scouting combines take precedence. When I was a college coach, I frequently received messages from overly anxious parents concerned that their child might miss out on a scholarship opportunity. The desperation was palpable. All their son or daughter needed was more coaching, mental work, or a special magic sauce to turn their child into a star.

It's not just sports. We see it in the classroom. The 2001 No Child Left Behind Act enacted sweeping reform, establishing outcome goals tying school funding to performance in standardized assessments. Ever since, a growing emphasis on teaching to the test has dominated the education system. Educators are a nervous mess come assessment time, as an entire year's worth of work is about to be judged by how a bunch of kids perform on a single test. The kids feel it too, in a pressure-filled battle to move up their high school ranking and accumulate accolades so they can choose a prestigious college versus a more practical choice.

Once we're out in the real world, our obsession with achievement and outcomes continues. It's embedded in our motivational systems. We get bonuses and financial rewards for hitting certain metrics. In the 1980s famed CEO of GE Jack Welch popularized the "rank-and-yank" performance review. Employees were ranked from best to worst, similar to the class rankings high schoolers face every year. The lowest performers were let go. The modern incarnation of stack ranking is still used by companies like Amazon and IBM, where employers believe that it harnesses people's competitive nature.

In the United States, striving for success is wrapped up in our ideal of the American dream. A belief in upward mobility and that through hard work, we can all achieve success. It's an important and hopeful message. One that is at the forefront of our nation's collective consciousness for a century. Yet it all rests on our definition of success.

In 1931, historian James Truslow Adams coined the term "American dream." But he did so not to give the US a pat on the back but to show how we'd gone astray. Adams warned that the original noble ideal had transformed from focusing on well-being, moral character, and opportunity to a "dream of material plenty." The definition of a good life had changed: moving from the internal to the external. Adams used the phrase in response to an America that had gotten lost during the opulence-filled Gilded Age and ended up in a calamitous Great Depression. As historian Sarah Churchwell explains, "The original 'American Dream' was not a dream of individual wealth; it was a dream of equality, justice and democracy for the nation." It was a hopeful, unifying message, one that had been transformed into an individualistic commercialized one. We've stuck with the materialistic version—two cars, a house in the suburbs, and lots of stuff—rather than the original version.

We've adopted the view of the parent on the sporting sideline: a relentless focus on the external, almost at all costs. We've Instagramified the American dream, focusing on the appearance without any underlying substance. We have oriented toward outcomes above all else. It can be summed up as valuing the external—accolades, achievements, money, status—as a way to succeed. We believe that unbridled striving is the path forward.

In some cases, such an approach seems to work. American athletes dominate many sports across the globe. And the college scholarships, and more so the salaries of those who make it to the pros, are used to justify the youth sports madness. On *Fortune*'s global list of the 500 companies with the highest revenue, 136 companies are from the US, which only trails China. Even in the classroom, research shows that having a performance orientation is a direct predictor of schooling success.

Yet, there's a hole in this approach. It leads to abhorrent drop-out rates in youth sports and to burnout and languishing in the workplace. It's why a 2022 survey by Deloitte found that 77 percent of workers experienced burnout in their jobs. And perhaps most interestingly, of those who were incredibly passionate about their work, 64 percent reported feeling stressed out from it. In other words, people felt burned out and at a loss, despite a strong desire to succeed. In the classroom, researchers Robert Rudolf and Dirk Bethmann found an interesting paradox: rich countries had sadder children. What was causing the rift? They concluded, "this apparent paradox can largely be attributed to higher learning intensity in higher-income countries." Rich countries tend to have a heavy achievement focus, and there's a tradeoff with living in that kind of culture. The competition, and the need to measure up that follows, is making kids miserable.

It also leads to poorer overall performance. South Korea provides an important cautionary tale. Their fifteen-year-old students rank first in the world in math and reading. They reach the top with a pressure-filled system aimed at mastering entrance exams to get into prestigious universities. It's so absurd that parents of kindergartners are dropping $25,000 on private tutors to prep for future tests. But early obsession comes with a cost. Their early academic lead fades as they enter the workforce. Research shows that their scores on cognitive ability peak earlier and decline faster than their peers from similar countries. As economist Ban Ga-Woon summarized, "Korea is caught in a trap of its own success. Education has played a crucial role in bringing the nation this far, but may now be sabotaging its economic future." South Korea's approach is akin to the eight-year-old youth basketball star whose parents pushed her to early success, only to fall back to reality once her peers started taking sports seriously later on.

We've messed up the balance between being driven by the outcomes and pursuing things for interest and joy. In an aptly titled study, "A Meta-Analysis of the Dark Side of the American Dream," psychologists Emma Bradshaw, Richard Ryan, and colleagues reviewed more than one hundred studies with seventy thousand participants. They found that when individuals' extrinsic aspirations dominated their intrinsic ones, it was "universally detrimental" to their well-being. It's not that we need to have solely intrinsic motives. It's the balance that matters. When we tip too far to the external, we languish instead of thrive. When winning is all that matters, it might work in the short term, but over the long haul, we increasingly play out of a place of fear. And perform worse.

In chapter 1, I outlined why so many of us can't perform up to our potential. We feel stuck, and we self-sabotage, shrink away, or choke. It's time to dive deep into why we've moved from thriving to surviving. It's not our lack of willpower, grit, or tenacity. It's not because kids or people these days are soft, undisciplined, or lack motivation. It's largely that we've pushed to chasing and fulfilling our self, *with the wrong ideals*. We've fallen for the wrong American dream version of success, which has overemphasized the external and neglected the internal. We've created an environment that:

- focuses on achievement above all else;
- narrows our drive toward obsession, to win at all costs;
- amplifies comparisons that are downright impossible to measure up;
- prioritizes extrinsic motivation over intrinsic;
- pushes us to find security and stability in the wrong places, overidentifying with jobs and pursuits; and
- mistakes superficial and transactional relationships for genuine ones.

As a result, many of us feel lost and isolated despite living in the most connected time in history. We feel unfulfilled despite a society brimming with excess and abundance. Anxiety is through the roof, and paranoia is on the rise. We can't stop chasing the external. We have the wrong view of competitiveness, success, motivation, and connection, and it's making us miserable, lonely, anxious, and afraid.

The solution isn't to stop striving for greatness or to stomp out our competitive fire. It's recognizing that the deck is stacked against us. That our culture, mindsets, and environment push us from competing to trying to win at all costs. And in doing so, we lose perspective on what matters. We need to counterbalance that by getting clear on who we are and what matters. It starts with defining what success actually is.

THE MISTAKE OF MAKING SUCCESS AND FAILURE A VIRTUE

For much of history, failure or just about anything bad that occurred was attributed to something else. If we lost a child, we attributed it to God's will. If our crops failed or our town flooded, we blamed it on fortune turning its favor elsewhere. The ancient Greeks blamed the god of luck for major catastrophes that were unexplainable. Ancient Romans blamed bad fortune on the gods being upset that we didn't worship them enough. Offloading our failures onto fortune wasn't perfect, as it prevented finding a solution, but it did allow us to have space between failure and our identity.

As we made our way to modernity, something changed. Failure took on a deeply personal note. As Scott Sandage outlines in his book *Born Losers*, starting in the nineteenth century, our language shifted from "I failed at . . ." to "I am a failure." Sandage traces this history to the rise of bank credit ratings. As banks went from local to national, answering whether Mr. Smith could repay his loan became increasingly difficult. In came credit reporting to judge whether someone was trustworthy or not. Phrases like "good for nothing" didn't start out as insults, but as credit reports meant to relay that the person was likely incapable of paying back a loan, so don't take a chance on them. With reports and ratings mainly based on our business dealings defining whether or not we were worthy of trust, our identities became intertwined with our jobs. Any success or failure was a reflection of our sense of self.

Failure moved from an event to a representation of our character, a label that reflected who we were. This simple shift in our story, ironically, pushed us not toward a story of growth but one of prevention and fear of failure. This internalization of outcomes caused us to hand over power of our self-worth and sense of self to others. The bank decided if you were worthy. We began to do the same with success.

In 1905, German sociologist Max Weber proposed the idea of the "Protestant work ethic" as a way to explain the rise and impact of capitalism in society. Weber's theory was that capitalism grew from the idea of work ethic as a virtue. It was a short step from the Protestant ideals of work to glorify God to accumulating wealth. Whether or not Weber's thesis on capitalism is correct is debated in academic circles. Yet, the impact that such a belief has on us is substantial. In 2013, economists André van Hoorn and Robbert Maseland analyzed over 150,000 individuals from 82 societies to see the impact of making work ethic a virtue. To answer the question, they examined how much *not* working impacted happiness and well-being. Their logic was simple. If work is seen as a virtue, then not working would harm well-being.

And that's precisely what they found. While unemployment caused distress in every group, Protestants felt even more distress from not working than their counterparts. Unemployment hurts

Protestants about twice as much. But it wasn't just about being Protestant. Living in a Protestant society, even if you weren't religious yourself, resulted in individuals feeling higher levels of distress. In other words, societal belief shapes the impact of not working. Our overarching stories around success and failure matter. They impact our psychology and biology.

The virtue-izing of success and failure points not to the hope they are meant to inspire but to a burden we all bear. We let outcomes become a surrogate marker for our character. Those who succeeded represented all that was good. Those who failed lacked the will, work ethic, and virtues to obtain success. We intertwined our sense of self with our achievements, and in so doing, we've pushed ourselves to activating our avoidance systems.

We can simplify how we respond to stimuli in our environment by what behavioral motivation system is activated. In chapter 1, we talked about fighting, fleeing, freezing, and so forth. But here, let's simplify it further: Do we approach or avoid? An animal might approach prey but avoid a predator or go toward an edible plant but avoid one that looks poisonous. In humans, as the threat level increases, areas in our brain that help regulate stress and emotion engage and nudge us toward avoidance. In the modern world, the same fundamental drives are expressed in our pursuits. Are we driven to play to win, where we want to take on the challenge before us? Or are we trying to survive via playing not to lose?

When researchers evaluated the impact of motivational style and goal setting on academic performance, they found that an outcome orientation predicted students' grades. But there was a downside. While an outcome orientation activates approach motivation, it also activates avoidance. It is a double-edged sword that pushes us toward a challenge but simultaneously engages our fear and protection system. We are pulling on both sides of the rope. With the tug of avoidance, even if it was moderate, came another important finding. A results orientation didn't impact enjoyment or interest in the material. While grades might have increased slightly, the underlying intrinsic motivational fire wasn't stoked. When both systems conflict, we are more likely to default to ambivalence or indecision, and if that avoidance system outshines the approach, performance starts to drop.

It's why if we dive deeper into the impact of a results orientation on performance, important nuances emerge. In a 2017 study out of Portugal, an outcome approach positively predicted grades but only for a subset of the college students—the ones whose parents were higher in the social class. Follow-up research found that in low-uncertainty situations, performance goals worked well. As uncertainty rose, not so much. A similar story holds in the workplace. Research shows that acute low-level pressure can improve performance, but chronic or high-level pressure—from rank-and-yank systems, for example—degrades performance. Other research shows that bonuses shift our morals, moving us from concerned about right and wrong, to being strategic about our self-interests. An outcome focus activates both our approach and avoidance systems. In low uncertainty or pressure situations, our avoidance motives can stay at bay. If we live in survival mode, seeing everything as a personal threat, guess what system takes over?

In my coaching practice, I've seen this across the spectrum of sport and business. An outcome-focus can help an individual climb the ladder. When they are young or moving up in their career, pressure and uncertainty are relatively low. They are the rising entrepreneur who isn't yet beholden to investors and can take risks because if she fails, she can start anew without too much damage to her reputation. As pressure rises or her public profile increases, that avoidance rope gets tugged a lot harder when stuck in outcome-orientation mode. The tighter the bond between our self-worth and our results orientation, the more susceptible we are to letting that avoidance side grow.

The problem isn't outcomes or results themselves. It's what we do with them. We've swung too far to one side of the spectrum, making winning the soccer game or being named salesman of the month an essential part of validating ourself. It's not about not keeping score; it's that we've made the score the only thing. We need to rebalance the equation. To find the middle ground between the Ancient Greeks' absolving blame and placing it on fortune and our modernistic tendency, asserting winning is the only thing. We must hold on to the idea that outcomes matter, but we should decouple our character from the result and recalibrate what is truly important to ourselves, our pursuits, and our relationships.

MAKING THE GRADE

Norway is a sports giant. They've won more Winter Olympic medals than any other nation. And recently, they have had tremendous success in summer sports. Karsten Warholm demolished the 400-meter hurdles world record. Kristian Blummenfelt broke the Ironman triathlon record and won Olympic gold. His training partner, Gustav Iden, won the 2022 Ironman World Championship. Casper Ruud reached world number two in tennis. Viktor Hovland is a top ten golfer in the world. Erling Haaland set the record for the most goals in a season in the Premier League. By any metric, Norway's elite athletes are achieving on a global stage. Yet, if we turn to their youth sports, their programs are the opposite of what I described early in this chapter.

Norway doesn't allow for official scorekeeping until the age of thirteen. They dissuade early national travel teams in favor of local leagues. You can't even post the results of youth games online without being fined. And almost sacrilegious in certain American circles, Norway doesn't allow trophies unless everyone gets one. As Tore Øvrebø, Norway's director of elite sport, told *USA Today* writer Dan Wolken, "We think the biggest motivation for the kids to do sports is that they do it with their friends and they have fun while they're doing it and we want to keep that feeling throughout their whole career." Their youth sporting model can be summed up with their chosen slogan, "Joy of Sport for All."

While youth sports in America aren't going to adopt the Norwegian model anytime soon, we can rebalance the equation. In the previously mentioned research on performance orientation and grades in school, I left out one crucial finding. A teaching environment that supported and emphasized *mastery*, where students focused on the process of learning and comprehension instead of a comparison to others, was also linked to better grades. But it wasn't the direct relationship that an outcome orientation had. Instead, in one study on college students, a mastery approach was linked to challenge-seeking, which in turn predicted end-of-the-year grades. In another study, mastery goals predicted higher levels of interest and enjoyment. Mastery works on our approach system without activating avoidance. It frees us up to take on a challenge and pursue our interests without getting bogged down by the pressure or judgment that often comes with an obsession with outcomes. The same findings hold true when looking at sport or the workplace. In a large meta-analysis that analyzed the impact of goal setting in sports, process-orientated goals had a large effect on performance. Outcome goals had little to no effect.

These two paths represent a fast versus slow road to success. Both a mastery or outcome focus can lead to better performance, but the latter is akin to taking a shortcut. Obsession over outcomes is the most direct path to improvement, but it comes with some downsides that shift us toward avoidance. The slow path takes a longer, indirect route. It helps improve our performance not by focusing on the results themselves but by supporting the foundation that ultimately leads to better performance. It stokes the fire of enjoyment and interest to sustain our curiosity and work ethic over the long haul. It pushes us toward challenge-seeking so that when we inevitably hit a roadblock, we'll take it on instead of trying to protect our ego. Both approaches work. One is more sustainable, providing success with less angst. And as we'll learn in this book, both are needed at different times. But society has thrown us so far out of balance that we can't even see the slow route right in front of us.

You're right to be skeptical. To quote former UCLA football coach Red Sanders, "Winning isn't everything; it's the only thing." Sure, you might think this may work on the playgrounds and entry-level jobs, but it can't work at the top of the top. Winning matters! In 2023, I sat down with three superstars to discuss how to achieve peak performance. Chris Cassidy is in a group that only includes three people in history. He started his career as a Navy SEAL, before becoming a NASA astronaut and spending a collective 378 days in space. Roberta Groner was an average college runner who took a decade away from sports to work and have children. Upon her return to competition, as a full-time nurse and mom, she placed sixth at the World Championships in the marathon. She accomplished that at forty-one, an age often considered past our athletic prime. Olav Aleksander Bu is a science whiz who revolutionized training in the endurance world. He's known for tracking and measuring everything—from frequent blood pricks to measure lactate to collecting feces samples—in order to improve performance. He coached the aforementioned Norwegian triathlon champions, Blummenfelt and Iden. When we sat down to chat at the MIT Sloan Sports Analytics Conference, I was sure the conversation would head toward how to use science to innovate. After all, we were at the mecca of data analytics in sports.

After an hour-long discussion, we ended up elsewhere. "It's about love," stated the physiology guru Bu. "The human element is key." He detailed that the love of the pursuit, process, and team were how he helped keep two teammates who are also rivals performing at a high level. Cassidy echoed his comments, discussing the impact of teamwork, connection, and purpose. Groner outlined that her key for going from mediocre to world-class was "finding joy." It sounds nebulous and unmeasurable, but here were three people who had pushed the bounds of what is possible at the highest level, all conveying the same message. They all put in tremendous work; they wanted to be great, but they found the balance to not let their striving get in the way. The late Kobe Bryant echoed the same sentiment when asked what quality all the greats share, "It's love. . . . And it's a pure love. It's not the fame. It's not the money . . . it's not even the championships." The Beatles may have been on to something. All you need is love.

After this experience, I surveyed over seventy-five high performers across sports and business on what allowed them to perform at their best and what prevented them from reaching their potential. The preventors? Expectations, overly concerned with outcomes, letting others or themselves down, and feeling like they "had to" instead of wanting to. They performed up to their potential when they felt secure in who they were and what they were doing, when their motivation was from joy, instead of fear. They felt free to perform. As Josh, an athlete turned entrepreneur, reported, "When I was where I wanted to be, pursuing what I wanted to pursue out of joy. When I wasn't worried about if I would succeed, rather I was seeing what was possible and simply learning and adjusting if I fell short. That's where the magic is."

What I'm arguing for isn't a complete flip to the other side of winning not mattering. It's finding a middle path, where our foundational approach is mastery, with a bit of results orientation when needed. It's going back to the original definition of the American dream, one founded on the process of improving holistically. We need to stop playing the external game and chasing outcomes and start focusing on the internal. To realize that success is only as powerful as what you become on the journey toward it. Don't take my word for it. Listen to the man who popularized striving in our world, the founder of capitalism.

RETURNING TO OUR ROOTS

When most of us think of modern capitalism, some variation of Gordon Gekko's "greed is good" speech delivered by Michael Douglas in the film *Wall Street* comes to mind. Capitalism is about competition, a sometimes ruthless, self-interested obsession that propels us toward progress. Yet, the founding father of capitalism warned of this individualistic, transactional path to success.

Adam Smith was a moral philosopher whose lasting legacy came in economics. With the publication of *The Wealth of Nations* in 1776, he helped usher in a new era of economic growth. But he did so with poignant clarity. Smith was the rare individual with an eye for seeing nuance instead of dogma. He saw the potential drawbacks of the wrong kind of striving while acknowledging that it was a deep-seated part of human nature and brought much good to the world. He wrote, "The pleasures of wealth and greatness, when considered in this complex view, strike the imagination as something grand and beautiful and noble, of which the attainment is well worth all the toil and anxiety which we are so apt to bestow upon it. And it is well that nature imposes upon us in this manner. It is this *deception* which rouses and keeps in continual motion the industry of mankind." Smith saw value in the drive to obtain wealth and status but also highlighted that it was a deception.

Smith wasn't against ambition. He thought it was vital. As political scientist and author of *Our Great Purpose,* Ryan Hanley, told me, Smith thought, "It's good that people care about our results. It helps us achieve. At the same time, Smith believed it can be corrupting. It can be beneficial for society but really dangerous for the individual if they lose themselves and lose a sense of their compass."

Smith got at the central tension. Part of us wants wealth and attention, but another part needs tranquility. As Smith wrote, "In some deep sense then there's a discord between what our world wants us to want and what our beings in fact need. Living our lives well requires that we figure out a productive way to navigate this divide between what the world says is good and what is in fact genuinely good for us." Or, as Hanley summarized to me, "Smith thinks when we're always chasing the externals, we develop a little bit in one way, but we also often suffer because we lose sight of what's actually going to make us happy as we're just chasing results."

Earlier in this chapter, I outlined two paths to success: the quick and the slow. The former focuses on chasing status and external rewards. The latter is based on enjoyment and intrinsic drivers. Smith outlined a similar idea centuries ago. "To deserve, to acquire, and to enjoy the respect and admiration of mankind, are the great objects of ambition and emulation. Two different roads are presented to us, equally leading to the attainment of this so much desired object; one, by the study of wisdom and the practice of virtue; the other, by the acquisition of wealth and greatness."

While capitalism may have ushered in an era of competition, winning at all costs, and greed is good, it's evident in Smith's writing that he is pleading with us to develop balance and safeguards that push us toward the long road occupied by wisdom and virtue. Smith implores us: "Examine the records of history . . . and you will find that the misfortunes of by far the greater part of them have arisen from their not knowing when they were well, when it was proper for them to sit still and to be contented." We don't need to abandon striving for success or our capitalistic ideals. On the contrary, we need to embrace capitalistic thinking. We need to bring it back in line with Smith's original intent. The man who pushed the world to strive is commanding us to balance our natural inclination to chase the external with an ability to be content. In other words, the secret to thriving in a world that has tilted the balance heavily toward the external is to master the internal.

HARMONIZING WITH OUR INNER WORLD

Smith's idea of balancing tranquility and striving has gotten a boost from modern science. According to the latest theories in affective neuroscience, we have several emotional regulation systems that guide our perception and actions. Three of the key systems are:

1. Threat and protect
2. Drive and strive
3. Contentment and soothing

Our threat system is tied to emotions such as anger, anxiety, and disgust. It pushes us toward protection, defending, or attacking, which we discussed in chapter 1. Our drive system is about wanting, pursuing, consuming, or achieving. It pushes us toward finding rewards and resources. Our contentment system moves us toward kindness, security, compassion, connection, and being okay with not pursuing or wanting. It's turning down the stress and alarm. All of these work in concert, feeding off of and sometimes counteracting the other.

As we go through life, we train the sensitivity of these systems. Some become more attuned and easily activated. Others are seldom called upon, and we forget how to utilize them well. As neuroscientist Jaak Panksepp noted, these emotional systems "behave like the sinews, and muscles of our bodies. The more they are used, the stronger they become, the less they are used, the weaker they become." Our environment, pursuits, and goals have done precisely that.

The external game is amplifying our threat system and mistakenly believing that our drive system will help us avoid feeling rejected, insignificant, or alone. If we just reach the top of the mountain, our threats and insecurities will disappear. They won't. All the while, we've forgotten our contentment system. Allowed it to wither away like a muscle that's been stuck in a cast for months. Think back to the protestant work ethic research that found that not working caused distress in people who saw work as a virtue. We've made being content seem threatening instead of soothing. We've deliberately detrained our contentment system.

The inside game is about having these three systems work in harmony. It's not turning off your threat system. We need a functional protective state, just not turned up to eleven. It's not forsaking our pursuits. We need to be driven, just in a way that facilitates growth and mastery instead of seeking to numb the rest of our experience. And more than ever, we need a contentment system to balance the world out. Not so that we are complacent, but so that we can be the person who competes like crazy in the game but then turns it off. So that we aren't bringing that same vigor to playing Go Fish with our seven-year-old. Or, as Adam Smith wrote many years ago, "Happiness consists in tranquility and enjoyment. Without tranquility there can be no enjoyment;

and where there is perfect tranquility there is scarce any thing which is not capable of amusing." We are no longer in harmony.

MAKING THE INNER AND OUTER ADD UP

Success is complicated. It's not as straightforward as most self-help books make it seem to be. It's also important. This book is about wrestling with that nuance, to find a better, more sustainable way to strive, one that doesn't make us miserable. How do we navigate potential, expectations, motivation, apathy, work ethic, and failure? How do we make progress over the long haul?

We've got to deal with the mismatch. The fact that we've over-weighed the external and neglected the internal. Until we do, we'll see threats everywhere and flip to attack, protect, or choke whenever we are in trouble. I'm going to show you how to do just that. To build a secure self, to pursue success without falling for obsession, to connect with others without losing your values. It will take a two-part approach:

1. Build up: We need to fill your basic internal needs with quality content instead of junk food. We need to find significance, coherence, direction, and belonging that is genuine.
2. Dislodge and realign: We need to ensure that when we knock ourselves out of that rut, we are able to find a new path that doesn't lead to delusion.

In practice, building up means the business professional moving from defining their self-worth by their job title to a more holistic view of whether they are doing meaningful work to help others. It's the social media influencer who counters the pull to gain followers by keeping their content and focus on making actual change in their local community. Building up is fulfilling your basic psychological needs with real things in the real world. Dislodging and realigning is about altering our perspective. It's Roger Bannister, who after months of trying to break the four-minute mile barrier, left training behind for a weekend hiking trip in the mountains—only to finally break the barrier shortly after. It's the middle manager who has convinced his brain that punching numbers in a spreadsheet and responding to emails is life or death, who volunteers at the homeless shelter and sees struggle in a different light. Sometimes, to get out of a rut, to feel and see clearly again, we've got to radically alter our perspective.

We need to make our inner and outer worlds add up, to ensure that the story we tell ourselves aligns with our experiences. The solution to survival mode—to getting us unstuck—is dislodging and realigning our protection, striving, and contentment systems. To shift from fear-based avoidance to joy-based pursuit. That means building a foundation based on clarity and coherence in ourself, our pursuits, and our environments. We'll learn how to navigate success (and failure) in a world that increasingly pushes us toward the wrong ideals. It's about how to free ourselves up to perform, to not be overcome by our insecurities that seem to push or pull us toward performing out of a place of fear. It's about fulfilling your potential in a world that continually signals that you aren't good enough—not because success is what defines our self-worth but because we find joy in the pursuits. Music producer Rick Rubin, who has worked with a who's who of successful artists, agrees, writing, "How shall we measure success? It isn't popularity, money, or critical esteem. Success occurs in the privacy of the soul. It comes in the moment you decide to release the work before exposure to a single opinion. When you've done all you can to bring out the work's greatest potential. When you're pleased and ready to let go. Success has nothing to do with variables outside yourself."

FROM COWARDICE TO COURAGE

"This is a disaster waiting to happen," was my reply to fellow coach and friend Shayla Houlihan when she asked about the latest news: a young high school phenom named Mary Cain joining Alberto Salazar and the Nike Oregon Project. We both knew why. It was November 2011, a few months after I'd departed and still a few weeks before I'd hit send on an email to start my journey as a whistleblower. Shayla was one of the few people in the sport who had an inkling of what I and others had been through. She was one of the reasons I came to my senses and got out of there, after a meet when I was delicately explaining the situation, she replied, "Steve, this isn't normal. It's crazy."

Cain was a teenage girl entering a world I'd left a few months earlier. Beyond the worries about anti-doping, my mind flashed to the obsession with weight and the discussion I'd had about a female with 12 percent body fat on the team, where Salazar screamed, "I don't give a damn about the science. I know what I see. She needs to lose weight." The poor teenager was doomed and she had no idea.*

It was Monday, December 10, 2012. I was staring at three short paragraphs I'd typed into the email application on my computer.

---

* Sadly, our inclination proved true. Cain suffered greatly in the program. As she outlined in a 2019 *New York Times* op-ed, "I joined Nike because I wanted to be the best female athlete ever. Instead, I was emotionally and physically abused by a system designed by Alberto and endorsed by Nike." Years later, Cain told me that reading the USADA report that came out of the whistleblower case I was involved in was a catalyst to opening her eyes to see that what she had experienced wasn't some justified pursuit of performing at the highest level. It was wrong. I only wish that moment had come sooner and that I did more to make that happen.

It started, "Look into the Nike Oregon Project . . ." before briefly detailing what I knew about testosterone use and L-carnitine injections. I'd been staring at that email all morning. No one knew I'd written it. I didn't tell anyone I was sending it.

After I left in May 2012, I followed the advice of pretty much everyone: move on. "It's not worth it," was the consensus among close friends and family. And from an individual standpoint, they were right. The best thing for my career and future was to shut up. More than a decade later, I can confirm that.

Contrary to the proclamations of the accused, whistleblowers do not prosper from the act. They almost always are the sacrifice for hopeful change. That's not just the case here. It's what research shows. The vast majority lose their jobs and face mental health struggles. According to one study, 85 percent of whistleblowers suffer from severe anxiety, depression, or other mental health problems, with 48 percent rising to clinical levels of the issue.

The logical thing is to stay quiet, and that was the plan. But over time, not acting ate away at me. I felt it viscerally. It was the hopelessness and worry when the teenage Cain joined. How could she handle that environment? It was the despair I felt when I had a conversation with the spouse of an athlete who was looking at the team. I tiptoed around the specifics, afraid that since they were in conversation with the program I'd be exposed. But I did say, "There was shady stuff going on, ethically and performance-enhancement wise, and if I were you, I wouldn't go." They joined anyway. I couldn't blame them. They were seeing the glittery exterior, rationalizing the seamy interior underneath. I had been there, too.

I felt both helpless and hopeless. The feeling that you could do something, that you were one of a handful of people who could warn others, but instead, you sat in your office twiddling your thumbs, ignoring phone calls from journalists sniffing around was tormenting. Finally, I'd had enough. Mary Cain joining was a catalyst. It got me to stop thinking about myself and to see others. What pushed me over the edge from cowardice to courage was a singular thought: *People needed to know.* The world didn't have to believe me, but the truth had to be out there so others could make their own decisions. That thought moved me from inner debate to taking action. At 1:50 p.m., I hit send. But this was an act of courage, not a way of being. You can act courageously by standing up. That is hard. Going against the easier choice, to stay silent, move on, or let someone else deal with it. Acting is the first step. But *being* courageous is different. I was not there yet.

It takes something else: *clarity.* Clarity on who you are and the complexity that comes with that. We need to stop playing the external game and start focusing on the internal, and realize that success derives its power not from the result itself, but from the transformation we undergo during our journey toward it. Let's begin our journey.

PART ONE

BE—CLARITY ON WHO YOU ARE

CHAPTER 3

SPEND LESS TIME SEEKING AND CHASING, MORE TIME EXPLORING

E ight laps to the mile, the 200-meter dirt loop with small red cones marking the interior curb of the track seemed large and daunting. Outfitted in the latest No Fear shirt that dominated 1990s playgrounds, I was ready to take on history. I was eleven years old, about to run the mile for the annual Presidential Fitness Test. I'd given up hope on ever achieving the coveted Presidential Fitness Award as the dreaded V-sit reach proved insurmountable to my naturally inflexible body. Instead, I turned to the event that I knew I could win: the mile.

The record board hung over the cafeteria as a reminder of who was not only the fastest in the school but the fastest person who ever graced Haude Elementary. The time to beat was 6:01. With my friend Chris positioned to call out splits, which, at the time, made no sense to me, I set out on my quest to break the record. I ran in the traditional way an eleven-year-old with no experience racing does. I went out hard, held on for dear life in the middle, and then gave it everything I had in the end. As I crossed the finish line, I collapsed. I'd used every ounce of energy to run as fast as my untrained body would allow me to. But it wasn't enough; six minutes and ten seconds was the best I could muster. While most of my other class walked away from the dreaded mile, I lay there, exhausted. Minutes passed before my faculties returned, and I was able to walk in to transition from P.E. to classroom work. I'd learned one thing that day: running was hard.

A few days later, my P.E. teacher, Mrs. Passmore, asked if I wanted another shot. She knew I was going for the record and felt bad I'd missed. Encouraged by the possibility, I decided to train for the event for the first time in my life. What better way to prepare than to run a mile hard, I figured. I set off running lap after lap. My initial enthusiasm soon wore off, and I wondered why in the world I was running in circles, causing myself such agony. As I ran round and round, a thought popped into my mind, *Was the record worth it?* When I finished, I came to a conclusion. Decades later, I still remember the thought, *Training is really hard. If I ran one mile every day, I could drop two to three minutes off my mile time in a few years. Then I'd have the world record.* Yes, as I walked into my house tired and hungry, I was convinced that if only I could train one mile a day, I would not only get the Haude Elementary school record but soon the world record.

When I returned to school the next day, I pulled Mrs. Passmore aside and told her, "I don't want to run another mile." I didn't need a record; it didn't mean that much to me. The training wasn't worth it. That day, I knew one thing for sure: Running sucked. I didn't want to go all-in on chasing the record. I went back to playing soccer and baseball. I was still exploring.

—

"I want to be a policeman," your four-year-old pleads before requesting toys, a costume, and books all related to the work of a cop. That may switch to a firefighter or a doctor a month or two later. And it doesn't have to be a profession. Ask any parent, and they'll regale you with stories of their child's latest craze: animals, books, superheroes, music, sports, princesses. Whatever the activity or identity, children are masters at exploring. They dabble until they find something that interests them, and then they go a bit deeper. Sometimes, they even move toward obsession, becoming enraptured with the thing, making it a central part of their world and who they are. Before suddenly abandoning it and moving to the next interest.

Forming our identity follows a similar ebb and flow. We move between different levels of exploration and commitment. During exploration, we dabble, trying on different roles, while in commitment, we tie ourselves to a particular role. A child moves from policeman to veterinarian, partially because she is exposed to different roles through books and interacting with peers and teachers. She's creating a broad base, which allows her to launch off in multiple directions. And if one doesn't fit, she can double back and head down a different path. Especially early on in their development, kids hang on to their interests, passions, and identities loosely. They stay in the exploration phase for much longer than their adult brethren. Children can sit with more uncertainty in their passions. It's not yet self-defining.

As we age, we go through a progression of broad exploration, deep exploration, reconsidering our choice on depth, and ultimately, a deep commitment. It's a process from broad to narrow, from uncertainty to security. At some point, as the uncertainty of broad exploration becomes unbearable, we search for stable moorings and start to lock in on who we are, what we believe, and with whom we identify. In our kindergartener example, it's when we fall in love with the idea of ourselves as a police officer. The deep dives function to spark curiosity, to transform the unknown into the known, and to find out that there are deeper layers that we were previously unaware of.

Narrowing allows us to do the work to spend hours practicing or understanding. It leads to expertise and security in knowing that you have something that makes you unique and special. And the further down the path you go, the fewer others you have to compete with. Everyone wants to be a firefighter; few in your class know as much about orcas as you. Kids dabble, follow their interests, and go deep, but often not enough so that they get stuck.

As we grow and develop, the commitment piece becomes ever more important. We can't handle the uncertainty of broad exploration. It often turns from productive to ruminative. We worry about whether we are a lost wanderer, unsure of what life has in store for us, or if we are following the correct path. We look to our left and right and see our friends head off to medical school or toward the standard progression of marriage, then kids. Wandering loses its luster. We need to be firm, to know who we are, to be committed to our job, our beliefs, our groups, and our entire sense of self.

Forming our inner narrative is like writing a book. Exploratory mode is great when we don't know exactly what we will cover. We need to read a lot, interview experts, or maybe even travel and try different activities. That's broad exploration. Eventually, we need to narrow, to start to take whatever it is we've researched and experienced and try to put it into a coherent structure. We start to outline the book and its chapters. That is deep exploration. When we start writing, we convert our outline to crafting our narrative. When we put pen to paper, we start to reach commitment. Occasionally, we might change our mind or reconsider our outline, or in the case of identity, renegotiate with our current self. Every once in a while, even deep in the throes of the writing process, we may get stuck or be convinced by an editor that we went the wrong way. A new or perhaps stubborn writer presses on, ignoring the advice. They are cemented to the original concept, unwilling to waver. But when we get stuck, a better strategy is often to zoom back out, to do a bit more exploration, to dabble to keep the creative juices flowing and not get wedded to a particular path. And at the end of the project, when their work is cemented into a printed book, they zoom back out—committing to exploration again. A good writer is like a good identity, a mixture of breadth and depth at the right time.

When we're young, we have a lot of flexibility with little security. We suffer through the angst-ridden preteen years, unsure of who we are. As we move through the game of life, the script often flips. We get more rigid and committed. But when we occupy a world filled with uncertainty and a comparison point that is impossible to achieve, we often overcompensate. We don't just move toward commitment. We move toward a much tighter bond. One that is harder to escape.

GETTING CAPTURED

"How about five miles?" Matt Cobb quipped as I stood there contemplating what he'd just asked me to do. For Matt, five miles represented a short and easy run, akin to going for a walk. The six-foot-two, rail-thin senior was the fastest runner in our high school, and if the cards fell right, he had a legitimate shot at qualifying for the state championship. For me, a fourteen-year-old novice whose longest run in my life up to that point was two miles, he may as well have said, "Let's run a marathon." I saw myself as more of a soccer player who occasionally ran than someone who enjoyed running. Yet there I stood about to go on a five-mile tour of neighborhoods.

Matt was there as a favor. His parents were family friends. When he learned that I'd be giving cross-country a try as I stayed in shape for soccer, Matt volunteered to take me for a run. As we set out on our jaunt, I deeply regretted this connection. As Matt peppered me with questions, as if clicking off six-minute miles in the humidity of a Houston summer did not affect him, my answers became shorter and shorter. I could barely breathe.

As we passed two miles and I ventured into the depths of the unknown, he was completely comfortable. I was trying not to die. We hadn't even reached halfway, and it was clear I was in over my head. "Just make it to the turnaround, just make it to the turnaround," was my only thought. I fought on until just past the three-mile mark, when I could take no more. I stopped, turned to my side, and let the contents of my stomach spew out on the manicured lawn of some unfortunate suburbanite.

Embarrassed and disappointed, I could hardly look up. I was a lowly incoming freshman, wearing calf-high socks and old running shoes, who had just let down the captain of our cross-country team. Matt came over, put his hand on my back, and offered sincere encouragement: "Don't worry about it. You're doing a good job. It's your first run. It'll come." I looked up and saw Matt standing there, finger on his watch, waiting to start back up. Seeing me looking up, he stated, "This is what it takes . . ."

That's when it hit me. It didn't matter that I had just puked my guts out. We had a run to do. For the next one-and-a-half miles, I listened to Matt as he told me that throwing up was a good thing. "Running is about exploring your limits. You found what your body and mind thought today's was. Now you are going beyond that."

As we trotted back to my parents' home, I was sure this was a one-time run. A favor completed. And I'd failed the test. Yet,

Matt showed up the next day. And the next. He was offering me a choice: either run or don't, but if I did, training would be the norm. And we'd repeat the same ritual the next day, the next, and the next. Only without the throw-up. My journey in running had begun. I fell in love with exploring my limits.

Within a few weeks, I'd go from two miles to easily running ten. That first year, I'd vault from a soccer player to one of the fastest freshmen in the country. A few years later, I'd turn that into the fastest high schooler in the country, as I concluded my high school career with a 4:01 mile. Along the way, I'd go from a reluctant runner to an obsessed one. At one point, I was averaging fifteen miles per day and crafting my entire world around the mind-numbing activity of putting one foot in front of the other for miles on end. Everything else was secondary: school, relationships, vacations, none of it mattered except for running. I was hooked. I was captured. This phenomenon isn't unique to me. It's a hallmark of high performers.

Steve Williams was driving down a highway when the passenger commanded him to stop. Was there something wrong? Williams pulled over. His passenger got out of the car, opened the trunk, grabbed a golf club, and began practicing his swing on the side of the highway. The passenger was Tiger Woods.

Williams was Woods's caddy at the time, and as he described in the HBO documentary *Tiger*, "Here's Tiger Woods on the side of the freeway in Toronto, swinging a golf club." He went on to explain, "He's got this thought in his head, 'If I can just do this,' and he couldn't wait until the next day or until he got back to the hotel or wherever it was. It had to be now."

Tiger's story mirrored an experience I had with another sporting legend. It was 2010, and I was sitting in a café that doubled as a video rental store—an odd combination, even back then. But we were in the middle of nowhere, or more precisely, Grapeland,

Texas, with a population of 1,493. Sitting across from me was Tom Tellez, the then seventy-six-year-old former University of Houston track coach and my current coach, known as one of the best sprint coaches in the world. After all, he'd coached Carl Lewis, Leroy Burrell, Mike Marsh, Joe DeLoach, and numerous others to Olympic medals or world records. We were eating our sandwiches, filling the space with idle conversation around sports, but it was clear Tellez's mind was elsewhere. Midconversation, he blurted out, "Let's go outside. I think I figured it out." I wasn't quite sure what he meant, but as I followed Tellez out the door, it quickly became evident.

"Do a stride. I want you to shorten your arm swing." Dressed in khaki shorts and a T-shirt, I ran down the dirt parking lot as Tellez observed. This was not an unusual circumstance. Tellez is a biomechanical wizard, helping not just runners but athletes in all sports, like when he worked with Andre Agassi. It wasn't unusual for me to get a late-night call that went something like, "Steve, I was lying in bed, thinking about your foot strike. I think I figured it out, you need to think more about pressing the ground instead of getting quick." With instructions to try out his suggestions and then get back to him. That day in Grapeland, Tellez was his trademark self, helping me finesse my running stride. When it came to the mechanics of running, Tellez would have appreciated Woods's highway pit stop.

The near obsession around their craft is a hallmark of high performers. They have this desire that borders on an addiction to improve, to get things right, to perfect their craft. It isn't just normal motivation; it's something beyond that, an almost manic-like intensity brought to drawing, reading, writing, piano, golf, or whatever the endeavor. The pursuit could be anything, but the intensity of concentration and persistence is consistent throughout. Woods and Tellez aren't unique in this regard. Stories abound from professional athletes to artists to executives, from the young to the old, and across the board, the drive is self-initiated.

THE DRIVE FROM WITHIN

In her groundbreaking work *Gifted Children*, psychologist Ellen Winner aimed to explore what set apart the prodigious and gifted. In exploring those who excelled early in music, math, art, or reading, some commonalities arose. There was the child whose life revolved almost entirely around drawing who would scream, "Bring me my markers!" as he'd draw morning, noon, and night. Winner wrote, "I saw this kind of thing in every one of the kids I studied. There was a mathematical kid who did nothing but mathematize the world—tried to turn everything into mathematical problems. There was a composing prodigy who not only composed all the time but also read orchestral scores for bedtime reading." It's not just young prodigies that are built this way; maybe you've heard stories of the NBA star who wouldn't leave practice until he made ten, twenty, or thirty shots in a row. Hockey fans will remember Wayne Gretzky's immense work ethic and dedication. As a child, Gretzky would practice for hours on end in the makeshift skating rink in his family's backyard. Regardless of the pursuit, these gifted individuals seem to have a trance-like ability to relentlessly focus on a task. They were obsessed with their craft. They were captured.

When it comes to high performers, we make a crucial mistake. We see the endless hours of work, the so-called ten thousand hours of deliberate practice, and we assume that is the secret sauce. The driver that converts the ordinary into the extraordinary. If the work is what matters, then by logical extension, it only makes sense to poke, prod, and push people to get their hours in, to mimic Gretzky's maniacal routine out on the ice rink. We see

Tiger Woods and can't imagine how a child would want to put in all that work by himself. We assume that someone behind him—a parent, coach, or teacher—was pushing them along. We make the same mistake as children transform into adults and playing fields convert to cubicles and offices. Our bosses adopt the position of presumed overbearing parent, and the social media gurus command us to grind and hustle.

But the secret isn't in the work. The work is often necessary, of course, but the work is a by-product. The takeaway from the stories of Woods and Gretzky isn't maniacal practice. It's finding something where interest, motivation, and talent align to light a fire that propels you to do the work. Professional ballerina Gavin Larsen described the experience to me, "It wasn't a conscious thing where I woke up every day saying, 'God, I love this!' I was just magnetically drawn to it. At the beginning, it felt more like a really intense curiosity, a kind of fascination. A feeling of having to be like a scientist and exploring, experimenting, and inspecting. I was drawn to it." Getting captured can't be forced from the outside; it comes from the inside.

Consider the aforementioned Woods, who is often held up as the poster boy for fathers to push their children to success. When asked for advice for parents eager to have their child follow his path, Woods replied, "Don't force your kids into sports. I never was. To this day, my dad has never asked me to go play golf. I ask him. It's the child's desire to play that matters, not the parent's desire to have the child play. Fun. Keep it fun." The spark comes first; the rage to master isn't prodded or pushed on a child from his father. Another famous prodigy, Wolfgang Amadeus Mozart, initially had his desire to play the violin rebuked by his father. It was only after Mozart displayed a spark that his father commenced formal lessons. Or, listen to Gretzky, who replied, "No one told me to do it," when asked about his marathon-like practice sessions growing up.

The inner drive to figure out how to swing a golf club or play an instrument doesn't come from an overbearing father or a tiger mother. It starts as a discovery process, one that evolves through natural play and exploration. Sure, after that fire is lit, support and structure facilitate development. You can't master hockey without having access to a rink, skates, and a stick. But it's getting captured that paves the way for you to handle the hours of practice. The rage to master occurs thanks to a combination of talent and interest aligning, with just the right amount of challenge and support to keep you invested and able to pursue the activity over a sustained period. It's a match problem. Dabble through interests, explore different pursuits and identities, and see how long the "thing" holds your attention. Think back to my experience as a runner. In fifth grade, I wasn't ready to be captured. Running sucked. A few years later, opportunity, talent, support, and challenge aligned, and I was off to the races.

As Winner points out, the drive must come from within, and if you are in the right place, with the right pursuit, you can find yourself in a virtuous cycle. "[They] are intrinsically motivated to make sense of the domain in which they show precocity. They exhibit an intense and obsessive interest, an ability to focus sharply. . . . They experience 'states of flow' while engaged in learning—optimal states in which they focus intently and lose sense of the outside world. The lucky combination of obsessive interest in a domain along with an ability to learn easily leads to high achievement." While prodigies might experience this to the extreme, we're all familiar with the slightly less obsessive cousin.

We get absorbed in an activity. Maybe it's rock climbing, playing video games, or figuring out the answer to the crossword puzzle. An initial spark of interest turns into a mostly joyful absorption. You spend hours crafting the newsletter or playing the musical instrument. You aren't playing the piano because you aspire to perform on stage. It's just something that takes you away. You aren't quite captured, but your attention and interest are sustained without much effort. It's this combination of interest, inner joy, and the freedom to choose the activity that creates the deep inner drive or curiosity that fuels the pursuit.

It's in this balance of exploration and deep dives, or going broad and narrow, where the magic lies. The broad allows us to have more potential paths to explore. The narrow allows us to be absorbed, to use the knowledge and skills we've developed. Or in the case of our identity, the broad allows us to see what interests us; the narrow allows us to define what matters and what we value. Both are vital.

GOING ON A HOT STREAK

Starting in 1984, everything that Rob Reiner touched turned to gold. He directed seven films over the next eight years, with the lowest ranked among them scoring 83 percent on the review aggregator Rotten Tomatoes. They weren't just well-received; they included timeless classics like *This Is Spinal Tap*, *When Harry Met Sally . . .*, *A Few Good Men*, and *The Princess Bride*. Reiner would direct a few other hits in the following decades, but nothing came close to this prolific period.

Reiner's hot streak isn't unusual. Other directors, from George Lucas to Greta Gerwig have experienced similar periods of unerring quality. Artists like Frida Kahlo and scientists like Albert Einstein follow suit. In almost every profession, individuals go through a creative or hyperproductive period where their talents, motivation, and luck collide. Northwestern University professor Dashun Wang has spent the last decade attempting to understand the science of hot streaks. In a 2018 study, Wang and his team analyzed more than twenty thousand artists and scientists, finding that over 90 percent of them had a period where their work had a much greater impact. Contrary to our expectations, these magical periods weren't related to how productive they were or even at what point in their career they were in. The young and old could experience hot streaks. On average, the hot streaks lasted 5.7 years for artists, 5.2 years for directors, and 3.7 years for scientists, though for some individuals, the streak could stretch upwards of 20 years.

Having identified that hot streaks were real, Wang and team set out to understand how they occur. They analyzed the career trajectories of thousands of artists, directors, and scientists. This time, looking at what the individual focused on before and during their streak. They discovered a surprisingly simple pattern: explore, then exploit that accumulated knowledge and experience. Broaden, then narrow. Explore, then commit. Artists experimented with different brush strokes and techniques for years before narrowing in on one style. Scientists branched out, working in different fields and collaborating with a diverse array of experts before narrowing in on the field that ultimately led them to their Nobel Prize. Wang provided the example of director Peter Jackson who, before his *Lord of the Rings* trilogy, had directed movies that fell in the horror, comedy, biography, and musical genres.

The magic was in the sequence. Exploration or commitment on its own didn't lead to a hot streak. It took both—in the right order. As Wang reported, "Our data shows that people ought to explore a bunch of things at work, deliberate about the best fit for their skills, and then exploit what they've learned." Or, as we've learned in this chapter, broad exploration opens the door for a deep, narrow dive. In sporting terms, specialization fails unless you've got a broad base of skills and development behind it. Take it from Tiger Woods, who, though seen as the poster child of early practice, played baseball and ran track and cross-country. Or Gretzky, who once said, "I played everything. I played lacrosse, baseball, hockey, soccer, track and field. I was a big believer that you played hockey in the winter and when the season was over you hung up your skates and you played something else."

Our modern world often discounts the exploration phase as pointless wandering. We romanticize the grind, emphasizing the value of hard work. Society, and achieving success, all push us in that direction. But when we go narrow too early or for too long, we cement not only our performance but our identities, our avenues for meaning and purpose. This changes everything—from our underlying motivation to how we see our future. The narrow allows us to become experts, to achieve success in a field. But narrowing, especially too early, comes with a cost.

As we climb that pyramid of success, we see the world through a very narrow lens. The top—status, money, fame, or whatever outcome we desire—becomes the only thing we see. Long gone are the days of dabbling and exploring, and with them often go the intrinsic fuel that started the journey. Joy is replaced by external motivators and outcomes. Before you know it, we are trapped on the top of the pyramid, unable to remember how we got there and unwilling to return to the base and shore it up. We're stuck.

FROM CAPTURED TO CEMENTED

In 1960, a woman named Nelle released her debut novel. It was a monumental effort that reached completion, thanks in part to her friends and family scrounging up funds to support her for an entire year so that she could complete the project. It was a gamble, as her editor warned that the book set in Alabama during the Great Depression probably wouldn't sell well. But it paid off. Within a year, it had sold over five hundred thousand copies, was translated into ten languages, and even won a Pulitzer Prize. A blockbuster Oscar-winning movie soon followed.

To Kill a Mockingbird has gone on to sell over thirty million copies. Yet Nelle Harper Lee struggled to produce a follow-up novel. In the years after her initial success, she had only a handful of short essays to her name. For the rest of her life, she would shun much of the world. As one of her close friends, Thomas Butts, relayed, Lee told him that one of the reasons she didn't write a follow-up right after was, "I wouldn't go through the pressure and publicity I went through with *To Kill a Mockingbird* for any amount of money." Her follow-up novel wouldn't come until fifty-five years later, when *Go Set a Watchman* was released in 2015, shortly before she passed away.

If Lee was a musician, she would have been labeled a one-hit wonder, those musicians who had the fortune of having a smash hit but struggled to capture lightning in a bottle again. We all know the songs: "Tubthumping" by Chumbawamba, "Ring My Bell" by Anita Ward, "Take on Me" by a-ha, "Ice Ice Baby" by Vanilla Ice. Years later, the tunes still get stuck in our heads. Musicians inevitably put out a follow-up album, but they struggle to regain that success, often trying to mimic the sound that made them famous. Or, out of frustration and a desire to put space between them and their defining song, they go in a completely different direction. Why do artists or creators, many of whom have enviable levels of talent and determination, get stuck, never to recreate their success? In 2023, Markus Baer and Dirk Deichmann provided us with an answer in their unique research on success in the world of cookbooks.

In a series of studies, Baer and Deichmann first found that only 50 percent of cookbook authors go on to produce a follow-up. The more creative that initial book was, the less likely an author was to put out another book, even if the first one had been highly successful. In fact, if a cookbook was given substantial recognition or an award for being novel, the likelihood of a follow-up dropped significantly. The reason was simple: authors were protecting their identities.

The recognition shifted the author's identity. They weren't just a cook or a writer; they were a creative. Their story had changed. Producing a follow-up puts that identity at risk, so many creatives don't. Or they shift genres and fields so they don't have to try. As Baer explained, "This newfound identity, which is special and rare, is then in need of protection. Essentially, once a person is in the creative limelight, stepping out of it—by producing a novel idea that disappoints or pales in comparison to earlier work—is threatening and to be avoided. One way to do so is to stop producing altogether. You cannot compromise your identity and reputation when you do not produce anything new." In other words, once our identity cements, we narrow and protect. The initial creativity driven by intrinsic motivation gets replaced. Success, and more so awards and recognition, pushes us to stop exploring.

"There's this thing people say about celebrities, that they're frozen at the age they got famous," Taylor Swift expressed in the documentary *Miss Americana*. Swift was lamenting the extreme end of cementing. You get stuck and stop exploring, partially because the world around you ceases to permit you to grow. It's not just celebrities or prodigies that experience this. When we get stuck in narrow mode for too long, we slowly shed the potential paths in our periphery. In the identity development literature, this early cementation is called identity foreclosure. We stop seeing other possible selves and get stuck on the one we have. Our brain's prediction of who we are gets trapped in a deep predictive rut. And we start acting accordingly, creating a self-fulfilling cycle that we can't see beyond. The more of a public self we have, the more we get pulled toward cementation as a way to handle the newfound exposure and instability. And since we now occupy a world where most of us feel like mini-celebs in our social media world, we are increasingly primed for identity foreclosure.

Intensive pursuit of a singular role often results in a unidimensional identity, with our personal and social selves converging on the same thing. We occupy a narrow world, a kind of identity tunnel. We can't see beyond the singular item. While our peers were trying on different hats, we missed out on the dabbling and exploring. Before you know it, as our cognitive capacities reach fruition, we start questioning, *What I am missing, and who am I?* Welcome to an achiever's version of a midlife crisis.

This doesn't just occur in athletic or artistic phenoms. According to a recent study, adults labeled as intellectually gifted are at a much higher risk of suffering from a crisis of meaning, an anxiety and depression-filled experience that is partially due to a loss of coherence and direction in one's life. When we suffer from a crisis of meaning, a slew of mental health issues follow, from compulsions to immune-related diseases to a rapid decline in our overall well-being. When researchers contrasted these individuals with similarly talented individuals who had recently achieved success, the risk for a crisis of meaning significantly dropped. It's the potential, without fulfillment, that does the damage.

Who we are, what we pursue, and what we identify with all provide meaning and direction for our lives. In the short term, a narrow fixation can work out. As we saw in the research on hot streaks, it's necessary to exploit our knowledge. But if we stay there for too long, we often cement and face a crisis of meaning—a sharp point in our life where we start asking if this is what we signed up for, if this is who we want to be.

When we narrow and cement, there are two main consequences. First, we close off other potential pathways and become incredibly fragile. For most, the common advice to "go all-in" or "burn the boats behind you" so that we have no other option but to succeed is terrible. It puts us in a place of playing not to lose and responding out of fear of failure. We're susceptible to any signal that indicates potential failure or mismatch between who you are and where you're going. Look no further than the curse of potential.

Second, our internal motivation and experience shift. Gone are the days of intrinsic joy and wanting to play or perform. They are gradually replaced by external drivers. Ellen Winner noted that the prodigies who failed to translate early talent to success in adult-hood experienced "excessive extrinsic control and pressure, leading to a decline of intrinsic motivation." She went on to conclude, when we push too hard "the intrinsic motivation and rage to master these children start out with become a craving for the extrinsic rewards of fame." In recent research involving the Swiss Olympic federation, when 155 youth athletes were evaluated in various sports, the athletes whose motivation was more intrinsically orientated were much more likely to make it to the international level a few years later. Those who adopted a fear of failure mindset were less likely to reach the next level. An overemphasis on rewards, accolades, and success sends a clear signal: achievement is what matters and is what is rewarded. Anxiety soon follows, and creativity and inner drive are often extinguished.

Achieving expertise often exacerbates the problem. In study-ing more than seven hundred thousand consumers, researchers Matthew Rocklage, Derek Rucker, and Loran Nordgren found that expertise leads to emotional numbness. As individuals achieved expertise in photography or wine, they had less intense emotional responses to the experience of consuming whatever it is they were an expert at. Their brain becomes sensitized to the thing that once brought them immense pleasure or joy. The researchers concluded, "Emotional numbness was a result of the application of domain-specific knowledge." When our predictions of self and the world narrow, we stop listening to our actual experiences. How-ever, Rocklage and colleagues found a solution: Get them to focus on and reconnect with the feelings of consuming art or drinking wine, and the numbness subsided. Or, put another way, to remember what it's like to explore, to play.

It's no wonder so many of us default toward choking. We can see it in artists and writers who feel stuck, trying to replicate their prior work to reach sales goals instead of exploring and growing as they mature. It's the young adult who carefully crafts a social media identity around a hobby, diet, or belief, only to feel trapped by their public persona. If you're known as the "carnivore diet guy," no matter what new evidence comes out, you're not changing your mind, because it's your identity at stake. You are stuck. The more expertise, or public notoriety you have, the harder it is to go back to exploring.

We have been convinced to narrow and cement, which then makes us incredibly fragile when our sole identity is even minorly at risk. While at the same time, we stop feeling and experiencing, tuning out the feelings and emotions that captured us and brought us excitement and joy to begin with.

Narrowing, or living in tunnel vision mode, can be great for performing in the short term. We can get work done. But if we stay too narrow for too long, we start to lose the ability to branch out. Potential paths fall away. Add in the double whammy of success, which pulls us away from our initial driver and toward a shiny object. (Picture Gollum.) Or the scientist who falls in love with a theory because that's where he gets the most likes and retweets. The news reporter who once went by the book gradually moves her reports more and more toward a particular bias because that's what gets the ratings. Success changes our incentives. And if our identity cements around our job or outcome, our behaviors and values will shift along with them. Success is like an undercurrent at the beach. Gradually, subtly pulling us away from our original location. If we aren't aware of its pull, it can be detrimental.

Philosopher Joseph Campbell called the items like success that pull on our self to get cemented the "hungry ghosts." Whether it's success, status, or some other insecurity, these ghosts lure us toward seeing only them. We get stuck. We desperately hold on to the items that promise to make us okay but are fleeting. As psychotherapist Mark Epstein described in *The Zen of Therapy*, "Look for clinging. However, it might manifest. Sometimes it shows itself in intimate ways, when someone holds on in a needy way; sometimes it shows itself in therapy, when people can't stop blaming their parents for ruining their lives." When we narrow, we cling to items that provide us comfort. We fall for the distorted success narrative. We cement.

When we are striving out of a place of insecurity, when we feel trapped, fear and protection take over. We move from a growth orientation to safety. We have nowhere else to go. We need these "things" to feel validated. We can't live without them. The hungry ghosts take over. They are in control.

BOUNCING BACK AND FORTH

Sustainable excellence is about balancing exploration and commitment. As we've seen throughout this chapter, we need both. In our pursuits, exploration creates a broad foundation for creativity and innovation. It emphasizes experiencing. In contrast, commitment allows us to focus and move from ideas to action. It's about doing. This is particularly important when it comes to our identities. Exploration frees us up to try on different hats and get a sense of what interests us and what we value. But we need commitment to give us a sense of security, continuity, and stability. With too much exploration, we feel lost and unmoored. With too much commitment, we are rigid, fragile, and numb. It's about holding on to both flexibility and security at the same time.

If we stay narrow for too long, it can change our relationship with our pursuit. We start to overidentify with our sport, hobby, or job. After all, we get so absorbed in the task that it becomes hard to create space between it and our sense of self. Success makes this even more difficult. We gain notoriety and status. People start labeling us as runner, cook, writer, or doctor. That success pulls us away from the initial interest and joy that served as our initial fuel. The external measures that tell us if we are successful or not become more important. And before we know it, joy is replaced by fear and anxiety. We've moved from want to need to have to. We feel trapped.

It can lead to living in survival mode, as we are overcome by apathy, as our intrinsic motivational power wanes. It can also lead to an incredibly fragile self. One that is susceptible to one loss, failure, or threat that dislodges our singular identity from its moorings. The secret sauce is balancing the broad and narrow—having security but also flexibility, and being able to fall in love and pursue something narrowly but zoom out and not get lost in a world of singular pursuits and lack of joy.

We can think of the broad versus narrow idea as what I call the attachment continuum: wandering to exploring to committed to cemented. If we spend too much time in commitment mode, especially with the wrong motivation backing it, we drift toward cementation. If we find ourselves in never-ending exploration, we drift toward wandering. We need to blend security and flexibility.

The key to navigating this cycle is to go in the other direction at the right time. To move from exploration to commitment, but then be aware that if we linger here for too long, we may end up in cementation. We need to be able to zoom back out to go exploring again. To find the joy in the activity that we are pursuing. If we don't, that joy will slowly fade and be replaced by fear and angst. We'll move from striving to simply trying to hang on. We need to be able to zoom back out and return to the basics.

Survival mode pushes us toward narrowing and cementing. We need to turn around and look the other way to ensure we aren't swinging the pendulum too far to one extreme. We need to bring back a bit of exploration, to refill our internal driver and be reminded of what it means to dabble in interests for the pure joy of it. Something that allows us to be without cementing, to form a robust and flexible identity. Adulthood might be great, but the key to mastering the balance between breadth and depth is not to leave our inner child behind. We need recess for adults. There are four keys to finding the right balance.

BRING BACK PLAY. BE A BIT OBLIVIOUS.

In 1968, Amby Burfoot won the Boston Marathon. Growing up, he was "a bona fide obsessive." But that early obsession wasn't in the sport that would bring him notoriety. "I spent about a million hours in my driveway in junior high shooting hoops. I taught myself the hook shot and could nail 90 percent from the free throw line." He was dreaming of Boston, just the Celtics, not the marathon. As he told me, "I was oblivious and blissed out at the same time. I played so many solo fictional mind games where I imagined I was a Boston Celtics star playing in the Boston Garden." All that came to a halt when he entered high school. "I quickly found out that basketball isn't a solo sport," he said. "They let other guys on the court! Guys who are tall, fast, strong, springy, and all sorts of things I was not. It was an embarrassment. They would steal the ball from me before I could get off one of my vaunted eighteen-foot jump shots." Running soon beckoned.

Burfoot's departure from basketball set the stage for his marathon career and his later work in journalism. Yet we can't discount those early years shooting hoops in the driveway. He was dabbling and exploring. He'd found something that was fun. He'd experienced getting captured, pursuing an activity for the joy it brought, and watching himself improve compared to a previous version of himself. He could experience all of this mainly because he was free from comparison. He was simply playing, and he was oblivious.

Fast forward to our present day, and we often lose out on both aspects: play and obliviousness. Everything is organized. We lose the natural scaffolding that occurs, from being the best basketball player on the block to best in our grade level to best in the city. We grow up, losing our obliviousness much too soon. We learn our place in the world, prematurely shutting the door on opportunities to explore. And we get sent a firm message that pursuing an activity, sport, or job is about productivity and success. Why try if we aren't very good? Without a bit of obliviousness, we miss out on the act of playing because it's fun.

Our inclination toward organized everything also takes away the natural aspect of play. We replace pickup games with leagues, natural play in the yard or local parks with structured and rule-bound activities. In schools, we increasingly limit recess. At home, we are scared to let our kids out of sight. It's survival mode run amuck.

Play counters this fear. Kids play kickball at recess, even if they are terrible, because there's no mom, dad, or coach there to critique. Adults can dabble in writing, without fear that their career is on the line. Play provides a space and environment to explore, mess up, and connect, without fear of failure taking over. According to psychologist Peter Gray, play functions to teach us to:

1. Develop intrinsically driven interests
2. Learn about rules and problem-solving
3. Regulate our emotions
4. Navigate relationships and make friends
5. Experience joy

Yet, we've increasingly eliminated it for both kids and adults, and the consequences for both are dire. In a 2023 paper published in *The Journal of Pediatrics*, Gray and colleagues compellingly argue that "a primary cause of the rise in mental disorders [in youth] is a decline over decades in opportunities for children and teens to play, roam, and engage in other activities independent of direct oversight and control by adults."

As adults, it's not much better. We often look down on the wanderers. We need our work to be directed, fulfilling some measurable outcome. I'll never forget one day when I was standing in the gym in Albuquerque, New Mexico. It was sixty degrees and sunny outside. The treadmills in the gym were packed, all overlooking a beautiful park with miles of dirt trails across the street. We see exercise as productive work, so we go to the gym and labor through the torture of a treadmill when nature is right there, calling us to explore. Research by Michael Norton and Gabriela Tonietto found that when we see leisure as unproductive, it reduces our enjoyment of that activity. It's no wonder adults are horrible at play.

Stuart Brown of the National Institute for Play defines play as "something done for its own sake," he explains. "It's voluntary, it's pleasurable, it offers a sense of engagement, it takes you out of time. And the act itself is more important than the outcome." With kids, play and obliviousness might be straightforward. But Brown's definition gives us a clue to how adults can utilize the same tactics to improve their mental health while keeping joy and exploration in their lives. We need to take time to do things that aren't meant to be productive, where winning and losing don't really matter, and where you pursue the activity for the joy itself. Join a rec league softball team, have board game nights with the family, and read fiction instead of only reading to learn. Bestselling nonfiction writers I know often dabble in writing fiction in their free time. It may never be published, but it's a way to play in their chosen field: to do something for its own sake.

In your career, give yourself "recess" a few times per day. If you're a musician, dabble with different instruments or genres. Or take note of 3M's 15 percent time rule, which essentially gave the company engineers up to 15 percent of their working hours to explore ideas that have nothing to do with their current projects. The side project time led to Post-it notes when in 1974 engineer Art Fry partnered up with Spencer Silver to figure out a better bookmark for Fry's church choir's hymnals. Google borrowed 3M's time rule, emphasizing 20 percent time in their early days. It's not setting an exact amount of time for side projects that matters. It's sending a signal that it's okay to be off task, to play.

We've convinced ourselves that everything we do has to have a productive outcome. Look no further than what we've done to living our life: we now track and measure everything with our smartwatches and devices. We've turned going for a walk with our dog, taking a nap, or eating breakfast into something we do to get a better score on our activity tracker. The cult of optimization and productivity has converted living life into a job scored by an external measure.

We need to let that go. To give ourselves time to play, even in work. For my writing, I instituted monthly "down the rabbit hole" days, where I spend a few hours going on a deep dive on a topic that caught my interest but wasn't related whatsoever to any project I was currently doing. It might not sound like play, but exploring an interest for the sake of it being interesting is freeing. Play rebalances the experiential and cognitive hierarchy, allowing us to feel and experience instead of becoming numb to our expertise. Taking time to do things with little point besides joy will remind you how to get back into exploration mode where you can be oblivious, free from the harsh comparison points that influence so much of our lives.

KEEP RETURNING TO THE PROCESS

Tom House is a former major league baseball player who, after his playing career finished, became obsessed with solving a specific problem: how to throw. In his illustrious coaching career, he's worked with many of the greatest in history: Nolan Ryan, Randy Johnson, Drew Brees, Tom Brady; it didn't matter if you were throwing a baseball or a football, House was there to help. When he looked at the commonalities between the greats, he noted they were all "Addicted to the process. Winning is a by-product. They get addicted to the process because it's what they can control." When I relayed that success often pulls us toward outcomes and the external, and the greats seem to have the ability to keep this at bay, he replied, "Yes, they stay in the process better than anyone. Wins only take them out of the process for moments." The people who master their craft and pursue it for a long time are able to stay intrinsically driven and point their rage to master on the process of getting better. They don't get lost in the pull of success and accolades. They don't get lost chasing despite achieving more than most could imagine.

In my writing process, I often start my next book project before the current one goes on sale. As you are reading this, chances are I've at least got an outline and am deep in the weeds of researching my next project. This is a simple mechanism to keep me grounded in the process of the work itself. Whether the current book succeeds or fails, I can remind myself that it was the excitement and curiosity of a new idea that propelled me to write the next one, not the outcome of my current book.

ADOPT A QUEST MINDSET

In 2014, performance psychologists Karen Howells and David Fletcher evaluated the history and life stories of world-class swimmers, and a pattern quickly emerged. They started with a performance narrative, a belief that results were nearly all that mattered. Getting faster and winning were prioritized above all else. Suffering and sacrifice were the name of the game. Yet, something changed when they came face to face with adversity. It dislodged the performance narrative.

The adversity didn't have to be swimming-related. For some, it was dealing with mental health issues such as OCD. For others, it was watching their family go through divorce or cancer. For many, it was the sudden overwhelming attention they faced as their stardom increased. At first, the athletes would attempt to maintain normality. They'd hide the trauma, compartmentalize it, push it away. Or double down on their athletic pursuit, escaping the chaos of life by swimming lap after lap in the pool. This sometimes worked in the short term but failed over the long term. As these coping mechanisms failed, they questioned the dominant results and outcome focus. As the prevailing narrative shattered, they started to switch mindsets. Their primary story moved from a performance to a quest narrative. The latter involves "individuals confronting their suffering, accepting the consequences and striving to gain something positive from the experience." The stress had freed them up to see their self and their pursuits in a different light. They were able to make sense of and find meaning in their journey.

It shouldn't come as a surprise that substance abuse programs like Alcoholics Anonymous adopt a similar approach. They take a quest or journey approach, giving people the support and tools to make meaning out of their experience, with recovery ultimately occurring in large part because of an identity change. Like the athletes moving from performance to quest, individuals who struggle with substance abuse make a similar switch. One study concluded, "recovery is best understood as a personal journey of socially negotiated identity transition that occurs through changes in social networks and related meaningful activities. . . . [Research] describing recovery journeys has pointed to the importance of identity change processes, through which the internalized stigma and status of an 'addict identity' is supplanted with a new identity."

When performance is the only thing, we are fragile. A much more sustainable way to make sense of our self and our journey in life is to switch to a quest narrative, which nudges us back toward exploration. Instead of seeking outcomes and any setback as an indicator that we aren't good enough or that we failed, we need to see our life as a bumpy, meandering path with more exploration. We don't know exactly what we'll face, but it's part of the journey of self-discovery. We can find meaning in anything. When we switch our mindsets to one that includes a bit more exploration, we aren't giving up on our performance. We aren't adopting a position where we never go narrow. We are just bringing our exploration versus commitment back in balance. We allow success to find us instead of obsessively searching, seeking, and chasing.

GIVE BACK TO MOVE FORWARD

One of the best ways to remember how to bring joy and to experience life instead of optimizing it is to surround yourself with people who are experts at that. Spend time with those who are starting their journey. Volunteering at a local youth program, team, or school can help bring back exploration and play. By giving back, we get to remember what it's like to be deep in the throes of curiosity and exploration. We get to remember what it was like to explore our interests without thinking about the money or accolades that may come with it. Mentoring helps to shift us from narrow to broad, from me to another focus. And it often reminds you why you got into a pursuit in the first place.

Working in professional sports, it's easy to get cynical and jaded. To prevent that from taking over, I periodically help out or run with local high school kids. Every time, it's a breath of fresh air, a reminder of a purer sport where kids just want to be a part of a team, challenge themselves, and get better. Similarly, I regularly volunteer at the local elementary and junior high science fairs. There's nothing better to realign your perspective than spending time with kids who embody curiosity. We lose our way when we forget what brought us down this path in the first place.

—

When we are young, we're experts at going broad and narrow. We dabble, try on an identity, give a pursuit a go, and maybe even get captured, but then just as easily move on to the next thing. We explore and get obsessed but seldom cement. We are masters of pursuing things for their intrinsic joy, creating games to play with others, keeping the ones that prove entertaining, and ditching the ones that prove dull. We are also a bit oblivious.

As we grow into adults, we become really good at going narrow. We strive for productivity. We deal with boredom and distraction. Our days get routinized and optimized. As we narrow, we get locked into seeking out success. We forget the intrinsic joy and play that pulled us toward getting captured. Instead, the pull of rewards, status, and prestige takes over. And society doubles down, incentivizing us to narrow, focus on performance, and seek out achievement and success. If we stay on this path, we often are met with a double whammy that sends us into survival mode: we lose the fuel that initially propelled us and put all of our meaning and significance into a singular identity.

Again, we need both: broad and narrow. In the right amount, at the right time. We need to be both secure and adaptable. To be committed, and even potentially captured, without cementing. We need to be able to explore and dabble without getting lost for far too long. The goal should be to identify where you are. Where do you fall on the continuum between broad exploration and narrow commitment? Then, put strategies and tactics in place to avoid getting dragged too far, either by your inclinations or the allure of achievement.

The best performers go broad, dabbling and exploring. They follow their interests when something tells them to go a bit deeper. If that subtle narrowing focus moves them from interested to captured, then they know to get out the shovels and start excavating in that area. But they don't get stuck, going deeper and deeper. They climb out of the hole for a break, look around, come up for air, and see if they want to continue down this narrow treasure hunt or explore another path. At some point, they move on and go back to exploring. And repeat this cycle of broad, narrow, pop out, and switch. Put another way, we must be a bit more like a kindergartner—never losing our sense of exploration, our capacity for surprise.

CHAPTER 4

ACCEPT THE MESSINESS OF WHO YOU ARE

I backed out of my garage in the same mindless way that I had thousands of times before. I turned the wheel to straighten the car, ready to head to work, when I heard a noise. *Knock, knock, knock.* Two men dressed in suits tapped on my driver-side window. I rolled the window down, a bit startled and confused. "We're from the FBI. Can we talk?" A flash of a badge, and I pulled back into the garage.

When we talk about courage, we often pinpoint the moment when we take action. When we move from uncertainty to standing up, speaking out, or doing the right thing. Like when I moved from staying quiet to whistleblowing. That moment is vital. But in many ways, we overstate its importance. It's a small step, and what occurs next is often much more difficult.

When I first blew the whistle, I was blissfully naive about what would unfold. I assumed I'd report what I knew to anti-doping officials, let them investigate, and in a year or two, move on with my life. That's not how it went. At times, my life felt like a movie.

There was the time a reporter staked out my house, and another wandered around my work harassing athletes I worked with, as I hid out in my office. There was the endless back and forth with officials, handing over my entire medical records, and taking my lunch break to a nondescript business tower to meet with the FBI. And there was that one time, at a conference where I was presenting in Virginia, when late at night, I snuck out of the dorm we were staying in to rendezvous with a stranger in the parking lot. I handed over my phone and computer so authorities could have a digital copy. Then met them at 6 a.m. the next morning to retrieve my digital life. All I remember thinking is, *someone from the conference is going to see this quick exchange at the break of dawn and think that Magness guy is doing a drug deal.* Ultimately, it culminated in several arbitration and appeal hearings. In total, it took nearly ten years from start to finish. From the age of twenty-six to thirty-six, it consumed my life.

As an athlete, I had the ability to single-mindedly focus on the task at hand. It didn't matter how school, life, or relationships were going; when I lined up to race, I flipped the switch to compete. Regardless of how the rest of my life was, I found comfort in the work. I reveled in it. I believed that my ability to compartmentalize and focus was my superpower that led to success. In other words, to deal with chaos, I'd learned to separate, compartmentalize, and put my head down and work.

I followed the same pattern with whistleblowing. The FBI or some reporter would stake out my house, and then I'd walk into work as if nothing happened. I'd go from meeting with USADA or having the other side's lawyers try to trip me up with a phone call to helping runners at a cross-country meet. I latched on to the approach I knew. I doubled down on the work, narrowing and constricting my world to focus solely on coaching. I'd keep my whistleblowing life separate from my actual life and try to deal with whatever came up. Before my story went public, this was difficult but achievable. But when things went public in 2015, compartmentalization became much more difficult.

I, and the other whistleblowers like Kara Goucher, found ourselves labeled as discontent liars or heroes. There was no in-between. Your friends and acquaintances within a sport that had been a central part of your life quickly split among those who wanted to associate with you, those who were scared to, and those who now hated you. There was no escaping the whistleblowing and the reality of the potentially life-changing impact it would have. I became a point of intrigue and controversy. Almost every job interview I had, from inside the running world to professional sports outside, ended with, "I have to ask you about the Nike situation." Or the time a major organization legitimately asked me if I saw something wrong at their corporation, "Would I blow the whistle to a regulating body or tell my supervisors first?" As one of my grad school advisors told me when the story broke, "Well, I guess you found that thing that you'll be known as for the rest of your life." And he was probably right.

To make matters worse, I was dealing with my own internal discontent. Sure, I did the right thing relatively quickly. But could I have done more or let people know earlier? Why didn't I say no to the infusion I received? Life goes from making sense, where I generally knew who I was, my values, and the actions that aligned with them, to a constant sense-making battle. Much of my strategy early on was to ignore and avoid. I attempted to prove my worth in the sport, to change the narrative from Steve the whistleblower to Steve the coach. I thought success would provide salvation. If I could achieve success in the sport that had become a large part of who I was, it would fill that void. The goalpost was ever-changing and never satisfying.

Compartmentalizing and separating provided temporary relief

but failed over the long haul. As I moved from the acute phase to the seemingly never-ending journey of not knowing when this part of my life would end, it began to feel like my life was on hold. I didn't know what would come of it or what would happen to me. Would I be punished, ostracized, or labeled as a pariah? Prospects within the sport to which I dedicated two degrees and thousands of hours of practice toward perfecting became severely limited. My motivation in my professional life plummeted. In my personal life and relationships, angst, anxiety, and discontent from trying to keep my worries at bay over what would happen seeped over. As an individual, I'd always been introverted and shy, but I carried around a level of inner confidence and security that I could turn on when I needed it. It's where the conviction to blow the whistle came from in the first place. That faded. I was anxious, filled with existential dread, and quite frankly, lost. I'd relied on justification and separation to deal with the messiness of my life. Whatever we avoid festers like a wound. It just grows, turning into a sensitive pain point that we protect. Avoidance turns up the threat alarm.

I was digging my own hole of misery. Instead of dealing with the thing and embracing the messiness of myself and the situation, I tried to flatten my world and myself. Further and further down the hole of living in survival mode, I went. I'm not unique. We are experts at flattening ourselves and others. It's a coping mechanism, just not a very good one.

People are messy. Yet, we do just about everything we can not to deal with the discord. As we learned in chapter 1, when under threat, we can fight and defend, avoid or shut down, narrow and cling, or accept, explore, and update. And too often, our default strategies are to avoid, separate, and narrow instead of accepting and dealing with the thing.

We flatten ourselves and our world so that we can deal with it. We move from 3D to 2D to provide comfort and security. When we flatten, we may temporarily turn off the alarm, as if we are hitting the snooze button, but that alarm will come back blaring. We've told our brain: This thing is so overwhelming, so disconcerting, that we want to get rid of it. Our brain makes note, becoming hyperalert to the threat. One athlete I work with put it well, "It's as if my brain knows that experience was so bad, I don't want to be there." We trade short-term artificial security and clarity for long-term fragility. We develop poor coping mechanisms for discrepancies in our self.

We need to find a better solution to dealing with the messiness of ourselves. One that provides security and flexibility over the long haul. We need to find coherence without full-blown delusion. To learn to coexist with our contradictory points without losing our minds. To free ourselves up to perform, to see the world clearly, we need to deal with our discrepancies in the right way. How we weave our contradictions, flaws, and missteps into our story impacts whether we live in survival mode or turn down the alarm. It's time to make sense of the messiness of being ourselves. Instead of flattening, we need to, first, get complex and, then, integrate the messiness.

MOVING FROM 2D TO 3D

"Be obsessed or be average," advises entrepreneur Grant Cardone. "Toss plan B overboard," suggests Harvard Business School fellow Matt Higgins. Centuries before these men, military strategist Sun Tzu wrote, "When your army has crossed the border, you should burn your boats and bridges, in order to make it clear to everybody that you have no hankering after home." Going all-in is common advice for pushers of all kinds, from athletes to entrepreneurs to artists. We see it in our religion of workism, in hyperspecialization in sports, and in the belief of many parents that their children need to have a future career path and college major decided at eighteen or else they will fall far behind.

For much of my life, I believed in this credo. In a September 2002 entry in my high school running log, I marked that I'd run fifteen miles that day and left a comment with the typical overly dramatic flair of a teenager, "I don't go out, I don't party, I don't live the life of a normal teen. Is this even living? Why do it? I want to be the best. I will not settle for mediocrity. I will take my body through hell, testing its limits." Teenage Steve was certainly obsessive, and he was convinced that going all-in was the key to success. He was mostly wrong.

According to a fifteen-year study of more than five thousand entrepreneurs, those who kept their day job were 33 percent less likely to fail. The same holds true for athletes. Those who specialize early, going all-in on one sport, tend to be worse off over the long haul than their compatriots who dabbled in other activities and specialized later. A 2021 meta-analysis evaluating over six thousand athletes across a variety of sports found that those athletes who made it to world-class, when compared to those who were good but not great, tended to have more multisport than specialized practice, start their primary sport later, accumulate less practice time, and progress slightly slower. As author David Epstein explained in his excellent book *Range*, diversity is an advantage.

It's not just about specialization. According to research out of Michigan State University that looked at over one hundred years of Nobel Prize–winning scientists, it turned out that what they did in their downtime, away from the lab, may have proved vital. Nobel winners were more likely to have hobbies or creative interests outside of their research. Compared to less accomplished peers, the distinguished scientists were twenty-two times more likely to perform, sing, or act; twelve times more likely to pursue creative writing; and about seven times more likely to participate in a craft like sculpting, painting, or glassblowing. Their less accomplished peers were more likely to be entirely focused on their scientific research.

Going all-in leads to a simple inner narrative. "I am a scientist." We turn down the volume on our other roles or versions of ourselves. Sure, we may still be a dad or enjoy playing poker, but it's clear to ourselves and others that what truly matters is the thing we are obsessed with. Our brain has gotten the message.

Singular focus isn't the only way we flatten ourselves. Take our use of labels. They help us make sense of our experiences and self, providing us with security and an explanation. When I learned what obsessive compulsive disorder (OCD) was, it offered a sense of relief that I've seldom experienced in my life. I went from the kid who was sure he was a bit crazy, thanks to the strange intrusive thoughts I'd had since the age of five, to someone who wasn't alone and had an explanation for why it occurred. It was liberating and freeing, moving me from crazy to human.

But, the same labels that help us can get in our way. They simplify the complex into bite-size usable pieces of information. And if we hold on to those labels tightly, making them self-defining pieces of who we are, moving from providing some security to being cemented and attached, they become a threat enhancer. I saw it with myself.

With a diagnosis, I could brush off any criticism of a behavior as just part of my OCD. It gave me permission to stop trying to work on some of the behaviors that came with it. It was as if my mind went "That's just my OCD. It's who I am. Deal with it" instead of realizing that I could still improve how I navigated many of the accompanying behaviors. On the flip side, for some time, I became hyperdefensive of what felt like "my" disorder. I'd get upset if someone referred to OCD nonchalantly, taking the downplaying of the disorder as a threat against me and everyone who shared the disorder. What I came to learn, though, was that it wasn't that person's problem. It was mine. The more possessive I felt of the label, the worse it made my experience with the disorder.

Recent research suggests overidentification with labels is pervasive in the social media generation. A number of studies have found that mental health interventions in schools, such as various behavioral therapies, either don't help or backfire. Researchers found that a program called WISE teens that delivered an evidence-based dialectical behavioral therapy to students led to worse symptoms of anxiety and depression. How could something that is supposed to help do the opposite? As clinical psychologist Darby Saxbe wrote, "By focusing teenager's attention on mental health issues, these interventions may have unwittingly exacerbated their problems . . . greater awareness of mental illness leads people to talk of normal life struggles in terms of 'symptoms' and 'diagnoses.'" Awareness is great, but when we're inundated with constant streams of information telling us to focus on a problem, our brain gets the message, turning up the volume to validate that label or identity. What we give attention to gains in value. Too much attention on just about anything can make it seem like the only thing that matters. There's value to knowledge and helping people understand. But if we let the label flatten us and become self-defining, all we're doing is priming our defensive mechanism, turning up our inner alarm. We need a balance of awareness, without attachment.

In survival mode, we overidentify to provide temporary security. It's not just our self-identities but also our social ones. Research shows we treat the groups we are part of the same way. We overidentify or resort to a dominance strategy where one group overpowers all others we belong to in terms of importance. Look at our social media profiles: Republican, Democrat, mental health disorders, trauma, pronouns, or athletic identity. We use labels in our profiles to describe who we are, where we belong, and what we care about. Many of these labels can be useful, but too often, in a world that pushes us to survival mode, we shift the balance from feeling secure to overly attached.

Labels get rid of the messy details so that we have a cheat sheet for understanding ourselves and others. They are a shortcut for judgment and understanding. But, often, those messy details are necessary. We can't throw them to the wayside without losing something important. There's a balance to be had. Overidentification with labels is a symptom of the flattening of our world and self. When we reduce ourselves to two dimensions, it provides temporary relief, but it makes us fragile.

When we flatten ourselves, we score low on two measures of complexity: social and self. Social identity complexity refers to whether we can hold multiple group identities at once. You can be both a jock on the football team and a science nerd on the competitive engineering club. They are a both part of you, instead of keeping them separate or letting one take over and denying the other. Self-complexity is at the individual level. It's the ability to see yourself in a multifaceted way. That you have different roles or sub selves, and that there are important distinctions among them. A woman might be a mother, a wife, an artist, a student, or a doctor, and with each one comes different traits (i.e., smart, funny, diligent, caring). The more varied and distinct the roles and traits that come with them, the more complexity we have.

When individuals score low on complexity, they have much wider swings of mood and emotions. Their self-worth is like a ping-pong ball, bouncing back and forth, entirely dependent on whether that narrow self gets validated or rewarded or not. They are more likely to be anxiously attached in relationships and have lower self-esteem. On the other end of the spectrum, higher levels of complexity buffer the effects of stress and any perceived threat to our status. We can withstand threats because our coaching self might be under threat, but our value of being a husband, teacher, or mentor provides us the security we need. We can be both content and determined, depending on the situation. We can move from one identity to another, turning up the dial and importance on one and minimizing the one that seems to be dragging us down right now.

We reaffirm our value. This turns down the threat by reminding us that we have worth elsewhere. It can be within the same field—after a rejection notice from an editor, we look at what people we admire have said about our work. Or it can be from something completely unrelated—we messed up at work, but we remind ourselves of all the good we did last week volunteering to feed the homeless at our church. We trade uncertainty in one domain for certainty in another. We might feel a bit of angst, but we deal with that by assuring ourselves that a different action we took supersedes the prior one.

Chances are you've had a teacher or boss tell you that your work just wasn't good enough. It happened to me my freshman year of college. An academic advisor suggested my writing wasn't up to par, that I needed to take a remedial course. As someone who thought writing was a strong point, I was left confused. In an experiment out of Saint Louis University, they put this common experience to the test.

Participants were given a test that they were told was predictive of career success. Little did they know, the test was rigged, with many of the questions unsolvable. After the test, experimenters told the participants some variation of, "You didn't do as well as we usually expect students to do, so I guess that was pretty tough for you." They were invoking failure and the emotional sting that comes with it. The students who saw themselves as bright coming in, now faced an academic telling them that they weren't as smart as they thought. And their future was dim. But the real point of the exercise came next.

They were given a second chance. Take the test again with some time to regroup and practice if they wanted. Researchers found that those with greater self-complexity practiced more, regardless of what they felt or were told by the researchers. Those who scored lower on self-complexity practiced less, and it was more dependent on their mood and what the researchers told them. In other words, when everything around them was telling them they weren't good enough, they listened. They stopped trying. The authors gave the conclusion away in the study's title, "Effort or Escape: Self-Concept Structure Determines Self-Regulatory Behavior." Those low in self-complexity hit the escape button.

When there's a discrepancy between who you think you are and the feedback coming in, those low in complexity default toward protect or avoid. They hear the academic advisor telling them their writing is poor, and instead of figuring out how to get better, they shield themselves from the angst. In my case, fortunately, I didn't see myself as a writer, so the critique didn't cut too deep. While I didn't take the course, I practiced with the help of mentors, which is partially why you're reading this book now.

Elite performers are experts at using complexity to enhance performance. Baseball superstar Aaron Judge transforms into someone else on game day. As he told writer Sam Borden, "I'm in here right now, and I'm Aaron—I'm hanging out with you, right? But you know, when I step out there, you have to be somebody else. Because maybe Aaron, in this moment, might be scared. But No. 99? He isn't afraid at all." He's putting space between his everyday self and his performing self. It's a way to ensure he doesn't take the full brunt of the pressure of performing in front of thousands of fans.

Judge isn't alone in this. Kobe Bryant had the Black Mamba persona, and Diego Maradona distinguished between his two names. As Maradona's fitness coach, Fernando Signorini, relayed, "I learnt that there was Diego and there was Maradona. Diego was a kid who had insecurities, a lovely boy. Maradona was the character he came up with to face the demands of the football business and media." Sports psychologist Dan Abrahams calls this putting on a game face. In order to adopt a game face, we have to recognize our complexity. To understand that we have different roles and that John or Hazel at home isn't the same person who steps out on stage. This allows us to protect ourselves from a loss on the field.

But there's a danger with game faces. As Abrahams explained when describing Maradona, "Occasionally that aggressiveness spilled into unfair and unnecessary play at times (sometimes even violence)." Or take the example of Johnny Manziel, who became Johnny Football, a free-flowing, risk-taking athlete. As Manziel described, "I wanted to be Johnny Football. Johnny Football never had a bad time." Unfortunately, never having a bad time meant excessive drugs, alcohol, and parties off the field. Our alter egos can backfire.

We all have different roles. They can work great in specific situations. Transforming into "99" can help during the three hours of a baseball game. But there is a cost to switching between father, writer, actor, or musician identities, much like there is a cost to switching our attention in an attempt to multitask. When we have to flip identities too frequently, it can make us feel lost or fragmented. And unlike with a baseball game, most of us don't have that distinct transition where we leave our persona behind. It seeps into the rest of our lives. Or if we create too much space between the person on stage and our everyday self, it can leave us feeling disjointed and fragmented.

We move from a persona or compartmentalized self to a facade. As actress Brit Marling reflected on her work, it's "the fear of revealing oneself honestly to someone. It's easier to take on a cover identity, and if that cover identity is rejected, then you—who you truly are—remains intact. Maybe on some level it's all connected to the idea that, if you go in honestly and you're seen as who you are, that might not be enough." For those of us who aren't performers, we may experience this as rationalizing our cheating in the workplace, with our attending church on Sunday. Our reaffirming that we are good, decent people on Sunday allows us to be a jerk during the weekday.

Research out of the University of Waterloo found that self-complexity alone isn't related to improved well-being, but the authenticity of the various selves is. It's not enough to have various roles that are important. We need them to be authentic, to feel like this particular aspect of our identity reflects who we truly are and that it makes sense holistically. This means that Aaron Judge and "99" overlap enough where they aren't butting heads. But the man who is godly on the weekend but a terror during the week, not so much.

We need complexity. In a world that pushes us to flatten, to avoid, or get rid of the messiness, to be singularly focused to succeed, complexity is more important than ever. It's like a safety net for our self. Look, if you are at war, you might want to burn the boats because it's either win or lose everything. But most of the challenges we face aren't life-or-death battles. It's akin to activating an extreme stress response as if a lion is in front of us. Most of us perform better when our backs aren't against the wall and fear isn't driving the ship. But as we've learned, complexity alone isn't enough. It sets the stage, but to thrive, we need to be complex and integrated instead of separated.

PUTTING THE PUZZLE TOGETHER

"When I was little, my uncle and aunt went to the airport and came back with a new person. I didn't recognize him. It was my dad." Jemal Wote grew up in Asasa, a small town of about 10,000 people that sits at 7,700 feet altitude in central Ethiopia. At the time, nearly 70 percent of Ethiopians were in extreme poverty. When Jemal was too young to remember, his dad left to find a better life for his family. When Jemal was in sixth grade, his dad returned, to take his family on a nearly ten-thousand-mile journey to relocate to Houston, Texas.

Jemal is outgoing and jovial, quick to crack a smile and a joke. He's at ease around people. Growing up in Ethiopia he was surrounded by friends and family. Connecting with others came naturally. When his family arrived in Texas, schools were closed for winter break. For the first time in his life, he felt alone and trapped. "It was hard. I was like an eighty-year-old man. It was just me and my sisters stuck inside. We had no friends. We were scared to leave the house." School provided hope, as Jemal recalled, "I was excited to start school, but while I knew how to read some English, I didn't know how to speak or understand it. I'd sit in the classroom, lost. I didn't understand what was going on. Everything was so different. I was also trying to fit in. I missed my home and friends." The toughest part, was just trying to find his place. He was plopped down into the fourth largest city in the US, inundated with American culture. It rightfully felt foreign. He was unsure how to navigate it. He desperately wanted to fit in, but didn't know exactly what that meant. How do you embrace the new without losing the old? This is the plight of the immigrant. Your world, culture, and self are violently shaken in an instant, and you have to decide how to put the pieces together.

At first, Jemal took refuge in a small community of Ethiopian ex-pats, where they celebrated traditional holidays and gave him the comfort of home. But in his school hallways his horizons and peer group slowly expanded. First, to a large group of immigrants from a variety of countries, who found common ground in their pursuit of trying to learn English and find their footing. He had others who understood the struggle. But Jemal didn't stop there. He kept expanding. First, through the common language of sports.

Initially, Jemal gave his sporting love, basketball, a try. Despite growing up idolizing LeBron James, the rail thin five-foot, ten-inch Wote didn't quite measure up on the court. Jemal found his footing when he blended old and new, taking up a sport with a deep heritage and pride in his native land: running. But he wasn't thinking about imitating Ethiopian running legends Haile Gebrselassie or Kenenisa Bekele. "The reason I initially ran wasn't to compete. I just wanted to be a part of the team. One of the seniors came up to me after my first season and said, 'We need you. You're the missing piece to help our team be great.'" He'd go on to qualify for the state meet, lead his team to much success, eventually earn a college scholarship, and complete his degree, while being named his conference's most outstanding performer on the track.

Every immigrant is faced with a choice: How do I navigate such a rapid and large change? How do I make sense of myself and the journey, holding both my heritage and the new place I'm thriving at? Jemal had expanded his horizons, but he didn't forget his heritage. He didn't try to keep them separate, either, making it a point to share his experiences with his friends and teammates. "It was a slow transition. I felt like I was growing, not leaving anything behind. Some items that I hold deeply, like my religion and values, have persisted with only minor changes. But I've also embraced American culture, music, and celebrations. I feel it's a bit like what I did in running. I just kept trying to learn and grow. At each new school, I'd try to bring with me what seemed to work, and then mix in whatever I was learning from others. The magic was when I combined those two together. It's the same with my culture and life. It's a journey to a cohesive story. I'm still trying to figure out who this Jemal guy is."

Our cultural heritage shapes who we are. It grounds us, providing norms and expectations for how we talk, what we eat, and what we value. But for immigrants or those who are multicultural, there's often a tug-of-war going on between their heritage and their new country or culture. How do you keep old traditions while fitting in with the new? There are a variety of hats to wear and narrative stories to pull from. Immigrants are undoubtedly complex. But how they deal with that complexity impacts their adjustment. Do they keep things separate, only bringing out the traditions around family while donning the new culture to peers? Or do they leave the old ones hidden away? Or maybe they mix the styles? How we handle our different roles impacts our well-being.

When dealing with our different cultural identities, we can categorize, compartmentalize, or integrate. Categorization occurs when you choose one identity over the other. It's the person who neglects their cultural heritage, choosing to adopt the norms of their new country. Categorization is about simplifying to avoid conflict and force coherence. It's a zero-sum world. I choose A so that I can ignore or not deal with B.

Compartmentalization is a slightly more complex strategy that involves acknowledging that one has two distinct cultural identities but keeping them separate and distinct. These individuals may celebrate their native heritage when family visits but make no mention of it when out with their new peers. They wear one hat at school or when out with friends another at home or church, carefully minimizing crossover. The context determines what identity is activated. Compartmentalization is about separating and narrowing to minimize conflict and achieve a more fragile variety of coherence.

Integration is about reconciling, connecting, and making sense of your different cultural identities. It's about acknowledging the differences but then seeing how they may complement and enhance each other. It's seeing power in the complexity. That these two sides of you can work together instead of battle. Integration occurs when individuals feel that they belong to different cultural groups and organize multiple identities within themselves to form one coherent supraidentity. It's having different roles but understanding how they fit together in a cohesive and unified way.

Research shows that those who integrate have higher levels of well-being and resilience, as well as a sense of coherence and meaning in their life. Psychologists Magdalena Mosanya and Anna Kwiatkowski summarized that "accepting all cultural paradigms within oneself can help boost competencies, leading to better adjustment." It's important to note that integration is a two-way street. It's not just dependent on the immigrant's understanding and growth. It's about those who interact with the migrants expanding, learning, and growing as well.

We all aren't immigrants like Jemal. But, we all face the same problem, it's the core of our identity. How we make it all fit together—from our job to hobbies to social roles—goes a long way in determining whether we can thrive, or simply survive. In the short-term, avoidance is much easier. But it leaves us fragile and less resilient in the long run. That holds true whether we're dealing with mistakes we've made, trying to find our place in a new land, or trying to fit together our drive to be great at work and home.

Integration is a sense-making process. It's coming to terms with the discrepancies in our lives. Not by pushing them away or avoiding the messy parts but by seeing how they fit in holistically. The problem is that we often amplify our contradictions. We cheated once; therefore, we are a cheater. Our essay got rejected; we must be a poor writer. In contrast with integration, we're trying to find the rightful place for our story. For many items, that means making it a sentence or a paragraph, not a whole story. For more critical items, it's understanding they may be a chapter, but they fit in with the rest of your life's journey. As psychiatrist Julie Holland wrote in her book *Good Chemistry*, "The only way not to fall apart is to come together; this is known as integration. Getting all the facets of the self to work together is a necessary step for emotional health and authenticity. You can't afford to shelter a saboteur among your fractured selves. This is why the idea of a unified self is so crucial. Self-hatred comes from a split somewhere."

In 2018, Kate Courtney won the mountain bike world championships. She was the first American to do so in seventeen years. As Courtney told me in an interview, "My superpower is being able to grind." But what often makes us great can transform into our worst enemy. Heading into the 2020 Olympics as one of the favorites, her cycling performance fell apart. With the delay of the Olympics and having to run through the media gauntlet for years instead of a confined period, when she reached the starting line, her energy wasn't there. She finished fifteenth.

Worn out and disappointed, Courtney didn't do what most athletes do in those moments, double down and work harder; she went the other direction. "When you have a more well-rounded life, it doesn't take away, it doesn't distract you as an athlete. It makes you stronger and better. And able to have a clear head when you get the opportunity to line up." To rebuild her motivation and to have a better relationship with a sport she loved, she went toward joy and mastery. A large part of that was expanding instead of constricting who she was. She told me, "Having a connection to that ability to be more than what you are on the bike. I bring who I am to the bike. But the bike does not make me who I am."

It's that tricky balance we've wrestled with this entire chapter. How much space is between who we are and what we do? How do we bring our diverse experiences and pursuits to our other aspects of life? Courtney explained, "It's important to recognize the broader picture. Not just of cycling but as me as a person . . . [There is] what you do and who you are. That what you do, I'm a bike racer, I do all these different things. The who you are is, I'm a daughter, a wife, a dog mom, is not as important as how you are. The ways of expressing yourself through the what and who is what really matters. How do I want to show up on the bike. And how do I want to show up as who I am?" As Shannon Lee, the daughter of famed martial artist Bruce Lee, expressed in *Be Water, My Friend*, "What you do and who you are is not as important as how you express your 'what' and your 'who' in everything you do. How are you being . . . To embody an idea, a practice, a value or concept is to integrate it into your being."

Courtney found her joy in training and competing again. As of this writing, she's moved from being ranked twenty-third in the world in 2021 to eighth in the summer of 2023. We might think of this as achieving balance in life, but I like to think of it as harmony. Courtney still trains an unbelievable amount. She still cares deeply about the sport and has an ability to grind. While balance implies being good at all things at once, or holding pursuits or roles relatively equal, harmony sends a different message. Harmony is about fitting things together in a way that amplifies or supports one another. In relationships and groups, harmony is about fitting different personalities, opinions, or interests together in a way that welcomes mutual respect and cooperation. We could call it coherence, harmony, or congruence, but what we are doing is making sense of the messy parts of our lives. We need to add up—not perfectly, but good enough so that our story makes sense. Not by narrowing, separating, or avoiding, but by embracing our complexity and integrating that into our story.

FULLY ADDING UP

When Doug Bopst was in elementary school, his parents got divorced. As he told me one afternoon, "It made me so anxious. I'd look around at my friends and ask, 'Why are their parents still together?'" So he did what many kids do and found a prized pastime: sports. Whether it was collecting trading cards, playing, or just simply obsessing over them, Doug was all-in on sports. But as he played a variety of games, he became aware that his love of them didn't translate into success on the field. His peers' skills were evident, even when they didn't care as much as Doug. As he reached his teen years, Doug felt increasingly less than. He started putting on weight and didn't know where he fit in at school or home. "Your identity at that age, as a boy trying to become a man is based on sports, status in school, if girls are interested or not. . . . I had none of that. I was the boy who got bullied, who tried to fit in but was largely the butt of the jokes. I remember asking, 'What's wrong with me?'"

At fourteen, Doug finally found peace. As he relayed to me, "The first time I was comfortable with myself was when I started smoking weed. It numbed everything. Soon, I was addicted to that feeling." At eighteen, he added cocaine to the mix, chasing the euphoric feeling that temporarily transformed him into a confident person who felt like he could do anything. Shortly after that, opioids took hold. A few Percocets to numb the pain grew to "enough to kill a horse."

Nothing knocked him off this path. Not when he was kicked out of his mother's house at sixteen, nor when he barely graduated high school. Not the panic attack and ER visit following cocaine use one day. Not even when because of drug use "half my nostril was missing, and I didn't have a bowel movement for nearly a month." Doug was in a dark place.

"Drugs filled a void," Doug says. It wasn't just the numbing of the world or the rush of energy and confidence that cocaine provided. "I was addicted to the community. . . . When I started dealing, it was the first time people started to say, 'Doug's the guy!' . . . I clung to the community of users to feel included. It was a place I felt at home. . . . It filled this void, a wanting-to-be-loved void."

At twenty-one, Doug got pulled over by a cop for driving his car with a busted headlight. Doug knew his life was about to change. As the police found drugs in his car, all he could think about was, "How did I get here? How did the kid who just wanted to be loved, who just wanted to fit in, who just wanted to feel like he was a normal kid, get into the back of a cop car?" He'd have plenty of time to wrestle with that, as a few weeks later, Doug was sentenced to ninety days of jail with five years of probation.

"Why are you here?" Doug's cellmate, Erik, asked him one day. Doug detailed his story, blaming his childhood, his parents' divorce, his peers, and just about anybody but himself. Erik interrupted, "You have two choices. You can look in the mirror and say you got yourself here, and it's up to you to change. No one's coming to save you. Or . . . you can go cry in the corner, blame everybody else for your problems, say woe is me, and feel sorry for yourself."

"That conversation saved my life," Doug says. Soon after, an overweight and out-of-shape Doug committed to changing his identity. "I wanted more. And it started with changing my habits and behaviors to become the person I knew I wanted to be." Following Erik's lead, Doug began working out. When he started, he couldn't even jog or do push-ups from his knees. But he committed to doing the basics a little better, to take action toward a better self.

Exercise allowed Doug to get comfortable with his feelings and emotions. It provided him a way to process what he was going through—"to transform pain into something meaningful, and to give me a way to cope effectively with stress." It allowed him to make progress at something to build confidence and self-worth. To show himself that he was capable of change. "I cried for obvious reasons because I didn't want to go in. And then when I left, I cried because I didn't want to leave."

Exercise had changed Doug's life. It gave him hope and a future. When he got out of jail, he started to put his life back together. He became a personal trainer, helping others transform their bodies and self. He lost nearly fifty pounds, stayed sober, held down a job, and got his life back on track.

On the outside, Doug was the epitome of success, overcoming an addiction and turning his life around. But the void didn't go away. "Eventually, the fitness identity got stale. I was still angry." Doug suffered from orthorexia, an obsession with healthy eating and living. He was chasing the ideal body and self. "I was afraid if I did anything that resembled old Doug, I would lose everything I gained." Fitness was wonderful. It saved Doug's life. But it became a crutch, striving for unrealistic perfection in a narrow area. "I was chasing external validation, a false idol."

Doug didn't find peace until he "made fitness part of my life, but not my whole life. Fitness became my identity instead of Doug being the identity. I had to change that." The thing that had helped save his life had also gotten in the way. Doug realized he was trying to fill that inner void and discontent with some version of external perfection. "I had to make peace with what I had done and been through. I had to reconcile my past, present, and future. . . . I had to acknowledge that there are still flaws in my personality, in my life, and it's just trying to dance with them the best that I can so that I can not only harness them but improve my relationship with them." Through acceptance, forgiveness, and gratitude, Doug was slowly able to find the inner peace he needed. He became spiritual and started *The Adversity Advantage* podcast to help tell stories of how to deal with life's challenges. He kept up his fitness and personal training but learned how to skip a day or indulge in dessert occasionally. He stopped chasing external validation and a false ideal of who he could be. He learned to let go of perfection and accept and control what he could. "I had to learn that it wasn't as much the fitness or pursuit I was doing that helped. It was the way I was fueling that pursuit." He learned to integrate what had occurred and what truly mattered most. In his words, it's "inner strength . . . I'm on a journey to discover more about myself every day."

The world is chaotic and stressful. We can head down the wrong path without even knowing it. Doug ended up in the back of a cop car, wondering how a kid who just wanted to be loved ended up sitting there. In my experience with whistleblowing, there were so many late nights where I asked myself, *How did I go from being a teenager who loved running and despised cheaters like Lance Armstrong to finding myself smack dab in the middle of a sporting scandal?* Perhaps you've experienced a similar conundrum at some point. Maybe it was crossing an ethical line or performing work you never thought you would. Or perhaps you saw getting into your dream college as setting you down a path that never materialized.

We like our stories simple, to make sense and to add up. But that's not realistic. We aren't in first grade anymore. Our journeys are bumpy, winding, and complicated. Often, they don't seem to make sense. We look back and wonder how that young adult ended up here. It's tempting to find coherence through simplification, avoidance, and rationalization, and to fill the void that comes with insecurity or lack of adding up with some external marker or measure. But as Doug shows us, that's a fool's errand. Contentment and the proper motivational fuel come from recognizing the messiness, seeing ourselves as complex individuals, and integrating those many selves. It's adding up, not perfectly like some fairytale, but in a way that allows us to learn and grow from our experiences. It's part of getting wise.

GET COMPLEX AND INTEGRATE

It's really hard to be real. Venture onto social media or spend enough time in the self-help aisle of the book store and you'll be inundated with the message to be yourself. Being authentic is a worthy endeavor, of course. But, as we've seen, too often we get to "real" by taking a short-cut. It's much easier to ignore, compartmentalize, and simplify our sense of self than to deal with the chaos. We need to learn how to embrace and deal with the messy parts, instead of creating this false requirement of an ideal self that simply doesn't exist. There are three keys to dealing with the messiness in a productive manner:

1. Accept with self-compassion
2. Be someone
3. Integrate the messiness

ACCEPT WITH SELF-COMPASSION

We are our own worst critics. We tear ourselves down with an inner voice that we wouldn't apply to our worst enemy. We beat ourselves up with a near barrage of "we aren't good enough" thoughts. Our inner dialogue spirals out of control, and we fall into a self-inflicted negativity cycle, where emotions and self-talk interact to continue pushing us further and further down.

When researchers out of the University of Manitoba set out to explore why we aren't kinder to ourselves, they noted a trend: We fear self-compassion. Being kind to ourselves, especially in a competitive world, is often seen as a sign of weakness. A signal that you are excusing yourself out of the failure and that the only way to get better is to harness your inner middle-school gym teacher who tried to "motivate" you by putting you down. It didn't work well coming from Coach Johnson, and it doesn't work well coming from coach you. And the truth is, being compassionate to yourself isn't a weakness. It's courage.

Clinical psychologists Neil Clapton and Syd Hiskey studied compassion in an unlikely place: the world of competitive martial arts. At first, combative sport might seem like a strange way to research something more associated with empathy and kindness. But if we view compassion through the lens of the affective neuroscience we covered in chapter 2, it's linked to our contentment and care emotional system. We see our newborn baby crying and jump in to soothe their distress. We see the competitor broken down, crying after a competition, and we put our arm around them and offer words of comfort. Compassion is seeing discomfort and helping relieve it.

According to Clapton and Hiskey, "at the core of compassion is *courage* and *wisdom*, in terms of (1) courageous willingness and emotional strength to turn toward, empathically engage with and tolerate distress; and (2) dedication to learn and develop skills . . . to take wise action in alleviating . . . suffering." It takes courage to have empathy, understanding, and care toward yourself and others.

Psychologist Laura Ceccarelli and colleagues found that when they taught athletes to utilize self-compassion, it changed not only their psychology but also their physiology. In one study, they had a group of national-level athletes visualize a time when they had failed, all while monitoring their nervous system reaction, along with a number of psychological surveys. The subjects' heart rate variability (HRV), a measure of parasympathetic nervous system (PNS) activity, dropped significantly when they visualized a past failure. This was a clear sign that they were experiencing a stress response, as the body generally sees a drop in the PNS and an increase in the sympathetic nervous system during times of stress. When athletes utilized self-compassion, their drop in HRV was dampened.

In addition, self-compassion led to more adaptive behavioral reactions (i.e., whether they would take steps to fix their performance or not) and fewer negative feelings and maladaptive thoughts. And what if the athletes had a mindset that led to fear of self-compassion, where they thought being kind to oneself was a sign of weakness? That was linked to maladaptive thoughts and negative behavioral reactions. Compassion, it would seem, allows us to stay with the discomfort or distress we are experiencing long enough to process or deal with it instead of avoiding it.

BE SOMEONE

As I drove into work, I'd often pass underneath a railroad bridge that went over Houston's busy and traffic-filled I-45. In giant teal block letters on the side of the bridge was a message: BE SOMEONE.

It showed up in 2012 and has become one of Houston's most photographed landmarks—a giant piece of graffiti that an artist had to complete in the middle of the night, with a lookout, while hanging off the side of a bridge that trains still use. It's such a cultural icon in the city that Houston rapper Paul Wall has the slogan tattooed across his chest. When asked about the graffiti, the artist behind it said, "I get it. It's vandalism, but it's in a different sense, too, if you just take those words and apply it to yourself, it might mean something to you."

What does it mean to be someone? We all have a need for significance, respect, or status. It's human nature. But being some-one reaches beyond status. It doesn't mean achieving fame and fortune. It's something much more basic and internal. It's feeling that our life is meaningful and that we are competent. When we lose or fail, our sense of being someone is often lost. Our sense of competency and self-worth plummets. Fortunately, there's an easy way back.

Ryan Holiday is a prolific and bestselling author. He's largely responsible for the reemergence and popularity of Stoic philoso-phy, bringing to light ancient wisdom from Marcus Aurelius and Seneca. Through his writing, he's become a source of deep think-ing and practical advice on navigating life's difficulties. When I interviewed Ryan, I wanted to know about something much closer to my heart: his exercise habits.

Ryan is not only an avid runner, but a quite good one. He was known to click off near six-minute miles for eight miles on an easy run, a feat that takes serious talent, training, and effort. Yet, Ryan doesn't race. "The activity is the goal. . . . I have enough compe-tition in my life through my work that trying to win at my hobby isn't one of my life priorities," he told me. Then what's the point of the near-daily run or exercise? "You want to have something that you win at every day that is within your control. And something that challenges you outside the mold of what you're doing profes-sionally every day."

We thrive in life when we are challenged but not threatened, when we have the freedom to take risks, to stretch our limits, to feel what it means to be alive. In our major pursuits, the balance between challenge and threat often sways toward the latter. As we've seen, if our job or craft means a lot, we derive our sense of self from it, even if we have learned to put a bit of space between who we are and what we do. Thankfully, there's another solution: diversifying your sources of meaning and competency.

According to recent research, our foundational needs are substitutable. If you are feeling down or despondent because your work lacks meaning, finding purpose at home with your family or in your spiritual pursuits stems the tide, dampening down the negative impact that lacking meaning in your work normally provides. Psychologists refer to this as fluid compensation. When a psychological need is under threat in one area, we look to satisfy it elsewhere, which largely works. This compensation helps us get through difficult periods of our lives. It's not a long-term solution, but it works well for dealing with an acute failure. It doesn't just work for attacks on our sense of meaning but also our sense of self-esteem, identity, competency, autonomy, and sense of belonging.

Choose something that consistently builds you up, that acts as a restoring and grounding agent to remind you that you are worthy, competent, and capable of doing difficult things. It doesn't have to be an exercise habit. As Holiday suggested to me, "If I had a very physical profession, you would want some relaxed still practice, like reading or meditating or yoga that forces you to be still in a different way." Or, as famed neuroendocrinologist Robert Sapolsky has noted, "We can be part of multiple hierarchies. And while you may be low ranking in one of them, you could be high ranking in another. You have the crappiest job in your corporation, but you're the captain of the softball team for the company. You better bet that's somebody who's going to find all sorts of ways that 9 to 5, Monday through Friday, is just stupid paying the bills. What really matters is the prestige on the weekend." We can use our storytelling machinery to our advantage. Not necessarily to delude, but to make sure that if we fail in the main thing, we don't spiral to oblivion.

Diversifying your sources of meaning and challenging yourself in areas that are within your control are all examples of building a robust self, one that can buffer against the constant attacks we face from living in a world that constantly reminds us that we aren't as good as everyone else. Take up a hobby where you don't face constant comparison. Adopt a practice that allows you to see consistent progress. Instead of striving to be the king of social media, try to become the hero of your neighborhood, the person who people can rely on to help fix a leak or the dad who is always up for a neighborhood pickup hoops game. If you don't feel like you are making a difference in your work, be a regular volunteer at your local food bank.

When there is little space between what you do and who you are, we go a bit nuts when we feel under threat. We flip out, throw tantrums, retreat, stop trying, or become apathetic. The way to fight back isn't to double down or further insulate. It's to diversify. A diverse array of experiences creates a resilient self, and research shows it leads to a happier, healthier you. Diversify yourself. That's the true key to being someone.

INTEGRATE THE MESSINESS

We're expert storytellers. We weave our behaviors and actions into a much larger story. We quickly explain why we did or didn't get the promotion or why our girlfriend broke up with us. We're great writers but very poor editors. A great editor takes what's there and makes it clearer, bringing out the author's voice instead of replacing it.

We see this in how we deal with traumas. A traumatic memory gets lodged in our brain, pushing us to panic or feel depressed whenever something triggers us. One of the more effective approaches to dealing with trauma is to write about it. Social psychologist James Pennebaker has been studying the effects of writing on trauma since the 1980s. Writing about our experiences and what we're feeling enhances well-being, helps us cope with stress, increases resilience, and reduces depressive symptoms. It's been used successfully to help with PTSD, depression, and life-threatening illnesses like cancer. Neuroscience research has found that expressive writing alters our brain activation in areas linked to processing negative emotions.

One of the reasons it works is that it allows us to deal with the emotional experience with some space. It doesn't feel as real as when we vividly recall the trauma. When we write, we have to slow down. We can take different perspectives, and we are in control. We can edit the story. It allows us to confront the things we've often tried to compartmentalize or ignore.

When it comes to benefiting from writing, the more expressive we are, the better. Expressive writing works via confronting the thing, not avoiding it. And most important, we don't just need to confront the experience but make sense of it. Psychologist Susan Lutgendorf found that to get the benefits of expressive writing, we must make sense of the difficult. "An individual needs to find meaning in a traumatic memory as well as feel the related emotions to reap positive benefits from the writing exercise," Lutgendorf told the American Psychological Association. She continued, "There has to be growth or change in the way they view their experiences." In other words, writing allows us to integrate and revise our experience.

Writing isn't the only way to integrate our experiences. Talk therapy works for the same reason. It helps us make sense of and gain a new perspective on our experience. The key to integrating and making sense is finding some way to deal with whatever is causing distress without activating your defend and protect system. Writing provides a bit of space that often lets us deal with the thing. Therapy offers a space that is nonjudgmental and safe. In a slightly different but innovative approach, you can use exercise as a buffer to the stress, so that you can work on editing your story. While processing whatever is bothering you on a walk, take off in a sprint whenever you feel the angst, fear, or anger rise. The physical action, and accompanying fatigue and heavy breathing, will often overwhelm the emotions that were bubbling over. It's why exercise helped Doug Bopst get comfortable with the rest of his inner world. Your brain has to prioritize the sensations it's experiencing, and often, a strenuous physical act taps into deeper and more primitive areas of your processing, pushing the emotions to the side for a moment.

—

In chapter 3, we discussed exploration versus commitment. We need both. They each serve a vital purpose. But success and the uncertainty in our present world often push us to cement and exploit. We need to counterbalance this pull by embracing play, perspective, and exploration. In chapter 4, we've learned the importance of complexity and integration. A robust self is both secure and flexible. That means holding on to the many yous and seeing how they all interrelate and connect. We need to move from a 2D to a 3D world. When we can integrate and make sense of our roles and contradictions, we take away power from our pain points. Complexity allows us to be open to change.

The magic happens when we combine these two ideas. Winning the inside game means being complex and integrated with an ability to bounce back and forth between commitment and exploration. We set ourselves up for better predictions when we integrate our expectations, experiences, and actions; our narrative and experiential self. Throughout the first section, we've lightly touched on our basic psychological needs: meaning, significance, coherence, direction, and belonging. The items that we need in our life that help us become happy, healthy adults with a high sense of well-being. This is called thriving.

When it comes to thriving, our first focus is often on happiness. We all know the feeling—that combination of joy leaves us feeling cheerful and content. If our life can contain more of these moments, we'll reach the good life. According to research, a happy life includes a mixture of joy, comfort, security, and stability. We seek out experiences, relationships, and work that lead to this much sought-after feeling.

The second, and perhaps deeper, level of thriving includes meaning. It occurs when we feel that our life has significance, that we are making a difference in something that matters. What we do, who we are, and what we believe all have a purpose. We matter.

Psychologists Erin Westgate and Shigehiro Oishi recently added a third layer to our conceptualization of thriving: psychological richness. They defined this quality as a life that includes varied, interesting, and perspective-changing experiences. It's when we are open to trying new things, to exploring and dabbling, to sitting with a touch of novelty and uncertainty. Those who are psychologically rich score higher on indexes of openness to experience, as well as having a greater degree of flexibility of thought. They approach life with an inner curiosity to figure things out. As Oishi and Westgate noted, "Those leading psychologically rich lives tend to have more complex reasoning styles, consider multiple causes for others' behavior, and do not believe that a few discrete categories can explain individual differences." Psychological richness frees us up from the duality narrative. The world is no longer right and wrong, good and evil. It's rich and full of details.

One key to developing richness is having our perspective changed. There are many ways to expand our perspective: from spending time abroad to taking on a challenging course or assignment, to diversifying our peer group, to something as simple as taking on the challenge of solving an escape room with your friends. Doing difficult, novel things that force us to rethink our assumptions contributes to richness. We get that aha moment that we might have had a wrong assumption or that there's another way to see the world or approach a problem. We don't obtain psychological richness simply by doing adventurous or novel things. Thrill-seeking or trying to experience that rush of dopamine or adrenaline doesn't do the trick. We need to integrate the experience. We need to be open to new experiences and perspectives but then work to make sense of them.

Striving for happiness and meaning improves our sense of well-being. They nudge us toward taking advantage of the familiar. Happiness requires comfort and security. Meaning focuses on a worthy pursuit and contribution to society. Both are vital. But they can cause us to narrow, to move toward a flat world that is predictable, coherent, consistent, and secure. Having richness offers something the other two often lack: expansion. It pulls back against the familiar and predictable, allowing us to see the world and ourselves through different lenses. And that matters even more in a world that pushes us to survival mode. It enables us to move toward updating our predictions with new information.

As Oishi and Westgate wrote, "In rapidly changing environments, a psychologically rich life might be most adaptive for learning and accumulating resources, whereas happy and/or meaningful lives might be more advantageous in stable, benign environments." We need happiness, meaning, and richness. We've neglected the third component of thriving. It's that component that frees us up, that turns down our threat-and-protect response. When it comes to our sense of self, we need a bit more openness and psychological richness.

Wisdom, self-complexity, and psychological richness all get at a similar vital component. When we expand our self and world, it makes us better, happier human beings. We need both breadth and depth, combined with the humility to recognize the complexity of ourselves and the world we occupy. When we explore with an openness to experience, we free ourselves up to not only be "captured" by an interest but also to add nuance and complexity to the way we see ourselves or the world. Our inner narratives move from *Brown Bear, Brown Bear, What Do You See* to *Ulysses*. Psychological richness helps us move from 2D to 3D.

It's time to realize that we are complex, adaptable, contradictory, messy human beings. The cheap way to achieve coherence is through a simplistic story. The better way is through becoming a better writer and integrating the complexity into a coherent story. We're on a journey, not only toward happiness and excellence but also for the joy of taking a walk in the woods and being surprised by what we find. Of living a psychologically rich life. Or, as Oishi and Westgate put it, a person on their deathbed "who has led a happy life might say, 'I had fun!' A person who has led a meaningful life might say, 'I made a difference!' And a person who has led a psychologically rich life might say, 'What a journey!'"

Dealing with the messiness lays the foundation for sustainable excellence. For security and flexibility. For holding two thoughts at once. For not pulling the alarm at the slightest hint of a threat. It allows us to get out of survival mode so that we can pursue what we want to pursue with enthusiasm and vigor, which is where we'll turn to next.

PART TWO

DO—CLARITY IN YOUR PURSUITS

CHAPTER 5

LEARN HOW TO LOSE

It was the fourth loss in a row. The University of Texas football team had entered the season with high hopes. They had a new coach, signing University of Alabama offensive coordinator Steve Sarkisian to a six-year, thirty-four-million-dollar deal. They had a roster of highly ranked prospects and rode the wave to fifteenth in the country. Then, it all fell apart, starting with a 30–7 drubbing by Iowa State, a decidedly mediocre opponent. The mighty Texas had gotten demolished. Frustration, despair, confusion, and anger boiled over. Nowhere was that more apparent than on the bus ride home.

"This is real!" shouted Bo Davis, the defensive line coach for Texas. "Some of you motherf—s need to get in the transfer portal. You wanna go? Get in the motherf—r! This shit ain't a game to me! You think it's a game? Get the f—k off of this bus! I got my ass kicked! And you motherf—s wanna laugh?" One of the players recorded Davis's tirade, and it soon went viral.

The responses to the leaked video were mixed, but many were surprisingly positive. "Fire 'em up! This shows passion!" was a common take on social media. Many condemned the player who secretly recorded the video. The "rat" was the real problem. Even national media pundits echoed the sentiment. "Bo Davis is a winner. Winners can sniff out losers," college football analyst Josh Pate tweeted. *College GameDay* correspondent Kirk Herbstreit said, "I'm giving Bo Davis a standing ovation for his passion and messaging. Can't imagine coming onto a bus seeing dudes laughing on their phones after a no-show performance." Davis's boss echoed the sentiment, "I think you could feel the passion and the want to get it done. I think that Bo exemplifies that."

There's no questioning Davis's passion, but was it helpful? After the speech, the fired-up Texas team went on to suffer their most embarrassing loss in over half a century. In a 57–56 shootout, Texas found itself on the wrong end of the final score. The team watched the win slip away as Jared Casey, a walk-on tight end who hadn't had a single reception all year, caught the winning pass in overtime. Texas lost to the University of Kansas, the worst team in their league, a 31-point underdog. In their entire history of playing one another, Kansas *never* beat UT in their home city of Austin.

We hold on to this belief that after a tough loss, a good ass-chewing is needed to right the ship. That tirades like Davis's show passion. And any display of the opposite, say laughing and joking on the bus ride home, shows players don't care. We should feel the pain. And if we don't, it's a major problem. The only issue with that narrative? It goes against everything we know about the psychology of losing. Joking around, realizing that it is, in fact, a game and not real, and moving on from sorrow to excitement are the exact behaviors that research shows lead to better performance the next go around. Davis's tirade tells us more about the dangers of losing than the player's reaction.

THE BIOLOGY OF WINNING AND LOSING

Two animals face off in a field, perhaps with a potential mate or food on the line. They snarl and growl, preparing to defend or attack. They are in competition. Ready to go to war for whatever vital resource is up for grabs. I'm not concerned with what contributes to victory or defeat but with what occurs after the battle. What happens to the winning and losing snake, mouse, or lion?

In the 1960s scientists noted an interesting phenomenon when animals were pitted against one another in the lab. From rats to chicks to fish, when competing for resources, the contest's result shifted the animal's subsequent behavior. The winner became more aggressive, attacking whatever opponent stepped into the cage next. The losers hesitated. They retreated and defended, hoping to avoid conflict. The behaviors translated into consistent outcomes. The winners kept winning at an alarmingly high rate, and the losers kept a streak of their own, succumbing to their opponents again and again.

With each victory or defeat, a few crucial changes occur. First, the animal receives feedback on their relative skill. They update their model accordingly. Are they better off taking on the challenge or running away? Winners learn that they should fight to gain resources. Losers have to come up with a different strategy. Adopting either dominance or submissive tendencies allows animals to survive. You might think that winners keep winning simply because they are better fighters, but research found that relative skill didn't explain the streaky ability. It's not just that winners tend to win because they are better fighters. The result changes the animal's biology.

A potential answer emerged when researchers investigated what was happening inside the animals' bodies. The winning animal experienced a surge of testosterone, and this surge was tied to dominance, aggression, and a willingness to take more risks. On the other hand, losers saw their testosterone flatline while the stress hormone cortisol skyrocketed. Submission and anxiety soon followed. In rhesus monkeys, the change in testosterone from winning or losing lasted for several weeks. It wasn't just that animals were learning their place and best strategy; their biology was following suit. The next time they stepped into the cage, their biology primed them toward victory or defeat.

Recent research has gone a step further. It's not just hormones that change with the outcome of a competition but our brain. In a study published in *Science*, researchers from Zhejiang University in China put mice in a tube and let them go at it. The scientists were able to both measure and then activate specific areas in the mouse's brain. They homed in on an area called the dorsal medial prefrontal cortex (dmPFC). They took the losers, who had become timid and submissive, and flipped a switch to activate the dmPFC. Almost like magic, the losers transformed, winning 90 percent of the shoving matches in the tube. According to one of the authors, "It's not aggressiveness per se, it increases their perseverance, motivational drive, grit."

What was going on here? The dmPFC is related to the decision to be dominant or submissive. According to the researchers, "synapses in this pathway store the memory of previous winning or losing history." Unsurprisingly, if the researchers artificially manipulated this memory via activation, the results often persisted. The formerly loser mice rose up the ranks of their dominance hierarchy, carrying forward their winning ways even after the scientists stopped flipping the switch on their dmPFC.

Whether via hormones or our brain activation, winning and losing have lasting effects. A surge of testosterone and a rise in status can push us toward confidence and persistence. A drop in testosterone and an increase in cortisol nudges us the other way; sending a message that it's better to retreat, lick our wounds, and not engage. This mix of biological and behavioral responses has been termed "the winner and loser effect." And it doesn't occur only in mice, beetles, or monkeys. It occurs in humans.

According to a 2017 meta-analysis, the winner and loser effect is apparent in people across a wide range of competitions, from video games to tennis matches to stock trading. Win, and you get a bump in testosterone and a better shot at succeeding in the next game. Lose, and a drop in testosterone and a surge in cortisol is headed your way, along with more debilitating competitions. For instance, Simon Fraser University behavioral endocrinologists found that when playing the popular video game *Tetris*, those who had been declared a winner saw a bump in testosterone and then performed significantly better in their subsequent game the following day.

Similar to animals, a surge of testosterone in humans following a win has been linked to increased risk-taking, putting forth more effort, and trying harder. And in terms of functional outcomes, it's linked to better endurance performance in both men and women. And just like in the animals, the effects aren't temporary. They linger. In a study on professional rugby players, a bump in testosterone levels after a game was tied to better performance in a game a week or so later. Higher cortisol levels were linked to worse performance in the subsequent game. Similar effects have been found across competition—from sports to Tetris to intelligence tests.

We don't even have to actually win to have the effect. In a study out of the University of Cambridge, researchers rigged a series of rowing races, selecting winners randomly. Unsurprisingly, the "winners" saw a bump in testosterone, while the "losers" saw a drop. It's our perception that influences our biology. Being convinced that they won was all that mattered. But the sneaky scientists weren't done. Following their glorious victory or disappointing defeat, they had the rowers respond to a questionnaire designed to see how highly these young males thought of themselves as a potential mate. The winners rated themselves significantly more likely to ask out an attractive stranger at a postrace get-together.

Competition is often about status. For college-age males, that might mean seeking mates. For others, that could be related to prestige and improving our social hierarchy. In a study on an Olympic-level female field hockey team, testosterone and cortisol levels predicted social status within the team. An athlete who was low in testosterone and high in cortisol was much lower on the team's totem pole when rated on leadership, popularity, and skill. On the other hand, those low in cortisol fared much better. This study points to another wrinkle in the world of hormones, status, and performance.

It's not testosterone or cortisol on their own. It's their interaction that matters. The dual-hormone hypothesis posits that while an increase in testosterone is nice on its own, it doesn't have the desired effects of boosting perseverance and performance unless accompanied by low cortisol. In research involving MBA students, group performance was only elevated when testosterone was high and cortisol was low. If stress was too high, forget it. Status-seeking, risk-taking, and other dominance behaviors don't occur when cortisol is significantly elevated, even if testosterone is through the roof. High cortisol crashes the party, overriding and negating the effect of testosterone and even winning itself.

The anxious winner may seem rare, but it happens to all of us. It's the person who is just thankful the game is over. They are relieved to be done with the presentation. It's the daughter who is playing scared out on the ball field because she knows her dad is going to offer harsh criticism afterward, or the consultant who fears his job is on the line, even though he's somehow making it through the pitch deck. When cortisol is high, even the bump in testosterone from doing well isn't enough. In such cases, status ceases to matter. Survival does. When we live in survival mode, we don't even get the biological perks of winning.

FROM LOSING TO SURVIVING

Biology doesn't always work so neatly. And that's good for us. Our hormonal response is impacted by our personality, sensitivity to threats, whether we lose in front of a crowd or a few onlookers or if we attribute our loss to bad luck or a personal mistake. While the complexity can overwhelm us, research points to a simple heuristic: We are more likely to have the classic cortisol-dominated response when we are under attack—when a loss threatens something important and meaningful to us, such as our identity, sense of competency, or perhaps the stability and coherence of our inner narrative. When losing puts things that matter in the direct line of fire, we spiral. We ruminate, experience frustration and anger, and if it's so intertwined that it feels deeply real and not a game, we may just unleash a tirade on the bus ride home.

What we do serves a vital role in crafting our inner story. It becomes part of who we are. It's where we partially derive our sense of meaning, connection, and purpose. We experience competency, showing ourselves and the world that we are capable and worthy and bring value to others. The more deeply intertwined what we do is with who we are, the more susceptible we are to the wins and losses. Wins feel validating. We get the surge of testosterone. We feel dominant and rise up the ladder of status. Our ego grows. When we lose, we shrink and get embarrassed. We lose a sense of not just what we do, but who we are. We lose status.

Status is a crucial part of being human. In many ways, we are not that different from our cousins, the great apes, that depend on a hierarchy. As Wharton School professors Adam Grant and Marissa Shandell wrote in a review on motivation, "Humans are achievement- and status-seeking creatures." The search and need for status seem deeply ingrained in all societies, even primarily egalitarian ones. In *The Status Game*, writer Will Storr outlined that we can achieve status in three ways: dominance, competence, and virtue. Losing dismantles the first two and potentially impacts the third. It should come as no surprise why losing in something that is meaningful and important can be so tricky. But there's something that makes it worse: when the assault on our status is there for all to see.

When we lose in public, we face humiliation. A direct attack on who we are, showing the world that we are incompetent and a failure. As Storr writes, "Humiliation is an absolute purging of status and the ability to claim it." Or, as professor James Gilligan noted, humiliation is "an annihilation of the self." How do we move from a small loss to humiliation? According to researchers, humiliation occurs when we make a bid at high status in a social circle or pursuit, experience public failure, get taken down by someone who has enough status to dismantle our claim, and find ourselves devoid of not only our status, but "more fundamentally the individual's very status to have made such a claim at all." After small losses we are able to bounce back and try again, or make another status claim. During humiliation, we don't even have a shot to get back in the arena.

When we lose, it can be hard to take. A board game defeat to our friends may leave us feeling a bit down or frustrated, but we can easily move on. If the same loss is to our family, it may sting a bit more, a sign that we aren't as clever as our younger sister. A slight knock on our familial hierarchy, but who cares about Monopoly, anyway? However, when we move from a game to our job, failure hits harder. If that loss is in a public arena, on the biggest stage, we've moved toward humiliation. The losing hurts more than it ever has before. It's easier to fail publicly because just about everything is public. We all can become Rick Ankiel, who famously went from starring in the baseball playoffs to an inability to pitch the ball anywhere close to the plate. Recalling the instance where his mind and body betrayed him, he reflected, "I made the mistake of thinking, being good at baseball is what made me who I was. When that glass is shattered, there was nothing left. Going from baseball's prodigy and poster boy. All of the sudden you are blindsided. You're the most vulnerable you've ever been, and everybody can see right through you."

When our status is under threat in the highest manner, we fall down the pathway of our old friends: defend, protect, or survive. We could shut down, like Manti Te'o, entering the ultimate protective state, a touch of dissociation where what we think, feel, and do no longer align. If we don't fall into an almost involuntary submissive state, we may try to justify or blame others to protect ourselves from the deleterious attack. We feel the surge of cortisol and the drop in status and look for someone to blame—the refs, the players, whoever it is. Or, we may choose another option. Ignore the status attack, double down, and work harder to ensure that no matter what happens, we win. This last option is what most "pushers" choose. But it often backfires.

I HATE LOSING

"I can't function as a human being after a loss. I can't eat. I can't shave. I can't hug my kids."

After uttering these words in 2003, football coach Urban Meyer went on to win a lot and lose only a handful of times. Over the next fourteen seasons, he captured three national titles, finishing within the top six an astonishing ten times. He didn't lose much and that was a good thing, as he later admitted, "I've never handled it well. Awful loser." Logically, he did everything to avoid this horrific experience. And he was remarkably good at it.

During the 2021 NFL season, Meyer's hatred of losing finally came back to bite him. During his seven years at Ohio State, Meyer lost nine times. In his first year with the Jacksonville Jaguars, he'd surpass that with a 2–11 record. During the tumultuous season, Meyer exhibited all of the classic signs of someone losing poorly. He started with a familiar tactic: doubling down.

After losing his team's first preseason game—a meaningless affair meant to get players reps and evaluate fringe players—Meyer tore into his coaches and team. As one Jaguars staffer reported to writer Albert Breer, "It was really over the top, and you could tell all this was new to him." As actual losses in the regular season mounted, Meyer's decision-making was increasingly questioned, and his hold on the team unraveled.

There was the constant public blaming of players, which led to an intense argument with his mild-mannered leading receiver, Marvin Jones; the benching of his best offensive weapon, running back James Robinson; and then, during a staff meeting, a berating of his fellow coaches, the ones he had hired. It was the ultimate sign of a sinking ship. As Tom Pelissero reported, "Meyer delivered a biting message that he's a winner and his assistant coaches are losers . . . challenging each coach individually to explain when they've ever won and forcing them to defend their resumes." When losing stings so much that it physically hurts, when who we are depends on success in a singular field, we default toward protecting ourself.

Kurt Warner—who famously went from sacking groceries to NFL MVP—summarized one of the problems the successful and driven face, "They're so used to winning, that once it starts to turn the other direction, they've never learned how to handle it." When we don't know how to lose well, we end up copying Meyer. Our motivation shifts from playing to win to trying to avoid that feeling of failure. Our source of status and significance fades, and we become hyperresponsive to threats. We start putting those around us "in their place," pushing others down to prop ourselves up. The stronger the emotion attached to failure, the more our defensive strategies are reinforced. Our striving emotional system gives way to our protection-based ones. We ingrain fear and avoidance strategies into our predictive algorithm.

As former chess prodigy and writer Josh Waitzkin outlined, "If a young basketball player is taught that winning is the only thing that winners do, then he will crumble when he misses his first big shot. If a gymnast or ballet dancer is taught that her self-worth is entirely wrapped up in a perfectly skinny body that is always ready for performance, then how can she handle injuries or life after an inevitably short career? If a businessperson cultivates a perfectionist self-image, then how can she learn from mistakes?"

Coming to terms with failure and saying we must "fail forward" is trendy in Silicon Valley culture, but we need more than slogans about embracing failure. We need to learn how to lose well—to shift from seeing any sign of failure as a threat to our sense of self to something we can deal with and learn from. The modern world inundates us with signs of losing, with the sense that we aren't measuring up. And many of them occur in a public forum. We don't have to be athletes playing in front of thousands to feel the burden. From Facebook to TikTok to Instagram, our failures are on public display. Combine that with the fact that we've moved from playing a local to a global game, and it's nearly impossible to measure up. We are all losing at something on a public stage. We are all having our status constantly questioned. We must learn how to lose well.

Contrary to what's often proclaimed, accepting a loss doesn't make you fragile. It hastens your trip from disappointment to being able to do something about the thing. It allows you to see things clearer, to move from a tantrum-throwing child to a space where we can make sense of and learn from defeat. No one enjoys getting their butt kicked, but learning how to lose better doesn't mean we aren't passionate or don't care. It allows us to perform at our best. From a place of love and striving to get better, instead of fear, shutting down, and a lingering negative emotional hit.

Research on quails provides a clue about how to turn the tide. In a study out of Bowling Green State University, researchers measured pecking and feather ruffling when birds were placed in a cage with a rival. Those who submitted kept on cowering when placed against a different opponent the next day. But there was an exception. The quails injected with oxytocin didn't submit the following day. They turned the tables on their new opponent. The oxytocin birds came back stronger, winning much more often after suffering an initial defeat. Oxytocin is commonly thought of as a "love" hormone, but it's more accurately involved in a mixture of bonding, connection, calming, and even confidence. Oxytocin tends to work against our other stress hormones, soothing distress and activating our calm and connect system, which researchers hypothesize clears the way for confidence to emerge. It has a similar effect in people. In soccer players, winners tended to have higher oxytocin and lower cortisol levels. Both of these were related to levels of anxiety and self-confidence. Researchers out of the University of Sydney found that giving participants oxytocin intranasally before being ostracized during a game increased their desire to play again. Similarly, acute stress often increases dopamine, the desire hormone that pushes us toward pursuit. Chronic stress blunts this hormone. Whether it's oxytocin, testosterone, or dopamine, what's clear is that if we linger in a negative state, our motivation shifts and we lose the ability to try.

Learning to lose is important for one more reason. Researchers found that how we handle winning and losing are connected. If we throw a tantrum and default to avoidance after a loss, we're more likely to settle into a protective state where we avoid challenging competitions after a win. Similarly, if we respond to a loss by aggressively trying to tear down the opponent to not have it impact our self-esteem, then we take the same approach when we win: defaulting to overly enhancing our "dominance," which then blinds us to seeing how to improve. Research shows if we are balanced in losing, we'll be balanced in winning. That doesn't mean not feeling the emotions of joy, sadness, frustration, or pride after a win or loss. It just means we keep them in perspective.

Even one of the best athletes in history, one who is notorious for his aversion to defeat, understood and accepted this lesson. As Michael Jordan told fellow NBA great Steph Curry, "I hate losing. I mean, it's not even a question. But I do respect losing because losing is a part of winning. You're never going to just win. You've got to lose to win." It is a subtle shift but an important one. You don't have to enjoy it, but you do have to respect it. Let's learn how.

LEARNING HOW TO LOSE (AND WIN)

Video games are often derided by older generations as a mindless entertainment diversion that makes kids dull and lazy. But seventy-seven-year-old pitching coach (and throwing maestro) Tom House has another take. "I'm envious of kids who get to grow up on video games today. Lose, then just restart. There's no better feedback loop to learn how to lose than modern games. This generation wipes away loss and failure faster than any I've seen." House continued, "Plus, they're losing with an audience of their closest friends. They get affiliation in loss. The forcing function of restarting with a slight pause in between leads to a communication flow state of how to prevent that mistake from being made again."

If video games seem too playful to learn from, we can turn to something far more serious. How do we develop resilience or the ability to bounce back from serious adversity? According to a review by psychiatrist Adriana Feder, resilience is an active process tied to a "rapid activation of the stress response and its efficient termination. Resilience is associated with the capacity to constrain stress-induced increases in corticotrophin-releasing hormone and cortisol." It's the efficient termination part that is vital. It clears the way for dealing with and hopefully learning from the actual thing. Feder and team found several factors that underpin our ability to be resilient:

- facing fears and active coping
- optimism and positive emotions
- reappraisal, positive reframing, and acceptance
- social competence and social support
- purpose in life, a moral compass, meaning, and spirituality

Whenever I've worked with professional sports teams, I've simplified this research into four key components after a game, win or lose:

1. Shift out of protect and defend
2. Keep it informational, not personal
3. Reframe
4. Revise

Let's look at how to put these components into practice.

SHIFT OUT OF PROTECT AND DEFEND

The half-life of adrenaline is less than five minutes. An adrenaline rush can be powerful, but it's gone quickly. The half-life of cortisol is around ninety minutes. Its effects linger for hours afterward and can compound with additional hits or reminders of stress, keeping us in a cortisol-driven stressed state for hours on end. There's nothing wrong with cortisol as a hormone. It does its job, freeing up energy and allowing us to handle difficult moments. But when it lingers or when we unleash a deluge when we just need a touch, bad things happen.

Step one is figuring out how to move on from stress. When we switch from stress-and-protect to repair-and-recover mode, not only do we escape the flood of cortisol, but we also prevent every moment from being a competition for dominance and status.

Research on professional rugby players found that watching what they did wrong after a game led to elevated cortisol and worse performance the next game. Watching what they did well had the opposite effect: a bump in testosterone and better performance in the games that followed. It's not that we want to avoid criticism forever. It's that after a tough match, we are in a sensitive period. Our brains are looking to validate our feeling that we are a bit useless. We are hypersensitive to any sign of a threat. It's why, when I asked University of Michigan psychologist Ethan Kross how he would handle a hard defeat if he was the coach at UM, he told me about creating a temporal buffer. "In the immediate aftermath of that loss, this is not the time to do the cognitive work to get better. This is the time to allow our emotions to hang out. It's phase one of allowing you to share what you're going through and not pushing people to heal more quickly than they are in a position to heal. I would share my disappointment but also what I'm proud about, getting to that big game. The next day or a couple days later is when we'd break things down, going over what succeeded and failed."

When we're down and out, we need to get out of the sensitive period, so that we can then give evidence to counter the doom and gloom loop that's playing in our head. As a director of performance science for an NFL team told me, testosterone levels were highest when athletes feel good. If you want to bounce back or prime yourself to perform, feel good! Reading your best writing before starting a new project, or having a "praise folder" on your computer to remind you that you're competent before stepping into a big meeting can work wonders. When your brain is searching for validating your incompetence, give it evidence to the contrary to help get you through the sensitive period.

This doesn't apply only in traditional performance fields. It occurs in our relationships and arguments. When in the heat of an argument—be it with a significant other or stranger over the latest hot-button topic—if anyone is in protective mode, only bad things will occur. We often force the other person into protective mode. A hint of a criticism of our spouse turns into a mountain. Or, in a debate, we turn into a prosecutor, causing the other person to stop listening. We've all experienced this. The quickest way to make things worse, to engender zero change, is to try to win an argument. Losing well and arguing well have a lot in common: getting out of protect-and-defend mode is crucial.

It's not just cortisol that lingers. It's your brain. Whenever we experience fear, pain, or loss, our threat-sensing area of our brain, the amygdala, goes on high alert. Amygdala persistence occurs when, well after the threat has gone, our brain is still latched onto it. Some of us are able to let go; some get stuck on the danger. Research shows that those who can let go and move on experience more positive and fewer negative emotions and increased overall well-being. We need to get out of protect-and-defend mode.

One of the ways to accelerate the return to baseline is by giving people time and space to decompress, especially with friends. After a tough loss, there's not much better than social support. Whether it's a postgame meal or happy hour with friends after a tough loss, friends help get us back to normal. Social recovery flips us into a positive hormonal and mood state. It helps in two ways. First, having social support dampens cortisol and pushes us toward affiliative instead of avoidance behaviors. Think back to the role of oxytocin in moving us toward calm and connection. A variety of research shows that oxytocin is released when socializing, giving hugs, or performing physical activity with others. Second, it gives us time to work through our losing experience with people who are supportive and not threatening. Decompress, debrief, and connect.

In a study on professional athletes, Christian Cook and Blair Crewther found that altering the social dynamics of the postgame review session shifted hormones and performance in an interesting way. Players who watched game film that showed strangers saw a significant bump in cortisol, while those who watched film that showed friends saw a slight decline. Even more interesting, the group that watched film that showed strangers who were much bigger physically saw a much larger increase in cortisol than those who watched those that showed smaller strangers. Reviewing game tape with strangers is scary enough, but we interpret them as even more threatening when they are physically more prominent!

Failure has a way of putting us in a sensitive period that we can either take advantage of for positive change and growth, or we can have it push us to double down and cement. Which way we go largely determines how we handle this critical period. When moving on from a tough loss, joking around with friends may be just what we need.

KEEP IT INFORMATIONAL, NOT PERSONAL

Once we are out of the acute threat phase, we need to figure out how to absorb and learn from the loss. Once again, let's turn to video games. When we lose in a game among friends, the failure is often seen as informational, not personal. There isn't enough time to linger on the friendly banter or trash talk; you have to absorb what went wrong and then get back into the game.

In fields far away from video games, researchers have noticed the same phenomenon when dealing with uncertainty in the real world. Personal uncertainty leads to being filled with negative moods and emotional states. When we take uncertainty or loss as something that undermines our personal view of ourselves or world, stress and protection soon follow. If, on the other hand, we can keep failure and uncertainty as informational, we are free to introspect, to make sense of, and to learn from what occurred.

Keeping something informational depends on creating space between what you're competing at and who you are as a person. As she outlined in her bestselling book *Educated*, Tara Westover grew up as one of seven siblings to parents who were extreme Mormon survivalists. Her family avoided authority, doctors, and even school. Her brother taught her to read while her dad steeped her in conspiracy theories. Even as she started to pave her own path, taking her education into her own hands by teaching herself enough to get into Brigham Young University, she held on to some bigoted ideas. It wasn't until a classmate sat with her at a bar until the wee hours of the morning, politely getting curious about her views, that she began to question them. The next day, she realized her conversation partner was right. How? He was curious. As she reported on Adam Grant's *ReThinking* podcast, the man at the bar "essentially separated me out from the ideas, and he was saying things to me that were, they were sort of like, 'You seem like a nice person. Help me understand how these ideas fit into your life.' And it was an amazing way of dealing with me because he didn't put me on the defensive. He wasn't attacking me."

It's the same approach that Daryl Davis takes. Davis is a Black man who has gotten more than two hundred people to quit the

KKK by simply befriending those who hate him. "If you spend five minutes with your worst enemy . . . you will find that you both have something in common. As you build upon those commonalities, you're forming a relationship and as you build about that relationship, you're forming a friendship. That's what would happen. I didn't convert anybody. They saw the light and converted themselves." We all can do a better job of this. If change is warranted, create distance between you and the role. Allow yourself or the person you are working with to put on another hat.

REFRAME

The Milwaukee Bucks were the number one seed, having won more games than any other team in the NBA. They were among the favorites to win the NBA championship. Yet in the first round of the playoffs, they fell to the number eight seed Miami Heat, who had barely squeaked into the tournament. After the final game of the series, Bucks superstar Giannis Antetokounmpo was asked if he thought the year was a failure.

Giannis responded, "Do you get a promotion every year? In your job? No, right? So every year your work is a failure? . . . You work toward a goal—it's not a failure. It's steps to success." He went on to say, "It's the wrong question. There's no failure in sports. There are good days, bad days, some days you are able to be successful—some days you're not. . . . That's what sports is about."

We're used to seeing success as binary. Win or lose. In his answer, Giannis is demonstrating self and performance complexity. We can evaluate performance in a number of ways. To move from seeing something as good or bad, success or failure, but along a continuum. Giannis is reframing his view of losing to include more nuance. This allows him to move from personal to informational and learn and grow from it. I saw the same reframing when sitting on a panel with WNBA superstar Sue Bird. When asked if she had ever choked, she said, "No, but I've missed a lot."

The sport of track and field teaches this lesson exquisitely. Only one person wins the race. If you judged yourself based solely on winning, 99 percent of us would be miserable failures. You're forced to move to the next level of judgment: comparison against yourself. Did you run a new personal record? Great, you succeeded, even if you finished eighth! This works well early on when progress comes easy. As we move up the ranks and progress stalls, new personal bests become fewer and farther between. You have to change or else just about every race will leave you disappointed. So you move toward evaluating your pursuits complexly. How was your effort? Did you execute your strategy? How did you respond when the pain was the highest? Your definition of success and competence becomes nuanced and complex. And that opens up the door for you to continually learn and grow instead of being miserable.

The best performers get this balance right. It's creating just enough space so that a loss doesn't cause you to spiral, to overcare, to be hypercompetitive at all times. But at the same time not so much space that you don't have that bit of tension pushing toward growth, or can self-delude so that you never see the lessons poor performances can teach you. That's what Giannis captures. Losing hurts. But it's part of the process. One that can't be avoided.

REVISE

I was seventeen. Sitting in second period German class. I'd just finished a six-mile run half an hour earlier. A classmate named Matt yelled from the computer, "New York City has been attacked." I vividly remember that classroom. Where I was sitting. The surprise turned to terror that washed over me. How school continued, but really stopped, as teachers rolled out TVs to watch what was unfolding. If you lived through September 11, 2001, chances are you recall where you were. The same goes for other national tragedies. So-called "flashbulb" memories feel vivid and real. The gist is that the flash of emotion tells our brain this is really important, so it becomes seared into our memory.

The problem? Researchers found that even within a year of September 11 occurring, 40 percent of people misremembered or altered significant details. How you felt was the most likely thing to change. As cognitive psychologist William Hirst reported for the American Psychological Association, "You tend to project your current feelings about 9/11 on what you felt then." We're used to thinking of our memories as inner pictures or videos that capture our experience as it occurred. But that's not how it works. When we remember something, it's more like we are recreating it, almost putting on a play instead of watching a film. This makes our memory a bit faulty at best. And research shows often our most emotionally salient memories are the most likely to be distorted.

But there's a benefit to this. Therapists use memory reconsolidation strategies to alter the power of traumatic experiences. In those who have PTSD, memory reconsolidation interference has shown some success. In this technique, individuals recall a traumatic experience while using either pharmacological, cognitive, or emotion-based strategies to disrupt and realign the experience. You can do cognitive rewriting, thinking your way through it. Naming it, seeing the logical inconsistencies, rationally talking our way through why the experience doesn't demand the reaction we are giving it. You can also attack it from the other side, the emotional or experiential. Psychologists have used drugs like beta-blockers that diminish the anxiety accompanied with recalling the traumatic experience. Or in other cases, using various strategies to calm down or replace the emotion.

One of my good friends who is a social worker, Andy Stover, utilizes Eye Movement Desensitization and Reprocessing (EMDR) in similar situations. EMDR was developed in the 1980s to help process trauma. It consists of going over a traumatic experience with a therapist, and then imagining or recalling aspects of that trauma (i.e., the shame or stress you felt) while you move your eyes side to side in a specific manner. While research is ongoing on how it works, current theories are that the eye moment helps dampen down the negative emotions associated with the memory. Turning down the alarm so we can reframe the memory.

Performance coach Tony Wilson relayed a similar tactic to me. He has athletes watch videos of their high-pressure performances, having them try to remember what it felt like to go through that at bat or race. Except, while going toward the pressure, he pumps in calm music to their ears and has them utilize a series of breathing exercises. The goal is to dislodge the connection between the pressure-filled situation and the body's ingrained threat response. I've used similar tactics, having athletes smile during the recall or having them watch a comedy routine or tell jokes after watching themselves mess up. Research backs this up: when we change our somatic state, we modulate the emotional punch behind whatever we are doing. Other research shows that reading a story right after recalling a traumatic experience disrupts that memory. Think of it like this. If our brain locks on to signals that send us toward threat, avoidance, or disconnection, all it hears is: This hurts, be sad, shut down. It knows that pattern. But if we add other sensory signals (feelings, emotions, muscular actions, vision), we can turn down the salience of the memory and remind the brain to wake up, and be aware of other experiential paths it can take. The link from feeling threatened to avoidance weakens as we become aware.

FREEDOM TO FAIL = FREEDOM TO PERFORM

I'm an expert at failing. And not just failing but a special kind: coming extraordinarily close to achieving the big goal, then falling just short. Consider the following: I was a phenom of a high school runner. But I never made it to the state meet in track until I won it my senior year because, for the first three years, I fell one place short in nearly every qualifying race. On the track, I ran a 4:01.02 mile, never getting under the elusive barrier despite years and dozens of races getting pretty darn close. In high school cross-country, I missed qualifying for nationals by two seconds, falling one spot short. In college, I cut it even closer, missing the NCAA championships by six one-hundredths of a second in a race that took 30 minutes.

My early coaching career was much the same. As you know, I received my dream job on the way to helping coach Olympians, only to have to rebuild because of what I saw. As a college coach, I helped a young man go from outside the top 100 in his event in high school to building a 20-meter lead at the NCAA championships heading into the final lap of the 3,000-meter steeplechase. Only to clip the barrier and fall less than 300 meters from the finish. As a team, we finished third, second, and third at consecutive NCAA championships. Phenomenal performances but always agonizingly a few points short of the title. The trend has continued in my writing. Collectively, my books have sold more than half a million copies, but I've always fallen just shy of making the *New York Times* bestsellers list. I'm an expert at near misses.

Early on, those misses left scars. The pain of not having my mile best begin with "3" haunted me for years. The feeling of just missing qualifying for nationals felt so visceral for too long. And it stung deep when I thought I had finally made it, and found my dream job, only to have it turn into a nightmare—one that I couldn't explain fully for years until it became public and the legal battle finished. Losses leave a mark.

We're often given trite advice to fail forward, but that misses the reality of failure. Whether on a large or small scale, failure and loss change us. But we play a role in how. There are two ways we can go when we fail. First is to protect and defend ourself, our ego. That's a one-way ticket to turning up our threat alarm and living in survival mode. It's what occurs when we berate others, lose our cool, or stew over the loss. If we push it away, our brain receives the opposite information: this hurts for a reason, remember it. And our predictive rut of connecting loss with fear starts to ingrain. Whatever we resist persists. I went this route for a while, trying to prove others wrong by doubling my effort to succeed. Trying to outrun, then outcoach my way to showing that those past experiences didn't define me. But ironically, trying to resist the definition ingrained it. Failure can distort our story. The other path is toward understanding and growing.

If we let it, failure brings clarity. It peels back the layers of pretense, cutting through our protective self-deceptions, so that we can see our self and pursuits as they are. We realize that most of our fears and insecurities are misplaced. That the world didn't end when we lost the game or didn't get the promotion. That we can go down a path that fear was previously blocking. Failure gives us a chance to own and update our story.

We craft narratives to make sense of our experiences, to find coherence by connecting the past, present, and future. We all walk around with stories that help guide our behavior and make sense of our experiences, but we ultimately play a role in how we tell those stories. How do we make sense of our failures? Do we freak out, compartmentalize, or accept and integrate them?

In studying how people navigate life's challenges, psychologist Dan McAdams found that how we tell our stories matters. Those who tell redemption stories, where we go from a low to a high, turning our suffering into something positive, score higher on measures of well-being than those who tell "feel good" stories, where everything is generally pretty good. The old adage that the bad makes the good better holds true. But in further research by psychologist Jack Bauer, it wasn't the sequence that mattered the most. It was the themes in those stories.

Bauer and colleagues found that growth themes mostly explained the higher levels of well-being. There needed to be signs of exploration and expansion. But not from a materialistic or outcome focus but, according to Bauer, from a more holistic and humanistic viewpoint. Growth themes lead to "strengthened senses of self, relationships, and philosophy of life." It's about having a secure sense of self but also being willing to explore. It's making sense of suffering, which sometimes means closure through acceptance and other times through change. As Bauer concluded, "It appears that well-being has more to do with interpreting meaning in one's life than with interpreting life as turning out well without a stated reason." It's about finding meaning in and making sense of the struggle. Years after his initial research, McAdams summed up what they now know, "It's good to tell life stories in which the protagonist is agentic, is engaged in warm close relationships, is resilient and forms a coherent narrative. Still, you can't just make those up. Lived experience needs to resonate with the story."

If we integrate, process, and move forward, failure can bring clarity by a "stripping away of the inessential." Failure frees us to take back control, own, edit, and rewrite our story, instead of giving over that power to someone or something else. When we hand over that control, the thing wins. When we lose poorly, we're giving over control and cementing the threat-prevention loop. We're telling our brain and body to get stuck. On the other hand, failure provides an opportunity to disrupt this pattern.

Learning to lose well means changing your story. It means lowering the defenses and the sensitivity to failure so that it isn't a threat. It requires learning how to move through the phases of fear or loss, first to go from stressed-and-protect mode to recover and restore, and then from recover and restore to learn-and-grow mode.

Failure can eat away at your soul. It can be uncomfortable and make you miserable. It makes us feel that way because we've ingrained the wrong story—a narrative that success defines us, and what we do is the outlet in which we feed that monster. To reach our potential, we need to let go of the success narrative, put space between what we do and who we are, and realize we are worthy. That advice might sound cliché. It might cause you to tense up, resist, and start talking about how "winners" must hate losing. That's the monster talking. The thing that's got a hold of you, that convinces you that your irrational tantrums after failure just mean you care. Sometimes, to achieve your potential, you just have to let it go.

CHAPTER 6

CARE DEEPLY BUT BE ABLE TO LET GO

M ichael Jordan's competitiveness is legendary. The best example may be the infamous flu game. Stricken with what we now believe to be food poisoning during game 5 of the NBA finals, Jordan went from puking all night to stepping onto the court and leading his team to victory with 38 points and hitting the game-winning shot. "I didn't want to give up, no matter how sick I was or how tired I was," Jordan said.

Even outside of official games, his competitive streak shined through. There was the time when, at one of his basketball camps, a seventeen-year-old O. J. Mayo, who was the number-one recruit in the country, started trash talking a retired forty-two-year old Jordan. He did not take it well. Jordan stopped the camp, sent everyone to bed, and told the young kid, "You may be the best high school player, but I'm the best player in the world. From this point on, it's a lesson." This continued when, as the owner of the Charlotte Bobcats and now in his fifties, he would take on players half his age in scrimmages. It even occurred at home. His son,

Marcus, relayed a story to the *Today* show about a time he was playing one-on-one against his dad as a freshman in high school, and "the game got so competitive to the point . . . I literally had to go call my mom because I was like, 'Dad's picking on me.'"

Off the court, it was the same. During golf matches, he'd wager thousands on the outcome, upping the ante and talking trash the entire time. "I considered myself competitive until I spent time with (Jordan)," actor Will Smith said on *Jimmy Kimmel Live!* A notorious workaholic with the accolades to back it up, Smith paled in comparison to his friend. He went on to say, "Michael will compete with anything. If we're drinking water, Mike will be like, 'I'll race you.'" If there was a winner, Jordan was going all out to be that person. Six NBA championships, five Most Valuable Player Awards, and on and on the accolades go. And more than just about any other person who has walked this earth, Jordan is known for coming through in the clutch. His competitiveness led him to greatness.

One of the ways in which Jordan fueled his competitiveness was to make nearly everything personal. Throughout his career, he used other people's slights of him as the gasoline for his motivational tank. His career is littered with stories of innocent jabs or comments that Jordan then turned into personal attacks and, ultimately, motivation.

During the 1996 NBA finals, the Seattle SuperSonics faced Jordan's Chicago Bulls. Going into the game, SuperSonics head coach George Karl was warned not to give Jordan any ammo. But before the finals, Jordan saw Karl at a local restaurant. Karl didn't come over and say hello. A small, innocent snub. As Jordan recalled years later, "That's all I needed—for him to do that—and it became personal with me." The Bulls won the championship.

But according to Karl, it didn't stop there. As he said years later, "At the end of his career, he was making up stuff. He was saying that I said he was old or he has a lousy golf swing or he always loses money on the golf course. I mean, I never said any of that stuff, but he made things up to motivate himself to reach a level of intensity that very few players ever got to."

Even Jordan's basketball origin story begins with an insult, the infamous story of him being cut by his high school basketball coach. It became the slap in the face that propelled him to future stardom. Decades later, Jordan reserved a part of his NBA Hall of Fame induction speech for rehashing the old tale and telling his old coach, "I wanted to make sure you understood: You made a mistake, dude." It didn't matter that Jordan wasn't actually cut. As a sophomore, he was put on the JV team instead of varsity. The entire Hall of Fame speech is a who's who of players and coaches who fueled Jordan by disrespecting or doubting him. As the sportswriter Rick Reilly wrote at the time, "Nobody was spared, including his high school coach, his high school teammate, his college coach, two of his pro coaches, his college roommate, his pro owner, his pro general manager, the man who was presenting him that evening, even his kids!" But for Jordan, it worked. At least when it came to performance, that is. It may have backfired when it comes to the other half of the equation; fulfillment and being able to be content.

CAN'T FLIP THE SWITCH

"I can't turn it off" is a refrain I hear constantly from high-performing executives and entrepreneurs. It starts with an acknowledgment that there might be a problem—an inability to stop thinking about the upcoming deal or adjusting the flow of a report. They might be at the dinner table with their family, but their mind is elsewhere. For many, this extends even further. "I can't stop competing. In every-thing," one entrepreneur lamented to me. It's not just about lacking the ability to leave work at the office; it's the inability to shift out of the competitive mindset that comes with striving. Game night with their family, the friendly pool game at the bar, the pickup basketball game in the neighborhood. They are overly competitive.

Dating back nearly one hundred years, researchers have noted the impact of overcompeting. Hypercompetitiveness is about needing to win at all costs to protect our identity and worth. It's linked to more physical and verbal aggression, and difficulty maintaining healthy relationships. In their book *Top Dog*, Ashley Merryman and Po Bronson describe this maladaptive competitiveness as "characterized by psychological insecurity and displaced urges. It's the person who can't accept that losing is part of competing. . . . He has to be the best at everything, and he can't stop comparing himself to others even when the competition is over."

Hypercompetitiveness can become a vicious cycle. We get caught up in maintaining our sense of self through winning. It's as if our brain has learned that we must win at any challenge to feel significant. It goes on a mission looking for ways to establish worth or alternatively on the lookout for any threat to our dominance. The preseason game becomes life or death. The board game with your family turns into an attempt to establish your intellectual superiority before unraveling into a frustrating screaming match. Researchers out of Slovenia found that students with hypercompetitive values were, unsurprisingly, more likely to self-handicap. To protect their self-worth, they had an excuse handy when failure hit.

Those who are hypercompetitive tend to need constant validation from the outside. Psychologists Jennifer Crocker and Amy Canevello divide our social motivation into two systems. An *ecosystem* motivation pushes us toward constructive and supportive relationships with others. We see other people as mutually beneficial and not threatening. An *egosystem* motivation pushes us to relationships with others and groups that allow us to defend or promote our self-image. As they explain, "Constructing, inflating, maintaining, and defending desired self-images becomes a means to satisfy their needs by convincing others of their value and worth." When we have an egosystem orientation, we tend to see competition as zero-sum. And for most of us, research shows that it doesn't turn us into Michael Jordan. It pushes us over the edge. As Crocker and colleagues discovered, we move toward self-preservation, where we are more likely to be "afraid and confused" than in the zone and performing to the best of our abilities.

The egosystem domination even prevents us from doing the thing we need most: detaching. In organizations that adopt an excessively high-pressure environment, stepping away and taking a break from work backfires. Researchers found that high-pressure workers feel more shame when they try not to work. This shame leads to more unethical acts and artificially elevates the impression that we are always working hard. When we feel excessive pressure, we self-preserve.

When our validation is too heavily weighted to the external, we often spend our time competing in minor things that don't really matter. As Will Storr writes in his book *The Status Game*, "We're routinely pitched into senseless competitions at the hyper-local level." We put our status on the line in grocery stores or airport security lines, losing our cool if someone inadvertently jumps the line. And our brains get the message that these small, inconsequential battles matter. We put our status on the line in situations that don't matter.

For most of us, the result of hypercompetitiveness isn't coming through in the clutch in game 7 of the NBA finals; it's survival mode. We start seeing threats everywhere so that we can fuel our motivational juices. We start avoiding situations where we can't win. Even Will Smith joked about this aspect of Jordan's demeanor: "You can't beat Mike in anything. If he can't beat you, he's not going to play." If we don't watch out, the same fuel that can push individuals to greatness on the field can leave us miserable and wanting off of it.

This is the central struggle with competition. We're told to care more and to make our work central to who we are in order to succeed, and we fear that we'll fall behind if we don't adopt such a mindset. In the short term, such an approach can work. Yet, it also sets us up to be miserable, to adopt a zero-sum winner-take-all attitude, to see success as self-defining, and to get most of our validation through external sources. There's a better way. Just ask Olympic and world champion pole-vaulter Katie Moon. In 2023, she claimed her second world championship title but shared it with Australian Nina Kennedy. After four hours of jumping in 85-degree heat, Moon and Kennedy tied at sixteen feet, one inch. They had a choice: jump off or share the gold. As Moon relayed, "Part of the reason we've reached the highest level is by listening to our bodies and knowing our limitations. We decided . . . sharing glory was just as good as earning it outright." When she received pushback on social media calling a tie an act of "cowardice," Moon responded, "Contrary to popular belief, you do not need a 'win at all costs' mentality to have a champions mindset."

In examining competitiveness, psychologist Gábor Orosz and colleagues defined four approaches toward competition. There's the person who lacks interest and is neither motivated to take on a task nor avoid it. They just don't care. Competition doesn't excite or intrigue them in the least. The second approach is the hyper-competitive person whom we've just discussed. They tend to need constant validation. Competition is where they derive meaning and value. The results matter . . . a lot! The third approach is the anxiety-driven avoidance orientation. These individuals shy away from competition. They often suffer from a need for perfection, and because that isn't achievable, they avoid situations that put them in danger of being exposed. The final approach is the self-developmental competitive style. In this approach, the internal matters more than the external. The desire for self-growth and improvement in relation to oneself is what keeps them going. Simplified, our approach toward competition can be by dominating to deal with our insecurity, refusing to play the game in either direction, avoiding the game to protect ourselves from the consequences, or seeing the game as being about our self-development, win or lose. We all occupy these four approaches to competitiveness at various points in our lives and pursuits.

This is the central tension, with not only competition, but performing well at just about anything. The more we care, and the more our job or pursuits feel a part of who we are, the harder we'll work. When our goals feel relevant to our sense of self, we're more likely to move from apathy to action. When what we are doing feels a part of who we are, it becomes more meaningful. Away from the sports fields, the same holds. If we transition from seeing ourselves as someone who dabbles in writing to someone who identifies as a writer, it helps our consistency in the craft. We write because that's what we do. When we move from a verb to a noun, from "I cook" to "I am a cook," we've signaled to our brain that this activity is a central part of who we are. We've moved from doing to being.

We see this pattern emerge in kids. In a 2014 study, when psychologists emphasized "being a helper" to a group of young children instead of "helping," the children were more likely to help pick up and organize a mess of toys and blocks. The researchers concluded that the subtle shift in vocabulary allowed the kids to take on a positive identity. Other research found that kids from low-income households were eight times more likely to do extra credit when they were primed with "education-dependent identities," by showing the value of becoming a college graduate. Similar results have been found in adults in a variety of activities, from the likelihood of voting to eating healthier to taking care of the environment. When something feels a part of who we are, we're more likely to make sure our actions align with our identity. We follow through.

Yet, as you're now aware, that's not the whole picture. In 2018, a group of NYU psychologists replicated the "being a helper" study with a subtle twist: They introduced failure. Instead of allowing the kids to successfully become helpers, the nefarious researchers highlighted when a kid messed up, spilling the crayons, missing trash, and so forth. After failure, those who had been told to be helpers had more negative attitudes and were less likely to help on effortful tasks. When it came to easy tasks they knew they could accomplish, the "being" group still helped more. In other words, after a setback, the group that tied their identity to helping, played not to lose. They were fine helping when the victory was clear but hesitant when a potential failure was on the horizon. Making things personal can lead to great success, but for most of us, it doesn't transform us into a clutch performer. Jordan, in many ways, is an outlier. Overly linking our identity with our actions makes us hesitant to take the shot when the game is on the line. There's a fine line between caring deeply and too much.

That's the central tension of performance. We need to care deeply, but not in a way that we lose control, becoming the hyper-competitive athlete who can't turn it off, or the executive who is blinded by the allure of winning. Or else we become Barry Bonds, who was one of the best in the game, but couldn't take getting overshadowed by others, such as Mark McGwire, who were cheating. So, the story goes, he joined them. The same could be said for Lance Armstrong. Or in the business world, companies like Enron or entrepreneurs like Elizabeth Holmes. When your identity is cemented to the pursuit, you become convinced the ends justify the means.

It's not about moving toward the opposite extreme of not caring. It's about finding the right balance between making everything personal and having space where we can handle setbacks without spiraling out of control. You move from *I am* to *I do* to *I like*. The closer you are to the being side, the higher the security and predictability. You are a cyclist or lawyer, and you see the world through that lens and act accordingly. But it comes with a downside: the security leads to attachment, which increases defensiveness when threatened and decreases flexibility or openness to change. After all, *I am* . . . is pretty definitive. On the opposite side, where you just like something, you are more open to changing. But that activity, group, or thing also has much less meaning to you.

For some items, such as our family, it makes sense to have them closer to the personal, or *I am*, side of the spectrum. For other items, like playing Monopoly or doing the laundry, it makes more sense to make that something we like versus a part of who we are. If innocuous chores drift too far toward being, we tend to see perfectionism (*I am an organizer*). We spend all our time organizing our sticky notes, and leave feeling burned out and exhausted for the actual pursuits that bring meaning or joy to our lives. Another way to think of this is, are you married, in love, or just liking something? With each increase in commitment, you decrease flexibility. But for some things, like a spouse, the tradeoff is healthy and worth it. For others, say "marrying" a group ideology or job, you are better off on the liking side of the spectrum.

When it comes to our jobs, we've often let our desire for success push us too much to the *I am* side. Our pursuits are going to be meaningful, but if we hold on to them too tightly so that they have a near full overlap for who we are, we start moving from a self-development approach to a maladaptive and hypercompetitive one. And if we're honest, if you are a pusher or striver, someone who cherishes the American dream model of success, then chances are you need to course correct.

LEARN TO LET GO

In the midst of the global pandemic, at the age of thirty-seven, Sara Hall had the breakthrough she'd long sought. She'd been a high school phenom, winning the Foot Locker Cross Country National Championship her senior year. She followed it up with a brilliant career at Stanford, where she was a seven-time All-American and three-time NCAA runner-up. In her professional career, she steadily improved, always a presence on the national level, but she could never quite make the jump to world-class. Her husband, Ryan, was the one who reached the next level, placing tenth at the 2008 Olympics in the marathon and running the fastest times ever for an American in the half marathon and the full distance. Hall was a great competitor, but she seemed stuck.

I had the pleasure of coaching Hall for a few years in the middle of her career as she moved to the marathon. Hall is one of the nicest people you will meet, but she also has an underlying ferocity when the gun goes off. While many runners shy away from competition until they know they are ready to do well, Hall wants to race all the time. She'd jump from running the US one-mile championship one week to running a half marathon shortly after. Competing fueled her soul.

It was in the longer distances that Hall found her calling. Once a 1,500-meter runner on the track, she started gravitating to and excelling at the marathon. But it wasn't until her late thirties, after she'd been a professional runner for nearly thirteen years, that she had her breakthrough. At one of the most competitive races in the world, the London Marathon, she finished second. The only person who beat her? The current world record holder. After her breakthrough in London, she said, "When you're secure in your identity you can celebrate others' successes and let them inspire you instead of threaten you." When pressed further on how she became secure in her sense of self, she replied, "It took lots of failure. Then, realizing I had built an identity around success. I had to realize I'm not what I do [and] learn I was worthy of love no matter what."

That wasn't the end of her journey. Two months later, she ran what at the time was the second fastest marathon in American history, a jaw-dropping 2:20. In 2022, at thirty-eight, when most athletes are either retired or on the downswing of their career, she broke the American record in the half marathon. When Hall first approached the race, setting the American record had been the audacious goal. As she got closer to the race, she and her husband/coach Ryan put it on the back burner. "We decided instead, the goal wasn't a time but the feeling . . . Flying along, stride fluid, flanked by amazing women, loving finally getting a cold day." As Hall explained after the race, "Sometimes you have to reframe your goal, because I never want to have a goal that's stealing my peace, ripping me out of the present and keeping me from loving the people in my life well." At thirty-nine, she finished fifth at the world championships. Late in her career, she had found her stride and herself. She balanced her extraordinary competitiveness with an ability to let go.

When I press individuals I work with who are incredibly competitive, there's a fear that surfaces. The mere mention of "letting go" shoots up a defensive wall. As one of my executive clients asked, "My competitiveness is what makes me great. If I turn it off, am I going to lose my edge?" It's often this fear that prevents us from performing to our potential.

Letting go can feel terrifying. It may feel like we are giving away our superpower. There's some truth to that. We can go too far. But for most strivers and pushers, we're so far to the being side of the equation that a bit of rebalancing enhances our performance and mental health. It takes security to let go.

Sara Hall didn't lose her competitive fire when she let go. She didn't stop caring about her performance or identifying as a runner. She just put it in its rightful place, shifting subtly on the spectrum. It's about finding the middle path, about being secure and flexible. It's about seeing what you do as important, even as a vital part of who you are, but not the entire thing. It's having a self-development view of competing. Even Michael Jordan had to learn to let go . . . just a little bit.

Jordan won six championships, but his first didn't come until year seven of his career. He was a bona fide star, winning Rookie of the Year, an MVP award in his third year, and leading the league in scoring multiple times. But he didn't start his streak of championships until coach Phil Jackson took over. Kobe Bryant is widely regarded as the heir to Jordan's competitiveness. He took a similar mentality to the game. Bryant played under six coaches in his twenty-year career. He won five NBA championships. All under Phil Jackson. Of course, the prime of his career was with Jackson, so we shouldn't attribute it all to Jackson's mystique. But it's a fascinating insight that the two players widely regarded as the most competitive in NBA history were coached by a man known as the "Zen master."

Jackson got that nickname for his penchant for bringing ideas from Buddhism into the game of basketball. Before mindfulness became mainstream, Jackson had his 1990s Bulls teams practice meditation before games. He experimented with practices in complete silence or in the dark. He preached staying in the moment and learning how to let go. In an environment that pushed brashness, bravado, and control, Jackson taught about the downfall of the ego and attachment. It's why Jackson asked one of his star players, Shaquille O'Neal, to read and write a book report on *Siddhartha*. Jackson felt Shaq was too materialistic and needed a dose of perspective on selflessness and what actually mattered.

Even his coaching style reflected this shift toward Eastern thought, as Jackson wrote in his book *Eleven Rings*, "After years of experimenting, I discovered that the more I tried to exert power directly, the less powerful I became. I learned to dial back my ego and distribute power as widely as possible without surrendering final authority." Or, as he concluded, "The most we can hope for is to create the best possible conditions for success, then let go of the outcome."

Too much ego involvement, taking everything personally, leads to hypercompetitiveness or avoidance. Our adrenaline and stress hormones overwhelm, and we move from playing to win to surviving. On the other end of the spectrum, too much detachment, and we occupy "why try" mode. What's the point of giving effort when we can rationalize or justify anything? After all, expert monks aren't winning many championships in competitions. Whether you are the best in the world or a novice, when it comes to competing, it's often about balancing these competing forces. I don't think it's a coincidence that Jackson had success with hypercompetitive athletes Jordan and Bryant not by converting them into some sort of Zen masters, but by gently, subtly pulling them in the other direction. Just enough, so their hypercompetitiveness didn't lead to their team's downfall. Just enough where they kept their egos in check.

Jackson and his star players found the balance that worked for them. Maybe they weren't Buddhist monks, but there's a reason Bryant gushed about the lessons learned from his mindfulness teacher: "George (Mumford) helped me to understand the art of mindfulness, to be neither distracted not focused, rigid nor flexible, passive nor aggressive . . . I learned to just be." The story is similar for another fierce competitor who combined insane drive with a bit of a temper. When Bruce Lee was younger, he didn't understand when his instructor, Yip Man, told him to stop being aggressive and instead to calm his mind and detach. One day, Yip Man even sent a young Lee home for essentially trying too hard and being too competitive, "Don't practice this week. Go home and think about what I've said," he commanded. It was during this period that Lee came to realize his now famous "Be like water" philosophy. Of being soft and strong, detached and powerful, or in our framing: competitive and being able to let go. Many of us are masters of pushing, striving, and attaching. But to reach our best without defaulting toward survival mode, we all need our own Phil Jackson, George Mumford, or Yip Man.

FINDING THE MIDDLE PATH

In the Buddhist tradition, suffering is believed to derive from attachment. The noble eightfold path provides the antidote. These eight items include understanding, thought, speech, action, livelihood, effort, mindfulness, and concentration. It's the sixth of these, effort, that provides clues to our conundrum of caring and competing.

The right effort involves understanding when and where to exert oneself. To illustrate what this means, Buddhist traditions tell the story of a man playing the sitar, a medieval guitarlike instrument. "What happens when you tune your instrument too tightly?" the Buddha asked. To which the musician answered, "The strings break." "And what happens when you string it too loosely?" the Buddha continued. "When it's too loose, no sound comes out," the musician answered. "The best tune comes from a string that is not too tight and not too loose." "That," said the

Buddha, "is how to practice: not too tight and not too loose." This parable demonstrates how the ego gets in the way, and the right effort is about giving attention and energy at the correct time to keep ourselves in tune. The ego will nudge and sometimes pull us away.

To reach that balance is no easy feat. Buddhism tells us to work on turning up or down welcomed or unwelcomed qualities. In our conceptualization, I like to think of it as the balance between identifying with a pursuit and letting go. Like the musical instrument, each individual might have a different balance in order to perform in the manner they desire. But we need to possess the ability to tune our inner world to meet those demands. Or as the poet T. S. Eliot wrote, "Teach us to care and not care." We need to be able to tune the strings for the situation at hand. That involves three steps.

IDENTIFY WHERE YOU ARE AND WHERE YOU NEED TO BE

Our goal isn't to be Zenned out. If we were, we'd recognize that pursuing a win in a random game is pretty meaningless in the grand scheme of things. Our goal is to find the right level of care. Remember the balance between *I am* and *I like*. Moving to "I am a runner" can help get me out the door because it's a part of who I am. But if I hold on to that too firmly, it can make running feel like a compulsion instead of something that I want to do. It can shift my goals away from something that is motivating and toward something that bring anxiety and a worry that I'll never be good enough in this thing that I really care about.

The first step is to identify where you are on the spectrum between making things personal and being wholly detached from them. One way to do so is to ask these questions:

1. If you walked away, separated yourself from the thing for a short time, how lost would you feel? Would the anxiety or stress feel overwhelming?
2. Are you overly reactive to minor comments about your job or pursuit? For example, if you love taking ice plunges every morning or love the keto diet, and someone casually says they don't work, do you immediately jump down their throat with why they are wrong?

These questions get at how trigger-happy your alarm is. In the first, your reaction to not being able to do the thing gives you an indicator of your attachment. Some level of sadness is expected. But if it feels like the world is ending if you can't lift weights for a few days or that you violate your diet for a weekend, that might be a sign you are too attached. The second gets at our inclination to jump into protect and defend mode. The quicker and more fervently we do, the more we identify with whatever is being "threatened." Again, it's natural to want to defend something important to you, but if you find yourself commencing World War III over a dietary choice, it's not a good sign.

The second step is to define where you need to be. Do you perform your best free of pressure, or do you need a tinge of stress to get the best out of yourself? In sports psychology, we refer to this as our individual zone of optimum functioning. Each individual needs a different combination of physiological arousal and even different emotions that come with it. For some, a touch of anger heightens their abilities, while for others, it sends them spiraling. It's the same when it comes to caring.

World-class coach Stu McMillan relayed a story to me about a unique athlete he coached for part of his career. Andre De Grasse went on to become an Olympic champion in the 200 meters. Still, McMillan found "he required super high levels of arousal just to get any sort of intensity out of him. . . . Andre would run at these low levels of arousal and look pretty trash. It's just not enough excitement for him. . . . He almost required a world-championship or Olympic final to compete at his best. And his championship record backed that up." Michael Jordan was likely wired this way. The only way he could get his body and mind where it needed to be was to make everything personal. At the other end of the spectrum, other world-class performers told me that they needed to minimize the role of their craft in their lives. They needed to detach from their work. We each need to make the determination about how we are wired. Once we do that, it is our mission to find where we perform best.

ADOPT THE RIGHT KIND OF CARING

Jonny Wilkinson is one of the best rugby union players of all time. He was part of the English national team for thirteen years, racking up an astonishing 1,179 points during his international career. Only one other player in England's history is within 700 points of Wilkinson. To cap it off, in the final seconds of the World Cup championship game, he scored the winning drop goal, bringing England its only championship in the tournament's history. Suffice to say, Wilkinson is a legend—someone who came through in the clutch, over and over again.

"It was pure panic. Chaos," Wilkinson described to Neil Squires of the *Express*. The lead-up to many games was torture to Wilkinson. He'd sit in his hotel room, searching for an excuse not to play. Other times, he'd find himself hiding away. "The team was outside in a huddle, waiting for me. I was supposed to be giving the 'come on, we can do this' speech, and I was a shivering wreck in the toilet." Wilkinson would find a way through, to get on the pitch and play his heart out, but the toll was grueling. The anxiety became overwhelming. Even the championship moment that was supposed to unleash unbridled happiness, failed to do so. As Wilkinson explained, that year was his most anxiety-filled, and the massive payoff never came. "There's guys who made the World Cup squad and never got picked who are as happy as anything, and there are some guys that played in the final and won it who are utterly miserable," Wilkinson said. He was the latter.

The joy disintegrated as his identity melded with the sport he was playing. "When I was playing rugby, I wore a rugby shirt and dissolved into what I was doing. The problem was my attachment to that idea of who I was meant I never took that shirt off. I became more and more attached to it," Wilkinson relayed to Squires before going on to conclude, "The massive gain—the 10 or 20 percent—came from realizing that if you want to explore your true potential, start learning to take the shirt off."

If one of the best athletes to ever play his sport is telling us that pressure and potential can be overwhelming, we should listen. We often think being obsessive and going all-in is the secret to success. We grind through the mess, believing it's the key. But it doesn't pay off. It doesn't work that way. Or, as Wilkinson put it in an interview with Andy Bull, "I lived a huge amount of my career thinking I was going to achieve joy through suffering, but all I did was create a habit of suffering."

Part of getting the right balance lies in how we care. Research shows that there are two kinds of passion that fuel drive: obsessive and harmonious. Obsessive occurs when we make the pursuits and the outcomes behind them self-defining. It fuels incredible drive but comes with the costs outlined in this book: burnout, cheating, and losing perspective. Research by psychologist Robert Vallerand found that obsessive passion is often a compensatory response to not fulfilling our needs. It's striving but out of desperation. We double down, trying to rigidly fulfill all of our needs through some pursuit, and it leads us toward being burned out, miserable, or cheating.

Harmonious passion occurs when we consider the activity or pursuit important but haven't attached our self-worth to the result. Instead, we focus on and enjoy the process. It's where the activity is seen as a way to holistically grow, instead of the near-singular source of significance and meaning. The relentless drive is still there. They want to win, but it's one that we can turn off when sitting down to eat dinner with our family or when congratulating our opponent after the game is won or lost. It's a passion that fuels their pursuit without distorting their self. Not surprisingly, harmonious passion is tied to being successful, without being miserable.

This subtle shift positively impacts our competitiveness. Care based on attachment often leads to obsession and a win-at-all-costs mindset where we are controlled by the thing. Care that comes from our internal values or focuses on the process leaves us with a similar intensity of passion but without the baggage. We choose to, instead of have to, do the work.

We have to take the jersey off, to learn to create space, to let go, all while holding the underlying joy of the pursuit front and center. Part of that is in setting boundaries, defining when you are focused and engaged and when you're not. Use natural boundaries like a car ride home or time in the locker room to debrief and switch out of stressed and focused mode. Reaching the top isn't about being obsessive all the time. It's about getting captured at the right time and then letting it go. Take it from one of the greatest rugby players in history, "The idea of who you are gets in the way of everything. It's the shirt versus the potential under it. You trap that potential with the idea you have of yourself." Stop trapping your potential. Take the jersey off.

The right kind of caring is from the inside out. It's liking or even loving your pursuit but not marrying it. It's holding on to your values tightly while keeping space between what you do and who you are. It's riding that line of being captured and passionate but in a harmonious manner. It's as if we need just enough of our ego involved, to care, to feel the pressure. But an ego concerned with our inner reflection, not our outer. That frees us up to perform.

LEARN HOW TO TURN THE DIAL

The final piece of the puzzle is to develop the tools to nudge yourself to either side of the spectrum. To be able to let go, or to make something meaningful and feel more personal. We can use various strategies, some of which we've already learned.

For instance, we already learned how changing our vocabulary from doing ("I like to write") to being ("I am a writer") can both turn up and down the dial. We also heard how Sara Hall learned to let go by changing her focus and goal. She ditched the time and focused on the feeling, making her goal more process-oriented and self-consciously driven. On the other side, Michael Jordan made himself feel like an underdog, like he was under-appreciated. He also engaged in a lot of trash-talking. He made it personal. For many, this would be too much of a burden, but for someone who probably was on the extreme end of physiological arousal needs, it worked for excelling in games.

We can learn from ancient wisdom, with Eastern religions and philosophies extolling the benefits of decentering. How does this process work? It starts with awareness of the situation and your thoughts and feelings, and then reminding yourself that you are separate from that experience. You aren't your thoughts or feelings. The practice of mindfulness is built on helping you decenter by increasing your ability not to react to or judge whatever arises.

Another way to turn the dial more toward letting go is by doing things that expand your perspective. That could be as simple as spending time in nature, reading fiction, or experiencing strong sensations like awe or flow. All of these pull us away from a self-centered focus to a reminder that whatever we are doing isn't all that matters. The same effect occurs when we spend meaningful time with friends and family. Research shows that doing interesting and challenging things with your significant others causes both of you to self-expand, seeing yourself and the world through a new perspective.

Even when we turn the dial up in the caring direction, we need to make sure it's the right kind of caring. And, perhaps more important, we can let go once that moment is gone. As we learned in chapter 5, resilience is tied to an efficient termination of the stress response. In other words, even when we occupy fight-or-flight mode, we need to realize when the proverbial lion has left. Far too many of us stay in hypercompetitive mode as if the danger is still there. In other words, it's okay to be Michael Jordan when in the game, but let's learn how to not compete in Monopoly when we get home.

RELAX AND WIN

The essence of this chapter can be summed up with an analogy: We need to strive to be like a world-class sprinter. They produce enormous amounts of power, putting nearly one thousand pounds of force into the ground with each stride. Yet, if you look at the greats such as Usain Bolt or Carl Lewis, they are as relaxed as can be. You see it in their faces as their cheeks bounce up and down.

They are trying to minimize tension because trying harder would lead to straining. And straining would slow them down. The key to sprinting is having your muscles work at maximum capacity while you are relaxed so that needless tension doesn't get in the way. It's in this balance of contrasts where elite performance lies. To be able to relax when the tendency is to tighten up and "try harder." Or, as famed sprint coach Bud Winter summarized it, "Relax and win!" Or, in Buddhist terms, sprinters have mastered the right effort.

The same holds true for the rest of life. Life tends to push us toward tension, often caused by putting our self on the line. We think bearing down, focusing obsessively on the end result, utilizing fear as our primary motivator, and trying harder is the way toward success. But the reality is that most of us need to go the other way. To counterbalance, societies pull toward attachment and obsession. To learn to relax and let go while giving our best effort.

Consider skateboarder Tony Hawk, one of the best athletes ever to walk the planet. Hawk revolutionized skateboarding, pushing the boundaries of tricks and artistry for decades. He climbed the ranks from phenom to a transcendent athlete. And behind it all was a relentless determination. He had an obsession that allowed him to practice the same trick over and over until he mastered it. In his own words, he was a "machine." Early on, his focus was success.

"I was singularly focused on skating and doing well at the events because that was the only road to success. It probably affected my emotional connections because I couldn't think of anything else. . . . I was just a machine," Hawk reported in the documentary *Tony Hawk: Until the Wheels Fall Off.* Partway through his career, he'd already reached the top of the skating world. He was the best in the world. Then he quit. The judgment and constant need to one-up himself and to impress others had taken its toll. It transformed an activity that once provided so much joy into one of despair. As he later reflected, "I felt like I was losing myself. Losing my passion. None of the money or fame or success was worth that."

It wasn't until his friend and fellow skater Rodney Mullen gave him some wise advice that Hawk returned to competing. Mullen told him to "risk not winning." Hawk explained, "I was like 'Oh I have all this freedom now. I'm not beholden to earning points and staying on all the time.'" When he returned to competing, Hawk said he "had a totally different approach to what I was doing. Started getting much more creative . . . I could still make it fun, and I could still do it for a living, and that was it. That was the turning point." After this, Hawk became the first person in history to complete a nine hundred in competition. He went from the top skater in the world to a worldwide phenomenon. By detaching from the competition and letting go, he freed himself up to perform.

That's the middle path. To recognize when we've been pulled toward tensing up—or attaching ourselves to the outcome, idea, or group in order to succeed—and instead, do the opposite. Like a novice sprinter, we might question, "How can I run fast by trying less?" As Tom Tellez once told me, "We have the wrong concept for effort. We think it means forcing, digging in, and trying harder. It doesn't. It means trusting our body to do what we trained it to do. Effort should be subtle. Not loud."

Some people need to make it more personal—to identify more as a lawyer so that they get rid of their imposter syndrome, or as an athlete so they get to the gym and train. Some need to let go a bit, to realize that teaching is what they do, and maybe even what they love, but if they identify solely with their job, they'll be burned out and quit in three years. In a culture that emphasizes the external and props up pushers, most of us need to be a little less like Michael Jordan and a little more like Sara Hall.

—

In part one of this book, "Be," I outlined the importance of going on a quest filled with exploration and commitment in order to pursue goals and identities that align with your motivation. I covered the importance of being the writer and editor of your story so that you can have an authentic and realistic inner narrative. In part two, "Do," I covered the importance of learning how to lose. How we handle and integrate our challenges and failures can either push us toward a fragile or robust sense of self. In this chapter, I've covered the role of caring in our pursuits. To learn how to compete without being deluded. Being and doing are deeply intertwined. We've separated them for the sake of organization, but what you do is often the primary driver for who you are. It's in our vocabulary.

It's about finding the middle path to have both security and flexibility—to be able to explore and commit, to try and let go, to feel secure in your story and be able to rewrite it—all while keeping intrinsic motivation, or pursuing joy, front and center. It's when our being and doing collide that we often get stuck. We force when we can't let go. We lose it and give up when protection and survival override anything else.

Up until now, we've mainly focused on ourselves. Who are we? What's our story? How do we compete? How do we handle winning or losing, trying or not? We've mentioned society's master narratives, which shape our expectations, but we've neglected the other, sometimes hidden, pull that impacts whether we are playing prevent defense or playing to win: our environment. The people, places, and things surrounding us have a much greater impact than we often admit. Spoiler alert: It turns out that the answer to the question that every mother asked, "Would you jump off a bridge if Suzy did?" is a resounding "yes."

PART THREE

BELONG— CLARITY ON WHERE AND HOW YOU FIT IN

CHAPTER 7

CRAFT YOUR ENVIRONMENT
TO WORK WITH YOU,
NOT AGAINST YOU

The tunnels underneath the McMartin preschool in Los Angeles, it was said, led to secret chambers where satanic rituals, secret meetings, and even animal sacrifices occurred. Most concerning, there were reports of an elaborate scheme of sexual abuse of children. All of this took place at a daycare. In interviews with nearly four hundred students, investigators uncovered horrifying stories, among the worst nightmares of any parent. Widespread abuse by daycare workers. A bizarre satanic sex cult in the middle of one of America's largest cities. It was so horrifying and widespread that one student even identified legendary actor Chuck Norris as a participant.

Devil-worshipping pedophiles were among us. And worse, they were working at our daycares and schools. While the McMartin preschool might have been ground zero, the concern spread far beyond Los Angeles. Around the country, more than twelve thousand allegations surfaced, and eventually, at least thirty people were convicted in relation to these satanic cults in daycares. The only problem? It wasn't real. Chuck Norris wasn't part of some occult practice, and neither were the daycare workers. There were no tunnels or secret chambers. The vast majority of those convicted by juries were exonerated, though some served over twenty years of jail time before they were released for wrongful conviction and rightfully awarded millions for their suffering. How does something like this happen?

In the 1980s and '90s, a large part of society suffered from a powerful collective delusion. As a child growing up during this period, I remember my suburban parents and schools being increasingly weary of "stranger danger." As elementary students, we had it drilled into our heads by teachers, police officers, and guest speakers to never trust a stranger. The fear was real. There were police training videos detailing how cops can identify satanic practices, bestselling books, and TV specials like Geraldo Rivera's 1988 special *Devil Worship: Exposing Satan's Underground*. It was the highest-rated TV documentary up to that point. Society was enraptured and delusional.

According to historian Sarah Hughes, the satanic panic occurred thanks to a unique combination of factors. First, the rise of infotainment in tabloids, cable TV shows, and more led to an erosion of the once-clear division between news and entertainment. The war for viewers meant an increase in stories that stoked people's fear and emotions. Second, it was a time of uncertainty and change. There was a rise in social movements, while fear around AIDs was at its peak. Video games, punk rock, and the emergence of rap were seen as corrupting kids' minds, so much so that Congress was involved to deal with this "crisis." And the world was locked in a cold war, with kids across the country taught to take cover under their desks if a nuclear bomb was headed their way. In other words, uncertainty was high, the country was rapidly changing, and people defaulted toward protection.

You might think we're not as gullible as our parents' generation. The '80s were a wild time. We've moved on. But substitute daycare centers for a pizza shop in the suburbs of Washington, DC, and you had the same story in 2020. Pizzagate, as it became known online, was a conspiracy theory promoted by the QANON movement that politicians were meeting in the basement of a DC pizza parlor to abuse children. That the pizza parlor had no basement was a minor inconvenience to the larger narrative. History rhymes.

When we are inundated with a message that the world is threatening, we start to believe it. A 2008 study found that media exposure explains why Americans, in particular, often see the rest of the world as dangerous. Other research shows a link between the amount of crime reported on the news and the degree of fear people have over crime. It's not just worry. News consumption is related to avoidance behavior as a way to deal with the fear of violent crime. It's not just traditional media that plays a role. A recent analysis found that social media consumption is linked to an increased fear of street violence.

This effect isn't limited to crime. A 2021 study in Spain found that the more news participants consumed about COVID-19, the more COVID was perceived as a major risk. A study following the Boston Marathon bombing found that individuals who had watched six or more hours per day of coverage of the bombing felt more stress than those directly impacted. Our perception is reality. Regardless of where you fall on the political spectrum, you aren't immune to a heightened fear or threat response driven by information consumption. In the 1970s, professor of communication George Gerbner coined a term for a similar phenomenon—*mean world syndrome.* Gerbner found that we tend to see the world as more dangerous and threatening than it is and that it was related to the overabundance of violence on TV.

It's tempting to call people dumb, but that's a mistake. There's something stronger pulling people toward believing in the crazy and delusional. When our environment screams danger, finding a place to belong, to validate our world, provides the antidote, even if that means accepting the crazy. In a series of studies out of Princeton University in 2017, psychologists found that social exclusion leads to conspiratorial thinking. Other research points to it providing purpose, meaning, and significance. We all want to belong, to have the world add up. Ironically, we fall for delusions precisely because we are trying to have things make sense under threat and uncertainty.

Our environment can either prod us toward delusion and grasping onto a false sense of fitting in, or it can help us see clearly with authentic connections as the backbone of our relationship with those around us. We've let our environments turn our threat alarms to eleven. Our environment—from the information we consume to whether we feel secure in it—shapes our expectations. And when everything around us is screaming fear and danger, is it any wonder we default toward survival mode and protection? Our brain is doing its job, predicting based on the information it has. To perform at our best, we need to learn how to turn down the threat, to feel secure instead of alone, to see the challenge clearly instead of through a distorted lens. It starts with making ourselves feel at home.

CREATING COHESION TO TURN DOWN THE THREAT

Matt Parmley is smart, with a wry sense of humor. He is a go-with-the-flow type of guy, who can flip a switch and turn into a ferocious competitor. Among his friends, he was the class clown, the one people could count on to break the tension before a big competition. But on one particular day, much more recently, he found himself in the hot seat. He was in a chair in the middle of a room, with forty peers circling around him. He had no idea what to expect. Then came the verbal beating. "You're not good enough. You're never going to make it. You choke on the big stage. You're worthless," were the words coming out of his coach's mouth.

Matt wasn't sitting in front of a Bobby Knight impersonator. He wasn't taking a verbal whiplash from a high school football coach who was drunk on power and control. He was sitting in front of me. I was berating him. I hadn't lost my mind; Matt was a willing participant in a mini-experiment. In his situation, most of us would have shied away, shrunk our shoulders, and maybe run out of the room. But Matt didn't flinch. He smiled. He was demonstrating the power of support and feeling like you belong. Behind Matt stood his girlfriend and teammate, Meredith, with her hand on his shoulder. It wasn't that the words didn't sting. They did. But with a physical reminder that he had others who loved and supported him, there wasn't a need to sound the alarm. This isn't wild conjecture. It's science.

In a study out of the University of Virginia, researchers put women through a different kind of threat: a painful shock while lying in a brain scanner. When a shock was imminent, the brain lit up in distress. But when the women were allowed to hold the hand of their significant other, the fear and stress were attenuated. Those who were in the happiest relationships had the greatest stress-relieving effect from holding hands. Psychologists at UCLA found a similar response when applying a painful hot probe to the forearm. When they showed participants a picture of their significant other, they reported less pain, and the pain-related brain areas were also reduced. The longer and more supportive their relationship, the bigger the effect. The researchers concluded that attachment acts as a safety signal.

Social baseline theory posits that we outsource much of our emotional regulation to others as a way to minimize risk and conserve energy. We share the load. Instead of feeling the full burden of taking on a challenge or figuring out how to get through a verbal beratement, our brain counts on others to help us cope. It has for a long time. Any parent knows that you bear your newborn's burdens, helping them soothe and manage their emotions. Sure, we develop a capacity to self-soothe, but the aid of another never truly leaves us. When we know we can share the load, our predictions of our capabilities change, shifting our perceptions of what we can handle.

With someone else there, the daunting seems manageable. For instance, when standing at the bottom of a steep hill, participants in a study at the University of Virginia judged the hill to be, on average, seven degrees shallower when they had a friend by their side. The same effect was found when subjects had to lift heavy boxes. Having a friend nearby led participants to perceive the boxes as lighter. Other research has found that forgiving others leads to judging hills as shallower, and being able to jump higher, while holding on to a grudge, made the hill seem steeper. Relieving the social burden frees us up.

Shigehiro Oishi, Jamie Schiller, and E. Blair Gross took this idea a step further, manipulating people's sense of being understood. After spending time conversing with a partner assigned to them, participants were handed a piece of paper where their partner had circled traits that described them. For half the subjects, the traits had been rigged to match precisely how they had described themselves (i.e., hardworking, friendly, etc.), and for the other half, polar opposite traits were circled. When the descriptors matched up, people felt understood, and they could tolerate the pain of sticking their hands in freezing water for longer. They also judged a hill to be shallower and the distances to a destination as shorter. These findings led the researchers to state, "The presence of a close other provides a sense of assurance that the world is a safe place."

When we feel secure and supported, the way in which we see the world changes. When we feel understood and connected, everything seems a bit more manageable, a bit more doable, and a bit less threatening. Instead of a big scary place ripe for insult or embarrassment, we walk around knowing that even if adversity rears its head, we will be okay. The world looks a little less dangerous and a little more conquerable when we have others in our corner.

We have an innate need to belong. A sense of belonging provides meaning to our lives, increasing our self-worth. It reinforces that our experiences or beliefs are normal and shared by others. When we feel like we belong, we can make sense of and cope with challenging experiences, while feeling like we have a place and people to retreat to if we fail.

A large reason we end up living in survival mode is feeling like we don't belong, both in terms of our social connection and the environment or spaces we occupy. When we feel comfortable where we live, work, or play, we turn down our alarms—not just because of the people who inhabit those spaces but because of the spaces themselves. If our workspace feels like home and reflects who we are, we'll be more productive. If we can decorate our home, or if we feel like the tools or instruments we utilize every day reflect who we are, we are healthier, happier, more resilient people.

We need to feel at home in all aspects of our life, including:

- with others,
- in our spaces, and
- in the direction we are headed.

THE LOST ART OF HANGING OUT

If you are standing in line at the movies or waiting for the waiter to come to your table, how do you deal with the boredom? If it's 1995, you converse with your friends or let your mind wander. As we learned in chapter 3, boredom pushes us toward exploration and can be a catalyst for creativity. Boredom is what fuels the pillow forts and made-up games of our youth. In the 2020s, we're more likely to fill that space by reaching for our phones and exploring in another way: by scrolling on social media. There's no bump in creative exploration. We've filled that boredom with something, but it's an artificial solution.

We've done the same with connection. We reach for a more superficial version. We listen to the feelings compelling us to affiliate, and instead, we mimic our psycho-biologic needs with a synthetic version. Sometimes, that means turning to things that feel like connection, such as watching our favorite Instagram, YouTube, or reality TV star. After all, we see more of their life than our actual friends. Our phones increasingly provide a temporary sense of ease, like a baby reaching for their security blanket.

Other times, it means reaching for a synthetic substitute. As psychiatrist Julie Holland wrote in *Good Chemistry*, "opiates mimic the body's response to feeling cared for. In animal studies, opiates very effectively relieve separation distress. They approximate that good chemistry of connectedness and attachment. Opiates are plugging a gaping hole for millions of Americans." When we lack a sense of belonging, or when it's under threat, our body goes on a panicked mission to fill this hole, and it impacts not only our health, but performance.

When Jaak Panksepp and colleagues gave opiate receptor stimulants to animals, they found that animals moved from being more submissive to dominant. Rats were more likely to pin their competitors during play. Panksepp came to the same conclusion Holland did. A small boost in opiate levels were "sufficient to generate feelings of social confidence, facilitate winning in playful competitions." We don't need drugs to get this boost; we need genuine connection.

How do we feel understood and connected in a world that feels so disparate and isolated? Part of our problem is we've killed the primary way we form bonds: hanging out. We've replaced it with either the superficial or the overly scheduled. We don't meet up and then figure out what to do; we put it in our Google calendars months in advance. We let some scheduler drive our interactions. And even when we do have those moments of being around others, we reach for a distraction to minimize the awkwardness, boredom, or filling time that dominated our interactions historically. We've taken away the glue that research shows us is crucial for maintaining relationships. By eliminating these feelings, we've turned our alarms up. It feels strange, almost threatening, to sit with other people, especially strangers. Casual conversations feel like an intrusion.

When I was coaching college cross-country, I quickly noticed a trend. While the rest of the world was hating on the conversational skills of teens and young adults, I was impressed. But they needed the right environment. When they were out on a run, they could talk for hours. The conversation would bounce from the deep (philosophical debates) to the mundane (favorite shows) to the absurd (who would win a fight, a lion or gorilla?). On runs, conversation flowed. And for good reason. Without headphones to distract, it was either be bored out of your mind or fill the time getting to know your teammates. If we want conversation, you need to create the space for connection.

During my time as a cross-country coach, I did my best to create space for the team to be together. I scoured the building I worked in and found a hodgepodge of chairs, a small cabinet people could sit on, and an abandoned couch. I crammed them all into my small office, transforming it into a place where nearly every inch of room was a place one could sit. I let the team know my office was always open to chat, sit around, do homework, or gather. Over time, it became the default postpractice and in-between classes place to hang out. Sometimes, we'd cram over a dozen people in, assuredly breaking some fire code. The point wasn't to talk track. It was to create an environment that allowed them to hang out. I let them shoot the shit. As it took off, we scheduled regular times to wrestle with deeper topics that people wanted to cover. Phones weren't banned. People still scrolled. But over time, young adults filled the space with conversation.

That conversation led to understanding, connection, and feeling like you found a place where you could be yourself. Belonging doesn't mean you are going to be everyone's best friend. It meant something more akin to what our ancient ancestors felt. I see you, know you, and support you. We're in this together.

I quickly learned that if you create the space, people will fill it. It's not about blaming younger generations for their lack of ability to converse or connect. It's our environment getting in the way. We need to create spaces that invite hanging out, conversing, and being ourselves. We've optimized our way out of the in-between moments that make and maintain genuine connection and conversation.

FEELING AT HOME IN OUR WORLD

Gina was isolated. It was freezing, wet, and windy. She was deep in the wilderness of Tasmania, in the midst of a winter "polar blast." And she signed up for it. Gina was participating in *Alone Australia*, a reality TV show that puts ten individuals deep into the wilderness of Australia, separated so that they don't come across one another. Only, this isn't American *Survivor*. They are truly alone. There are no TV crews, no other humans to interact with. They are given meager survival gear, and 150 pounds of camera equipment to self-document their journey. The person who lasts the longest wins $250,000.

Despite the freezing temperatures, rain, mud, and downright miserable environment, Gina brought a unique approach to the challenge. When she arrived at her site, she did a barefoot dance in the moss. Why? "That was my way of saying to the land, 'I'm here, and I want to dance with you.'"

Her main competitor, Outback Mike, took a different approach. He was a pilot in the Australian Defence Force. He was an adventurer, who had been on many solo survival expeditions. Such as the time he simulated a shipwreck escape by building a dugout canoe, then sailing one thousand miles along the Great Barrier Reef. He was a survivalist. And he brought that to the contest. Mike was determined, relentless, and hardcore. He wanted to win.

Mike created a shelter. He chopped down branches and small trees, stacking them horizontally and binding them together so that he had four walls. A tarp went over the top. It was sturdy, practical. Gina took a different path. She created a home. It wasn't glamorous. It was more of a hut, a few small trees and branches to hold the structure in place, surrounded by green grass, branches, and more to create the walls. That distinction was important, as Gina told *The Guardian*: "If we don't have a house, there's a part of us that freaks out. Think about how you feel when you're moving house. If we have a shelter that feels secure and cozy, like a home, there's a huge part of our nervous system that down regulates and therefore doesn't burn as many calories. And also, has that feeling of, 'I could be here forever because I am so comfortable.'"

It wasn't just the living arrangements that made the difference.

Mike was surviving. Gina was living with the land. "This whole thing wasn't a temporary thing where I was going to go and be 'on the land'; for me it was about being one with the land." And after sixty-seven days finding her own food and braving the severe winds Australians call the "Roaring Forties" that shredded Mike's shelter, Gina came out on top. Before she knew she won, at the tail end of spending a week inside her hut due to the rain and wind, she realized, "Oh, I don't feel trapped, I'm just here." Shortly after, producers let her know she was the last survivor, "They were like, 'You can go home now!' I was like, no, no, no! I'm just getting started!" Gina was at home. And that proved to be her advantage.

We're all familiar with the home-field advantage in sports. While the total effect and potential causes have been widely debated, from referees to the energy and excitement of playing in front of a home crowd, one small but important aspect is ownership. When we perform in a familiar place, it feels like it's our own. There's a sense of comfort to it, a sense that I belong here. It can even impact our biology. Some research on soccer players found that during home games, players had higher testosterone levels, especially during a rivalry match. While another study found that players are more likely to be assertive in home games. In many ways, we are all trying to create a home-field advantage. An environment that invites us to learn, grow, and perform.

The same effect holds away from the sporting fields. As I walked into the first-grade classroom, I was struck by subtle shifts in design from what I remembered of a classroom decades ago. As expected, students' work was all over the wall, along with a mixture of inspirational posters and reminders of the critical lessons for that week's units. But long gone were the rows of nondescript desks and chairs. A mixture of traditional chairs, stools, and even beanbag chairs and pillows littered the room.

There was a reading nook. As one educator told me, "Teaching is less and less about a teacher standing at the front of the room dictating. For a lot of our activities, like reading, that may mean lying on the floor reading a good book. We want students to feel at home doing their work."

Research validates the approach. In a series of studies out of the University of Salford in the UK, Peter Barrett and team found that the school environment had between a 16 and 25 percent impact on learning rates when analyzing thousands of students. There were three main parameters they referred to as SIN: stimulation level, individualization, and naturalness. A rich environment that was appropriately stimulating; felt personal and inviting; and had fresh air, appeals to nature, and good lighting makes a difference. It creates a space where kids feel more at home and free to learn.

The same holds true in our workplace. Markus Baer, a professor of organizational behavior, found that participants who took part in a negotiation performed up to 160 percent better when they felt at home in the negotiation room. The wild thing is that the negotiators weren't really in their own office. They spent all of twenty minutes making the office feel like home and became better, more confident negotiators compared to those who came into the room and started negotiation. In research by Craig Knight and Alexander Haslam, decorating an office increased well-being and productivity, but the effect was even more pronounced when workers had input on the decorations, even if the decorations were ultimately the same. They felt what is called psychological ownership.

Feeling ownership of your workspace leads to an increase in positive feelings and greater commitment to the work. Psychologists have tied the benefits of such ownership to fulfilling some of our basic psychological needs: self-efficacy, identity, a sense of belonging, and having a place to call our own. When our environment allows us to be who we are, we feel and perform better. As

Annie Murphy Paul wrote in *The Extended Mind*, "When people occupy spaces that they consider their own, they experience themselves as more confident and capable. They are more efficient and productive. They are more focused and less distractible. And they advance their own interests more forcefully and effectively." Therapists have long taken advantage of this effect. How they arrange the room's furniture can impact the therapy's quality. Research suggests there is a direct relationship between the space feeling personal, soft, and inviting and the patient's judgment of the quality of the care.

It's not just in sports, work, or the doctor's office where this idea surfaces and changes our behavior. If you feel a sense of connection and ownership to the lake you kayak on or the trails you walk on, you're more likely to take care of that public space: picking up trash, volunteering, or donating to the park. Experiencing awe out in nature also leads to a feeling of psychological ownership. Not because we think we own the mountain, lake, or forest that gives rise to such feelings. It's that we feel a connection to nature, that we are home, and that we belong to something much greater than ourselves. In other words, Gina's secret to outlasting in the wild is research backed. We've increasingly become disconnected from our space. The way back is to connect with our environment.

Simple and subtle changes can make us feel this sense of ownership in our work arenas, whether by putting up pictures of our family, organizing it in our style, or sticky notes of quotes that resonate. Decorating might seem trivial, but those pictures and posters send a constant subconscious message that you belong here.

Feeling ownership of one's space tells us that it's okay to take on a role that feels authentic. The space we occupy tells us whether we belong here, whether we are accepted, and if we can let our guard down. We feel more confident and invested. We approach challenges with a sense of inner security. Alternatively, if our space feels threatening, we need to be defensive and aggressive. Our space tells us which role to play and whether to approach or avoid.

There's a downside to ownership, one that any dog parent is well aware of. When the mail carrier approaches our mighty puppy's yard, it's as if everyone's life is at stake. A mixture of growling, barking, snarling, and pacing up and down the fence commence, all as a signal to the mail carrier to get off my property. The teeth marks on the windows of our house from our dog, Willie, reflect this hostility. The same attitude arises when Willie procures a new bone. Suddenly, in his mind, I have transformed from loving friend who is good for some much-needed scratching to a mortal enemy who, at any moment, might steal away this precious object. I'm a threat. He must defend his objects and territory at all costs. Ownership has a close cousin called territoriality.

Instead of feeling connected to the space, we become like the dog in the yard: extremely protective over our space or objects. We are afraid of others intruding. If someone disturbs us at our cubicle, comes in to borrow our stapler, or sits in "our" chair at the lunch table, we feel as if a mortal sin has been committed. Our space or objects have been infringed upon. We follow such indiscretions with behavior similar to Willie. Anger, resentment, or a berating soon follow.

Territoriality is one of the contributors to road rage. We lose our minds when someone cuts us off, partially because we take it as an infringement on our space. As neuroscientist Douglas Fields explains, "We tend to view the area around our vehicle while driving as territory. When a vehicle cuts in front of us, this can pull the Environment trigger to defend that territory." We move from Joe the commuter to Joe the fierce protector of our property. And before we know it, we are flipping off some mother and child.

When we adopt such a mindset, our coworkers start to see

us in a negative light, and it can significantly diminish team-work and creativity. Territoriality predominantly occurs when we see ourselves as separate, independent individuals and when our identity is attached to an outcome. We feel under threat, partially because we see our work as being zero-sum. We must protect our house. It's as if we've moved from a feeling of comfort and oneness with the space to an experience of mine-ness, greed, and protection. It's as if that desk belongs to you and only you. When we live in survival mode, we're more likely to become the dog viciously protecting his yard from the invading army of delivery drivers. In some situations, like sporting competitions, we might swing a little more toward territoriality, but moving too far in that direction moves us from assertiveness to unhelpful aggressiveness.

The ownership versus territoriality distinction follows the nuance we've wrestled with throughout this book. Sometimes, like in a rivalry game, we might turn the dial up, edging toward defending our turf. But if we go too far, we get stuck aggressively defending instead of proactively approaching. For the most part, we want to feel at home but with an expansive, cooperative mindset instead of a narrow, self-centered one. It's no different from what Adam Smith warned us of so many years ago. We need to counterbalance our self-centered view of the world with one that sees us as part of a greater whole, belonging to a greater community. We need to make our environments feel like home, while also welcoming to those around us.

The space we occupy can either reaffirm our sense of self in a positive way, telling us to feel secure and comfortable. Or it can put us on the defensive. What self is your environment inviting? There are two ways you can feel the right kind of ownership in your environment.

MAKE YOUR SPACE INVITING

While decorating might not be for everyone, it is vital for performance. Whether it's pictures, posters, or inspirational quotes on the wall, adding your personal touch to your space creates a home-field advantage. The key is that it is authentic and meaningful to who you are and the vibe you want to give off. If you want inspiration, walk into an elementary school classroom. It's a mixture of posters meant to inspire and help the students, with enough personal messaging that signals to the teacher (and others) that this is my homeroom. I've seen teachers with everything from Disney to sports themes. They reflect a little piece of the teacher, along with an invitation to come in and learn to all those who venture into their classroom.

The same can be said for meetings in the workplace. Research shows to increase interaction and performance of a group, simply follow a few tips. Make the meeting in a familiar environment, where everyone is sitting at eye level and can see one another. In other words, King Arthur may have been on to something with his large round table. In our offices, the same principles hold. A recent study found that simply having a higher number of desks in our visual field decreased collaboration and our sense of team cohesion.

USE OBJECTS TO INVITE ROLES AND ACTIONS

In the episode "And Maggie Makes Three" of the long-running cartoon *The Simpsons*, Homer is burned out at his job at the nuclear power plant. He quits in dramatic fashion, humiliating his boss, Mr. Burns, along the way. Soon after, Homer learns that his wife, Marge, is pregnant with their third child, Maggie. After realizing the nuclear power plant is his only route to providing for his budding family, Homer resorts to begging Mr. Burns for his old job back. Mr. Burns acquiesces but puts a giant sign that reads "Don't forget: you're here forever" in front of his workspace. In the episode's closing scene, we see that Homer has put pictures of his baby girl Maggie all over the sign so that it now reads, "Do it for her."

Objects invite action. They act as a communication system to our brain. Ecological psychology tells us that our perception is linked to the environment we occupy. The objects in our space are like a cheat code for the brain, allowing us to get to a behavior much more quickly and smoothly. If we see a chair, the motor program for sitting lights up before we've even taken our first step toward the chair. Our brain paves the way, nudging us toward the action.

We can take advantage of this by utilizing objects as reminders, or tying an environment to a specific behavior. A notebook on your desk invites creative thinking or writing. While phones invite scrolling. If you want to improve your likelihood of exercise, consider placing your running shoes by the front door so you see them every day. We can create mental nudges via our environment.

The objects in our environment don't just prime actions; they invite different roles. A picture of your family reminds you why work is important, activating your provider or caring self. An athlete wearing a game-day jersey can transform the shy kid into a competitor. In many ways, this connection can be seen clearest when researchers hand people a gun—their perception shifts. Just by holding a gun, people—including trained police—are more likely to misidentify objects that others are holding. We mistake phones, shoes, and even bananas for a weapon. Our perception of the world alters simply by holding an object. Innocuous items start to seem a bit more threatening. Research shows that drivers who have a gun in their car experience more road rage. They drive more aggressively, flip people off more, and are more likely to tailgate. A 2018 meta-analysis looking at over sixty years of research found that having a weapon nearby increased aggressive thoughts, actual aggression, and appraising the situation and others as hostile.

Why? Holding a weapon changes our expectations. Our brain stops seeing ourselves as Joe, the friendly neighbor walking down the street, but as Joe, the weapon-toting protector who should be on the lookout for a threat. As Jessica Whitt, the author of one of the aforementioned studies, explained, "When someone holds a gun they become a shooter, and this changes how that person perceives other people and things. . . . [Y]our perceptual system aligns with seeing yourself as a shooter."

We see the same effect in products we own. Marketers have long taken advantage of this. A study by psychologists Jaeyeon Chung and Gita Johar found that objects can prime or activate an identity. Meaning, if you give someone a notepad or a book, their writer or reader self would be salient. But in that process, we turn down our other selves. Chung and Johar found that our performance in tasks unrelated to the activated identity gets worse. For example, if our athlete self is active, we might not perform as well on an academic task or vice versa. This effect was even stronger in those who had lower self-concept clarity.

Objects tell us which role to occupy. They change our perception not only of the environment but of ourselves. Whether on the athletic field or in our office, objects remind you who you are and why you're doing it. We can invite the role of writer, runner, teacher, or student to be open to learn and grow. Or we can invite roles that make us feel defensive and under threat. We can use this to turn us into a fierce competitor or someone with road rage who lost their mind. Rig your environment wisely.

SEEING A FUTURE

"Princesses can't be black. They are white," a first grade student blurted out as my wife, Hillary, was going through her lesson on fairy tales. Hillary quickly retorted. "Cinderella can be any color. Look around the room. Aren't we all different? Don't you think princesses reflect all of us?" She then grabbed books showing princesses of all makeups.

Just about every elementary school teacher has experienced something similar when they ask their young students to draw a firefighter or pilot. Kids draw a male. It may seem like a small, innocuous comment, but it gets at something more profound: we can only be what we see.

We just learned that objects prime us for action. When we see a chair, a part of our brain is already primed to sit. But what if we don't know what a chair is? This example might seem absurd but think about an object familiar to one society but foreign to another. At one time, chopsticks, forks, or baseball gloves had no meaning in some parts of the world, while they invited a specific action in another. The first time we see an object, it doesn't invite a simple action. We had to understand what it could do, and if we were lucky, watch someone else show us how to use that object. If we don't know what an object is for, it's not inviting an action. The same holds for our environment inviting roles.

Our environment tells us which hat to wear and what role to occupy. We dress up, acting professionally and formally when meeting with a distinguished business client, and then drop the charade when we relax with our coworkers at the bar after the meeting. We pick it back up the following day at church, where we wouldn't dare utter choice words, but then invoke those same phrases when our football team loses the game a few hours later. We may be reserved and respectful to one client, but confident and brash to another. We move from shy and introverted to bold and boisterous, depending on the setting. Our language, dress, and behaviors all shift depending on what environment we are in and who we are around. This isn't rocket science. It's part of being human. Sometimes it's intentional. Other times, it feels like our demeanor shifts and changes without our control.

In the research lab, psychologists use priming to make different identities more salient. They remind participants of their ethnicity, gender, job, political affiliation, or past exploits as a way to move that self to the front of a person's mind and then see how their behavior changes. In a study out of the University of Michigan evaluating working in a large group, if individuals were reminded of their ethnicity, coordination and cooperation within the group declined. If they were primed with the fact they all attended the same college, cooperation increased. In other research, reminding college students that they were athletes led to lower self-regard and worse performance on a math test. Reminding a group of Asian females about their ethnicity improved academic performance while focusing on their gender decreased performance.

Not only does our environment invite different roles, but it tells us which future roles we could occupy. Often, the idea of representation gets thrown into the culture war dustbin, but research shows that it plays an important role: shaping our positive future roles. If an identity can't be seen, it's like the object that we don't know what it's supposed to do.

According to the possible selves theory, we all carry around possible future selves. It's a mixture of hopes, dreams, fears, and goals that contribute to our imagined future of who we want to become. These apply to our aspirations (e.g., a creative or successful self), our fears (e.g., an alone or depressed self), our personal pursuits (e.g., mother, friend, gardener self), or our occupations (e.g., teacher, doctor, etc.). The more salient these become, the more we are motivated to work toward (or avoid) that future self. If you grew up watching an alcoholic family member ruin their lives, you might have strong nonalcoholic behaviors. Or if you come from a family of teachers, that might be a strong future self.

We shape our future selves based on the information we have. When we see someone we can identify with pursuing a career, it opens up possible future selves. Think about your work. Chances are you were inspired by a teacher, mentor, friend, or family member to explore that field. It wasn't a potential path for you until you figured out what a genetic counselor, anthropologist, or social worker did. It's why schools have career days where parents and guests come in to talk about what they do. You are expanding possible future roles.

This is called the role-model effect. It's not just about modeling professions. It's seeing others who you can relate to as successful individuals. For instance, in an analysis of seven thousand students across seventy-nine schools, researchers found that if a Black student had a Black teacher early in elementary school, they were 13 percent more likely to attend college. If they had multiple Black teachers, kids were 32 percent more likely to enroll in college. Although the data isn't as robust, there's a similar effect with male teachers for male students. It's not just similarity; it's seeing a future. In a review of over fifty-five studies on the impact of role models on students' attitudes toward the science, technology, engineering, and math (STEM) fields, researchers found that psychological similarity, perceived competence, and perceived attainability of success were all positively related to student motivation. In other words, students were more motivated to enter STEM fields when they had a role model they could relate to and see themselves as in the future.

It's not just kids who need role models. As we age, our potential future selves get narrower. We start to feel locked in, as if aging is restricting our potential paths. There may be some truth in that a fifty-year-old isn't going to dominate the 100-meter dash. But what we often neglect are the future roles that are expanding. Research shows that while our mental agility might decline in older age, our crystallized intelligence, or wisdom, keeps growing. Our strengths shift, and in those changes are opportunities for new roles.

As organizational psychologist Adam Grant wrote, "The best way to find yourself isn't looking inward to see who you are. It's looking outward to see who you admire. Role models help you identify what you value and who you want to become." The more limited our role models, the narrower our future-self predictions are—and going back to chapter 4, the less self-complexity we have. We are like the first graders who don't understand yet that a firefighter can be a woman. When we live in survival mode, our future possible selves narrow. The antidote is to give evidence to the contrary.

INVITING THE RIGHT SELF

You're finally on vacation, ready to catch up on well-deserved rest and recovery, when you put your head to the pillow, expecting to drift off to a sleepy bliss, and instead, you're greeted with a restless night's sleep. You aren't alone. For over fifty years, scientists have known about the first night effect. We are initially more restless in new environments. In 2016, Masako Tamaki and colleagues gave us the reason why: half of our brain is acting as a night's watch. When in a new environment, it's on high alert, looking out for danger. When we're at home sleeping, no night watchman is required.

The environment we live and work in, the objects we hold on to, and the people around us signal whether we are safe, belong, or have a future path available. When we are surrounded by others and feel at home, our predictive brain goes, "It's safe here! I can contribute and have purpose." When we don't see a future, when we can't see ourselves in society, our brain goes, "I don't belong here. I don't have a positive future," and defaults to survival mode. Belonging is about seeing your role and future, and then inviting the appropriate self for the situation. It's giving your brain the goods to be motivated instead of protective.

We perform best when we feel secure, challenged but not threatened. We need to ensure our environment aligns with our desired future self, where our inner values align with our external actions. The space we occupy can either reaffirm our sense of self in a positive way, telling us to feel secure and comfortable and to play like we are at home—or it can do so in a defensive way, telling us that our home turf is under threat and that we need to live in survival mode. We need to craft an environment that invites actions that support and align with who we are and want to become.

CHAPTER 8

FIND CONNECTION AND BELONGING WITHOUT FUSING

'm not concerned. I know I would never do anything wrong. And if there was any temptation, I'd leave." It was a sentiment I heard from athletes. It's one reporters and coaches relayed top NCAA prospects had when asked about joining controversial groups. People were sure of their values, or at least professed that they were.

Yet, I watched it occur during my time at Nike. An athlete would come in, wide-eyed, enthusiastic, and ready to see what they could do. They had good intentions and lots of motivation. They were good, decent, ethical people. But over time, their boundaries would be pushed, and those attributes would erode. It started slow. A slew of unlabeled or sketchy supplements, then borrowing prescription drugs without a doctor's instruction, and finally trying to fake their way through testing to get that prescription inhaler a coach wanted. The same occurred off the track.

They'd go from a kind teammate, interacting with competitors as if they were on this journey together, to isolating themselves from competitors, to in some cases, ignoring verbally abusive tactics used on teammates. Athletes would come in and slowly, gradually succumb to the environment. Some went further than others. But it was rare for the person to escape unscathed.

They thought they signed up for the same game they played as a child. A difficult but enjoyable challenge to see how good they could be. That slowly changed. Maybe it was a coach who said they needed to be more serious. Or the pull of medals, championships, or status. The intrinsic joy slowly gave way as external forces dragged them toward different motivations, behaviors, and even ethics. What they wanted to do soon became something they had to do. Before they knew it, who they thought they were and who they were based on actions were misaligned.

Elite athletes are particularly susceptible. They are constantly judged. Their performance is public. Their identity is often wrapped tightly into one thing. They largely derive their sense of competence, belonging, and happiness from a singular pursuit. Their world has narrowed and shrunk. But it's not just athletes. We all have insecurities and an identity in need of validation and affirmation.

The lawyer who starts out wanting to fight injustice but finds their ethics shifting as the prominent firm pushes them for more hours, more cases, and more wins. The politician who wanted to change her country for the better succumbs to playing a different game: backing the causes of big donors and stoking fear and outrage to gather support. Staying in office supersedes all else. Our ethics and values become slogans, ready to be dismissed. The person who started social media to spread positive, accurate, and helpful views on nutrition and exercise ends up pitching sketchy products, demonizing others, and using outrage to build their platform. They get captured by their audience. Shifting to conspiracies and extreme dogmatic views because that's what sells online.

We don't just want to belong. We need it to be a healthy, happy human being. But that deep human need makes it both necessary and the place where we are most vulnerable to outside factors, where the external can take over the internal. We settle for fitting in.

When we're too entangled with a group, idea, or theory, we're more likely to get in our own way, to default to playing not to lose, to resist taking the calculated risks that often lead to breakthroughs. The nutritionist who proclaims herself a die-hard believer in keto diets, or whatever the latest theory is, but then can't dislodge from the theory because it's become a central component of who she is. The parent who lives vicariously through their child's sporting endeavors. The individual who gets consumed with a cause so much so that they can't separate reality from conspiracy. Belonging is vital. But if we aren't careful, it can create attachment that makes us lose perspective. We move from clarity to delusion.

We tend to think of our beliefs as fundamental aspects of who we are. We have strong ethical, moral, or core values that define who we are. When life gets crazy, when we feel threatened, we reflect on these foundational beliefs and values to help navigate the tumultuous waters of a chaotic world. A deep and consistent part of who we are that is immovable. That's the child's storybook version. It sounds good. It makes us feel like we are good, decent people who would never cross a line because our values are deeply ingrained. Reality and the latest science tell a different story. Our values, beliefs, morals, and ethics are deeply influenced by the world around us. And often, those who are so sure of their ethics and values are most vulnerable.

When we live in survival mode, we try to fill that void of connection any way we can. We reach for the dark side of belonging, where our sense of self becomes so enmeshed with our groups, ideas, and surroundings that the external takes over. We are so desperate to fit in, that our values and behaviors shift to match whatever group or ideology seems to offer a solution. It's a phenomenon that we think happens only to the outliers among us, but in reality, it can happen to anyone. And over the long haul, it leads to fear, avoidance, and protection, as we grasp onto the superficial.

Thriving needs a different kind of belonging, a more authentic version that leads to expansion and growth instead of isolation and narrowing. Chapter 8 is about finding belonging without handing over our thinking. It's finding the middle way between identifying with a group or person and getting enmeshed with them. It's finding meaning without melding. It's preventing the outer from taking over control of our inner sense of self, strength, and values in our attempts to perform well. We need to have a solid foundation of belonging and connection but the freedom to explore away from it.

HANDING OVER OUR THINKING

Southern Baptists are one of the most conservative sects of mainstream Christianity. Many congregations push heavily toward purity culture, abstinence, and a slew of traditional values. In 2023, the Southern Baptist Convention voted to disallow churches with female pastors in their leadership. If there's any group that would promote hardline conservative values, it's the Southern Baptists.

In 1970, a poll commissioned by the Baptist Sunday School Board sampled Southern Baptist pastors on their views on abortion— 70 percent supported abortion if it protected the mental or physical health of the mother, with about the same amount supporting abortion in the case of rape or fetal deformity. While not exactly pro-choice, these are far from the hardline pro-life views of the church today. In fact, finding a happy medium was the goal. In 1974, the Southern Baptist Convention put out a resolution that "reflected a middle ground between the extreme of abortion on demand and the opposite extreme of all abortion as murder." It wasn't just the pastors that held such views; the congregation echoed their leaders. During the same period, a poll found that over 90 percent of Baptist congregants in Texas thought the abortion laws at the time were too restrictive. Fast forward to our current time, and the views have flipped. According to one poll, nearly 70 percent of Southern Baptists think that in all or most cases, abortion should be illegal. The Pew Research Center categorized them as "opposes abortion rights, with few or no exceptions."

How did the views of an entire religious sect shift so dramatically? After all, the Bible hasn't changed. What happened was that, starting in the 1970s, there was a struggle in the leadership over abortion views. Those with a stringent view won out, taking leadership and speaking positions at their conventions. Views quickly flipped. The leadership established itself as firmly pro-life. The congregation soon followed. In the span of about a decade, an entire group shifted from against abortions but with reasonable flexibility to a fixed pro-life stance, with few exceptions. First leadership of the convention, then pastors at individual churches, and finally, those who attended on Sundays.

Don't like talking about abortion? Choose your hot-button political topic: gun control, immigration, taxes, or health care. We tend to think our views on such subjects are hardwired. We believe that we pick our political party partially based on our moral beliefs. We feel strongly about being pro-life, so we call ourselves a conservative. We feel passionate about bodily autonomy, so we identify as liberal. But that's not what occurs according to research. In a test of ideology and morality, Peter Hatemi, Charles Crabtree, and Kevin Smith found it was the other way around. Our political affiliation predicts our moral beliefs. Politics shape "how individuals rationalize what is right and what is wrong." Your tribe does more to determine your morality than your morality does to determine your tribe. The researchers summarized their findings: "We will switch our moral compass depending on how it fits with what we believe politically."

We may start out choosing our groups based on what we like or what we believe in. But over time, those groups become a large part of our identity. Going to church or synagogue every week becomes a central part of who we are. Being a Republican or Democrat seems increasingly important in defining what we care about. It's not just politics. It's any group we strongly identify with. Pick your poison: feminist, capitalist, Trekkie, whatever it is. The more firmly our identity is intertwined with the group, the more power the group holds. In many ways, it's no different than defining yourself as a Yankees or Red Sox fan. It starts as an interest but, over time, becomes a part of who you are. It's a cheat for our brain, a way to quickly make predictions without analyzing every single belief, behavior, or action. It's much simpler to say I'm a feminist; therefore, I should act this way.

When our identity becomes intertwined with our groups, we go where our tribe goes. We despise cheaters until our star outfielder tests positive for performance-enhancing drugs, then we are okay with it. Or, as one educator told me, "Parents who never paid attention to the schoolwork we sent home suddenly became passionate about what was being supposedly taught in their schools." Why? Their political tribe deemed it a pressing concern. If a tribe we are intimately linked to changes its stance, we get dragged along with it. Often imperceptibly.

Our identity is more powerful than our principles or values. Recent research found that we value our identity much more than the accuracy of information. So much so that psychologist Jay Van

Bavel concluded, "It turns out that if you insult and publicly criticize (someone), their identity needs increase, and they become threatened and less concerned about accuracy. You actually need to affirm someone's identity before you present information that might be contradictory to what they believe." The power of our group identity is why people believe crazy things.

LOSING OUR SELF TO FILL THE VOID

He was a champion who had overcome a rough childhood, to reach the highest heights of his chosen craft: swimming. He was a four-time NCAA champion who left school early to pursue his Olympic dreams. In an illustrious career, he competed at three Olympic games, capturing two gold, a silver, and two bronze medals. At the 2004 Athens Olympics, he brought glory to his country, anchoring the 4 x 200 relay and holding off Ian Thorpe, the best swimmer in the world at that time. Four years later, he helped Michael Phelps capture one of his record-setting eight gold medals by swimming the preliminary round in the relay so Phelps could be rested for the final. Klete Keller was in his element in the pool. But after three Olympics, it was time to transition to the next part of his life.

Keller struggled with retirement. He worked odd jobs, moving from one pursuit to another. He bounced around the country, living in North Carolina, DC, California, and Colorado. His marriage disintegrated. His wife divorced him, and he lost custody of his three kids. There were allegations from his wife of erratic behavior and of Keller being suicidal. For almost a year, he was homeless, squeezing his six-foot-six-inch frame into his Ford Fusion. Keller described himself as lost.

In 2018, USA Swimming wrote a piece on the journey of Keller and what he'd learned in battling the loss of identity, the feeling that he needed to live up to his swimming prowess in his next line of work, and the difficulty in never experiencing the rush of emotions that came from competing against the world's best and then standing on top of the podium in a moment of pure glory. He relayed, "I had a really difficult time accepting who I was without swimming in my life. Swimmer had been my identity for most of my life, and then I quickly transitioned to other roles and never gave myself time to get comfortable with them. I really struggled with things. I didn't enjoy my work, and that unhappiness and lack of identity started creeping into my marriage." Keller's experience, sadly, isn't unique.

Athletes die twice. Once, like the rest of us, of course, at the end of our physical life. And once when they have to move on from their sport. For most of us, we follow a simple path. Years of education culminate in a career that we can then spend decades perfecting. We pursue our career well into our fifties, sixties, or even seventies. For athletes, this isn't the case.

You start early, often in grade school, and ramp up through high school and college. If you have potential, while everyone else is figuring out what to do for the next fifty years of their lives, you are perfecting your sporting craft, doing what you need to stay eligible and compete. And then, depending on your sport and level, it's all over at eighteen, at twenty-two, or if you're lucky, in your thirties. Whenever that point comes, the thing you've tied your identity to and pursued with passion is over, and you have to start anew. You move from being at the top of the hierarchy to years or even decades behind. While you were inching out seconds in your marathon time, your peer group at your next endeavor was learning the basics of the job. Now, at twenty-five, thirty, or forty, you are a beginner. From among the best in the world to a novice in a moment.

You lose the thing that provided stability, status, competency, and direction in your life. It's no wonder that retiring from sport often leaves athletes feeling lost. Look at the best in history. Michael Phelps suffered from severe depression after retirement. So did boxing legend Sugar Ray Leonard, who once said, "Nothing could satisfy me outside the ring. . . . [T]here is nothing in life that can compare to becoming a world champion, having your hand raised in that moment of glory, with thousands, millions of people cheering you on." Even those who handle it well often struggle.

Sport often naturally fulfills our basic psychological needs. It gives us meaning and purpose, something to master, to get better at, a place where we belong and feel secure. Almost instantly, we leave that all behind. We lose our sense of self. And research shows those with a higher athletic identity struggle more. The tighter the bond, the harder it is to let go. As Keller told USA Swimming, "As I look back now, I wasn't a very good husband. But now, I feel like I've come through the darkness and found the light that I always wanted and needed to be happy. I'm getting there."

On January 6, 2021, as a mob of people infiltrated the US Capitol, it was hard not to succumb to the car wreck or gawker effect. Scrolling on social media, you were greeted with an array of pictures that had little comparison in our history. There were gruesome injuries and death from the calamity and chaos. There was the bizarre—the man dubbed the QAnon shaman wearing a Viking helmet and fur vest, sitting at the podium of the Senate chamber. And then, if you scrolled through the pictures, there was a giant of a man donning a blue jacket with large white letters "USA" on the back and an Olympic patch on the front. It was Klete Keller.

According to his friends and former teammates, Keller was never that interested in politics, but during the 2020 COVID pandemic, his Facebook posts became increasingly hostile. For most, the pandemic threw us for a loop. Suddenly, we were dealing with a lot of uncertainty in the world. Add in political chaos, and it's easy to see how someone like Keller would be susceptible to seeking order and connection somewhere. It's easy to hate on Keller. And some may be deserved. But what is more important, societally, is why so many people filled a significant gap in their lives by fusing with a group. As Olympian Gary Hall Jr. reflected on what happened to his former teammate, "He was struggling with identity and hard times. That's what these radicals prey upon. He got swept up in it."

GOLDILOCKS: FUSE, FIT IN, BELONG

We all want to belong. It's one of our most powerful needs and drivers. We need to feel at home and a part of something. Groups play a vital role in that. Even more so when the world doesn't make sense. But, as we just saw with Keller, there's a downside. We can go too far: our individual self can get subsumed by our group identity. This is called identity fusion. And although it's primarily seen with groups, it also occurs with individuals and ideas. It's when our individual self fuses with our group or social self. Two becomes one through narrowing and assimilating. Identity fusion is a last desperate grasp for filling the void. It's not belonging. It's the result of a close cousin: fitting in.

Bestselling author and researcher Brené Brown first talked about this distinction in 2012 when she wrote, "Fitting in is the greatest barrier to belonging. Fitting in . . . assessing situations and groups of people, then twisting yourself into a human pretzel in order to get them to let you hang out with them. *Belonging* is something else entirely—it's showing up and letting yourself be seen and known as you really are."

Remember our discussion in chapter 4 on how immigrants

make sense of their past, present, and future? They can assimilate, compartmentalize, or integrate. Connection works in much the same way. Researchers found that our social identities intertwine in similar ways: dominance, compartmentalizing, or merging. When we try to fit in, we prioritize the external to fill our connection needs. We change ourselves with a mixture of compartmentalizing and assimilation. We may even ditch our prior beliefs or values to fit in.

Fitting in leads to fusing. When our void is large enough, we don't just prioritize the external, changing to feel a part of something; the external becomes internal. Identity fusion occurs when we become dependent on the thing, group, or person to make us feel significant, hopeful, and connected. It's the fast food version of belonging. It might temporarily fill our cravings, but we'll pay for it over the long haul. It's belonging that is superficial and contingent. We narrow and cement so much that it's as if we are handing over the steering wheel to someone else. We separate, enmesh, and assimilate while leaving our individual self behind.

Research shows the higher our group identification, the more our emotional states and moods converge and spread within that group. Work in sports shows it's not just our emotions; it's our biology. Generally, after we win a game, we get a surge in testosterone, reinforcing that we are dominant and climbing the status ladder. But this surge doesn't just occur when the person who competed in the game takes victory. Their teammates on the sidelines can experience a similar increase. Researchers of out Nipissing University in Canada found that testosterone increases when we watch our teammates win a competition. But there's a catch. The surge only occurs if that teammate is "central to one's own identity." When our identity is entangled with others, our biology follows suit, even if we're sitting on the sideline. This can be beneficial. A spreading of a positive, energized sporting team can lead us to victory. Or it can be dangerous, turning individuals into a fearful and outraged mob.

It's also what leads to cheating and fraud. We've handed over our ethics and values to someone or something else. It's what I saw as a whistleblower. Identity fusing with a pursuit (i.e., winning a medal) or being part of a group (i.e., a part of a top professional team) lets people throw away whatever ethics or values they brought to the table and justify nearly any action. When our world narrows so much, almost anything can be deemed acceptable because we lose the ability to see anything beyond a small slice of the world.

Fitting in, or its more extreme version, identity fusion, is a shortcut for our brain. It allows us to make predictions easier. When there's near-complete overlap between our self and group identity, we look for where the group goes to understand the appropriate belief or action. Our brain, the expert rationalizer, then convinces us that it's our individual belief or idea after the fact. It's the shortcut to a false sense of stability. Our groups tell us what matters, what to be concerned with, and what to value. It's how gangs thrive.

In communities where chaos is high and socioeconomic status and opportunities are low, gangs step in to fill the void. In a review on the subject, law professor James Hardie-Bick suggested that "gangs can serve to reduce the existential uncertainties that accompany social exclusion and marginalization." Gangs provide a stable identity and form of social status when many in the community are without either. For the rest of us, the entanglement with others is just as powerful. We see the same effect with online "gangs." As psychologist Scott Barry Kaufman pointed out, "Some fans [reach] such an attachment to a celebrity that the celebrity can never do any wrong and even the most hateful things are justified, excused, and even adored . . . with individual relationships we call this toxic."

Belonging is different from fitting in. It's not about finding stability and connection through assimilation and handing over our self. It is about integration. It's being secure but open, connected but through expansion. It's getting to security and clarity through self-complexity instead of constriction. It's the internal guiding the external. We bring our values, ethics, and experiences to the table and make the group better because of it. In researching the benefits and downsides of groups, renowned psychologist Roy Baumeister concluded, "The decisive factor, we found, was the individual, responsible, differentiated self. The bad side of groups generally emerged when individual selves became submerged in the group." It's just what Adam Smith told us centuries ago: other and self, at the same time, in the right amount.

In the always-connected, seemingly chaotic world we now occupy, identity fusion provides an easy way toward a sense of security. But it comes with a steep price. When our identity becomes deeply entangled, we hand over our thinking to whatever defines our sense of self. We get lost, defensive, and incapable of creating space between who we are and what we belong to. We become ideologues, nationalists, conspiracy theorists, or simply trapped. And once that entanglement occurs, it's really difficult to see clearly and break free. If we do so, it feels like we are losing a large part of who we are.

In his 2005 commencement speech at Kenyon College, writer David Foster Wallace said, "In the day-to-day trenches of adult life, there is actually no such thing as atheism. There is no such thing as not worshipping. Everybody worships. The only choice we get is what to worship." Wallace went on to warn that most of what we choose to worship will eat us alive. When we experience a feeling of oneness, it might fill that hole of meaning, purpose, and belonging. It may validate who we are. But it blinds us, causing us to narrow so much that we can't see beyond the thing that we are fused with. And that delusion has drastic consequences. As social psychologist Jonathan Haidt stated, "When you're on a team, it makes you stupid because your thinking is: how can we win. Not what's true . . . If you embrace a good-evil framework . . . that's going to drop you by ten or twenty points on your IQ." Or as humanistic philosopher Erich Fromm wrote, "Once a doctrine, however irrational, has gained power in a society, millions of people will believe in it rather than feel ostracized and isolated."

BELONGING WITHOUT FUSING

Living in survival mode, and the loneliness that often comes with it, pushes us toward identity fusion. We need to find genuine, meaningful belonging instead of cheap, contingent fitting in. It means finding a balance where we can like or even love groups or ideas, but we can't marry them. It means finding belonging through expanding our sense of self instead of narrowing it. The keys to belonging without fusing are:

1. Balance individual and social self
2. Find security, not safety
3. Expand, instead of narrow
4. Activate your moral self

BALANCING INDIVIDUAL AND SOCIAL SELF

There was a major problem in a particular group. The group was thriving, expanding rapidly as more and more people joined. But as soon as the group hit around 150 people, chaos reigned. Insubordination, discontent, and even violence took over. Factions developed, once tight-knit communities fractured, and people left.

Years later, as new people joined the group again, the cycle would repeat—growth, division, separation.

Welcome to the world of our ancient ancestors. For a long period of time, hunter-gatherer tribes in the Neolithic era were stuck. Anthropologist Robin Dunbar found that once tribes hit a ceiling of around 150 members, they'd split apart. The reason? They hit the threshold for transitioning to what's called an anonymous society. When a tribe was smaller, you had a reasonably good idea of who was part of your community. You knew just about everyone. Anyone you didn't recognize, you could assume was an outsider. As groups grew, knowing everyone became impossible. Societies had to transition to an anonymous one, where there were members of your tribe you didn't know directly.

In a small local community, it's easy to understand who you are, what your roles are, where you belong, and who is part of your community. As a community grows, we lose individual distinction and ease of our sense of belonging. Dunbar found that it's less about maintaining cooperation than about coordination amid a growing society. Social cohesion erodes when we can't know all of our neighbors. To move to an anonymous society, societies had to evolve. They had to find ways to bring cohesion and stability via balancing the individual and social self. They had to manage this tension.

Our ancestors solved this via social institutions. In research analyzing how societies transitioned from hundreds of inhabitants to thousands, social institutions grew alongside the population. For example, religions became increasingly important, helping maintain social cohesion, compared to secular societies. Similarly, activities that facilitated group connection, like feasts and dancing rituals, played a prominent role. Monogamy and marital arrangements helped bring structure to an area that often led to competition and violence. And outlets for societies more volatile individuals (i.e., males), such as a rise in clubs or activities for men, were crucial. Even the proliferation of writing helped communities break through the approximately 150-person ceiling. According to biologist Mark Moffett, writing allowed for the proliferation of a common understanding or mental model. We could label ourselves and our tribes to help us make sense of ourselves and our groups. As Moffett concluded in studying human and ape communities, "I propose that anonymous societies of all kinds can expand only so far as their labels can remain sufficiently stable."

This trend isn't just reserved for our ancient ancestors. While violence may not be the result, ask anyone who has managed the growth of a company from start-up to large corporation. As the size of the company grows, you need more structure and institutions to allow for expansion. You are managing the same tension our ancestors felt.

This represents a modern battle, the balancing of our individual self and social self, of distinctiveness and cohesion. With the rise of social media and the online world, we're going through a version of what our ancestors went through: an anonymous society on steroids. The solution isn't to let go of our individual self. It's not to become collectivists. It's to balance it out. To learn from the past.

We need outlets for both sides of the coin. While much can be made of the decline of religion in modern societies, one of the often overlooked parts is a stable local community. It doesn't have to be a religious institution, but we need something that ties us to those around us. Similarly, as our ancient ancestors discovered, we need outlets for people to achieve status and significance in something meaningful. The "men's clubs" of the past were simply outlets for male status competition. For a long time, sports, bowling leagues, and other recreational activities filled this role. But increasingly, the only places where we fill our individual distinctiveness and status bucket are through either our job or a never-ending competition for followers online.

In our modern world, we've tried to solve the anonymous society problem by insulating, narrowing, and tying ourself to a group. We've reached for significance and belonging via attachment instead of balancing self and others by expansion.

FIND SECURITY, NOT SAFETY

"Crying. Lots of crying. The first day of pre-K is often a disaster," a close friend who is a teacher reported to me. Think of it from the kids' points of view. You've spent most of your life with your mom or dad by your side. They are there to care for you and provide for your physical and psychological needs. They are your core conduit to navigate the world you live in. They are your role models. And then, suddenly, you're dropped into this strange room with an adult you've never met and fifteen other kids you don't know. Mom drops you off, and you have little concept of when she'll return. Is it any wonder tantrums are a rite of passage for many preschoolers?

Over time, kids adapt. They bond with their teacher, learning that this strange new environment is okay. That the teacher will look out for them and let them know the rules of this foreign place. Gradually, kids move from fear of the strangers around them to becoming best friends. They start playing and exploring, and the concern that Mom or Dad might not return slowly fades. They feel secure.

In the 1950s, psychiatrist John Bowlby developed attachment theory to describe the impact that relationships and bonding have on children. He posited that parents who are responsive to a child's needs create a sense of security. That fundamental relationship gives kids the confidence to explore their environment, to interact with others, and figure out how the world works. They know that they can always return to mom or dad and that if they happen to deal with something they aren't prepared for, the parent will help them figure out what to do. A secure attachment is developed when parents are responsive to a child's needs. Kids feel comfortable pushing the boundaries of their world. They can handle moderate levels of distress and uncertainty.

There are three other attachment styles included in the modern theory. Avoidant refers to when a child tends to avoid or ignore the parent or caregiver, having little inclination to explore and little to no emotional response when the parent leaves. Anxious attachment is when the child explores a little bit but is wary of the environment and others, even when the parent is nearby. They become highly distressed when the parent leaves, spiraling toward a full-blown tantrum, as if they don't know what to do when mom leaves. And finally, the disorganized style, which is marked by chaotic behavior. They don't quite know how to respond to their environment and seem to be overcome by fear. Their brain's prediction software is haywire. Research shows that a secure attachment helps kids' social, cognitive, and emotional development. They learn not only how relationships work, but how to regulate their emotions and manage their inner and outer world.

In recent years, the theory has stretched from children to adult relationships. We can be secure, anxious, and overly dependent on our partners, avoidant of relationships to protect ourselves, or fearful avoidant, where we really want a relationship but are uncomfortable with connection, so we tend to close ourselves off. Similar to children, when we are secure in our attachments as adults, research shows we have less fear of failure and are more likely to approach goals and challenges with a mastery focus. We approach instead of avoid. In addition, secure individuals tend to show higher concerns for others and have lower levels of distress amid uncertainty.

We often confuse security with safety. And in so doing, we end up with avoidant or anxious attachment styles. Safety and security are not the same. Safety is preventative. It's making sure that there aren't monkey bars at a playground so that no one can fall. It's providing trigger warnings so that students can avoid something that may make them uncomfortable. It's stepping in and solving your child's schoolyard problems. Safetyism often provides the illusion of security when, really, it's avoidance.

And often, it doesn't work. Take, for example, trigger warnings. A large meta-analysis found that, at best, they make no difference, and at worst, they increase anxiety as our predictive brain prepares for disaster. Or take your child's experience at recess or in school. When adults step in too quickly, children don't learn. If a mom, dad, or teacher steps in when a child first struggles with a math problem, learning is much less effective than if the child is allowed to struggle on their own, even if that struggle gets them no closer to the actual answer. Similarly, playing touch football or tag at recess teaches kids to understand social interactions, solve arguments, and regulate emotions and behavior. An adult referee always being there to step in harms emotional and social development.

Safetyism turns up our alarm sensitivity. It sends the message that the world is dangerous, and we need to avoid conflict or threats. Or that to solve our frustration or anger, we need to appeal to someone else. It makes us hyperaware of threats. Adopting such an approach makes us more likely to default to survival mode and reach for cheap ways to cope with the anxiety. We anxiously attach to an individual, group, or ideology.

Security gives people the tools, confidence, and platform to take on challenges. When we're young, it's knowing that if we fall or fail, Mom will be there to help us get back on the horse. As we get older, it's understanding that we can take a calculated risk and not lose our job if we fail because our workplace understands the value of innovation. Security is about being able to explore.

Think of it like having a spotter while lifting weights. A good spotter is there, paying attention and maybe even encouraging you. But their hand is not on the bar. You are the one lifting the weight, doing the work, and navigating the pain. The spotter won't grab the bar to help you reach your goal. They only step in if things really go sideways. It's no wonder that research shows when we have a spotter present, not doing anything but standing there, we can lift more. In one study, participants completed on average four and a half more reps in the bench press when there was a spotter nearby. It's as if our brain goes, "Hey, we can take a bit more risk, and venture into the depths of fatigue because if we fail, we aren't going to drop a weight on our chest and crush us."

Good parenting, leading, and coaching are the same. We're not dependent on the spotter. They provide a sense of security that frees us up to perform. In our lives, this security could come from providing any number of psychological needs we've discussed. A sense of meaningful connection, competency, purpose, or significance gives us clarity to pursue excellence. Our groups and environment play a large role in filling those needs. When we try to fill them by fusing or insecurely attaching to a group, we get the superficial and contingent variety. It's as if our spotter talks a good game, but deep down, we know they will only step in if there is something in it for them. How do we create security without negative attachment? Make sure it's expansive.

EXPAND INSTEAD OF NARROW

The questions started innocently enough. ("Where are you originally from?") As I looked around the room, the individuals sitting directly across from one another seemed jovial and excited. After a long summer break, the first day of official practice had commenced for the University of Houston cross-country team. But before the athletes got to running, they found themselves face to face with a teammate they didn't know well or at all. As the questions progressed, those smiles turned to concentration. "Do you have any siblings you don't get along with?" Gradually, the questions got more personal, forcing individuals to go a bit deeper, to disclose more about themselves, to move beyond the outward projection and superficial answers, to get underneath the surface level. "What are your three a.m. thoughts? What's the most devastating thing that's ever been said to you?" By the end of the exercise, casual acquaintances were discussing their fears and anxieties. The atmosphere in the room had shifted.

As the coach in charge of this exercise, I knew it wasn't an original one. A decade earlier, in my twenties, as a single male with a bent toward science nerdom, I convinced a date to replicate an experiment I'd read about by psychologist Arthur Aron. He took strangers, sat them down in a chair, and gave them a list of questions to ask one another. They started easy but gradually got more personal. Aron believed that graduated exposure led to more connections. As we open up, we slowly learn to trust the person sitting across from us. The story goes that the first pair who underwent this exercise in Aron's lab got married. My first date did not end that way . . . but it did plant a seed on how to create team bonds years later.

Graduated self-disclosure works because it primes us to expand our self. We go against our instinct to tell only a carefully crafted sliver of our story and paint a more nuanced, deeper image. As the person sitting across from us takes in the information, they start seeing you not as some caricature or as a simple label or category, but as a complex human being. We've moved from someone who is partially anonymous to someone who is three-dimensional.

As we learned in discussing attachment theory, relationships provide the perfect backdrop for understanding the nuance. Research shows that with just about any relationship, be it with an individual or group, we include others in our sense of self. So much so that when we see or think about our partner being in pain, fMRI studies show our brain activation is similar to when we, ourselves, are experiencing pain. But as we've learned throughout this chapter, how we include others in our self is critical. Do we superficially fuse, or do we meaningfully integrate?

Similar to the research discussed in chapter 4 on immigrants, we do best when we integrate instead of compartmentalize or fuse. Research shows that healthy, genuine relationships tend to make it where we incorporate our partner's views and experiences into our own. Not abandoning our individual identity or resisting change, but acknowledging the difference, appreciating the benefits, and figuring out how to make our personal and collective identities work in concert.

Self-expansion leads to self-clarity. It allows us to make better predictions as we have a broader perspective. It increases empathy and decreases our protective, territoriality-like defense. Self-disclosure is one avenue to enhance self-expansion, but we can also get there by sharing novel and challenging experiences. When we do activities that push us outside our comfort zone, it moves us from the superficial and protective mode to showing a more complete version of who we are. This could be trying a new activity, traveling to a foreign country, or learning a new skill together.

The same holds true away from our relationships. Spending time in nature, volunteering, experiencing different cultures, and practicing gratitude and compassion are different ways to expand your perspective while creating connections with other people, ideas, and even objects. People who score higher on self-expansion tend to be less egocentric, more empathetic, more inclusive, and less likely to play the social status and power games that occur in groups, while relationships high in self-expansion report increased levels of satisfaction and commitment.

ACTIVATE YOUR MORAL SELF

"Everyone is doing it" is a refrain that works equally well for teenagers doing dumb things out of peer pressure, elite athletes doping, and corporate malfeasance. We rationalize and justify our transgressions by convincing ourselves that those around us are taking the same approach. But how do you combat this strong pull? As we've learned, part of the problem is that when we are surrounded by others pushing boundaries, our "group" identity is activated. We want to fit in. So we act how someone would if they were in that group. We cheat or cross the line.

There's a simple way to combat this: activate another, more powerful identity. In a 2013 study, sociologist Michael J. Carter put students' morality to the test when they were alone or pressured by the power of a group while playing a lottery-type game. Would they report being given extra bonus points that they didn't earn in the game, but that would lead to them receiving extra money? When pressured by the group to conceal the cheating, 67 percent of students acted immorally, compared to only 40 percent when they were alone. Peer pressure works. But Carter had an interesting twist. For half of the students, he activated their moral identity by having them write a story about themselves acting in a way that displayed characteristics that reflected their moral values. At the end of the study, these students were much more likely to turn themselves in. Carter found that for each standard deviation increase in moral identity from the activation, students were 43 percent more likely to act morally. Carter concluded, "The most salient identity operated to influence action."

In chapter 7, I discussed how putting pictures of your family on your desk at work improves performance by making you feel at home. It has another benefit, activating your moral self. Research led by Ashley Hardin out of Washington University in St. Louis found that having pictures of family in your office makes us less likely to commit ethical violations at work. We're reminded of a much more important role than winning at a game or making a few extra bucks; being the person our son or daughter can be proud of.

We have multiple hats we can wear. Our surroundings nudge us toward certain roles. But we have the power to interrupt this cycle. To remind ourselves that another, more important role might be more fitting. Having clarity on your values, ethics, and morals can help. But, regularly reminding yourself of them, and reflecting on how your behaviors align with those, can go a long way toward ensuring you don't get pulled toward a faulty group identity.

BE A TRACK AND CROSS-COUNTRY TEAM

In a 2018 review, psychologists Wim Meeus, Lotte van Doeselaar, and colleagues evaluated how feeling distinct impacts our adjustment and psychological well-being. They found that distinctiveness likely provides the foundation for our identity formation. Early on in our childhood, we understand that we are unique and different from our parents and our peers. But it's not as clear-cut as feeling unique and being better off psychologically. There's a Goldilocks zone for feeling distinct. Too much, and you are more likely to feel separate, lonely, and less securely attached to others. Too little, and you're more likely to feel lost and detached like your decisions in life are influenced and controlled more by others. You start to think, *No one gets me!* It's in the middle zone, kind of unique, where people flourish and function as adaptable, secure, and resilient individuals. We need some boundary between us and others but not a brick wall.

We need to feel connected and distinct. It's balancing self and others. It's finding meaning without melding and bonds without losing our mind. It's preventing the outer from taking over control of your inner sense of self, strength, and values. It's about having a secure but flexible sense of self and others. We need to have a solid foundation of belonging and connection but the freedom to explore away from it.

I like to think of this as being part of a track team. You compete as an individual but are also part of a diverse team, all with different talents, shapes, and sizes. You can have a 300-pound shot putter next to a 110-pound distance runner. A kid from the fanciest of American suburbs next to an immigrant from a country where half the country doesn't have access to electricity. It attracts individuals from all walks of life and all racial and socioeconomic backgrounds, and it puts them on the same team, imploring them to use their individual skills with a larger goal tying them together. You are playing both an individual game and a team one. Both independent and dependent. It's the perfect backdrop for balancing individual and group, through expansion instead of constriction.

The glue that holds sports teams together, especially those with a large individual component, comes from vulnerability. You get to see each other at your highest highs and lowest lows. You see guys who can bench press four hundred pounds crying after a rough performance. You watch people push their absolute limits, exhausted from fatigue at the end of a grueling race or workout. It's raw and emotional. In the crucible of competition, people are themselves. You can't put on a tough guy facade but crumble when a slight bit of pressure arises. Fatigue exposes us. We are who we are.

That vulnerability isn't a weakness; it's a strength. It helps to cement connections, relationships, and respect. There's no hiding, and that realness creates cohesion. In many ways, it's linked to the research we covered on relationships. It creates connection through expansion. When we do novel, interesting, challenging, emotionally charged things together, it expands our perspective, both as individuals and as teammates. We start to see others as complex human beings, instead of as robots on a field.

At the same time, in sports like track, you can't hide behind your teammates. You are responsible for yourself and your effort. Mixed sports with individual and team components take care of the high school group project phenomenon, where the hardworking group member gets stuck carrying the load of others. Psychologists call this social loafing, a backing off in effort because it's hidden from view. But in mixed sports, like cross-country, it balances the individual and team. You get the benefits of sharing the burden without the downsides of social loafing. You get support without being able to fully hide.

And as we learned in chapter 5, such sports invite complexity of judgment. You aren't only judged by the outcome but by the effort you give. You can lose the race but celebrate setting a new personal best. There's a continuum of success and failure. Lastly, there's a goal tying the group together. A realization that we often have to put our ego aside, or quiet it down, to give our team the best chance of success. We connect to someone we might not have much in common with because of a purpose that aligns us. This combination of factors provides the right balance of group and individual self. In summarizing the research, Roy Baumeister wrote, "Groups go bad when individual selves merge into the group. Groups flourish when they capitalize on individual selves, each different from the others, individually accountable and responsible, thinking for themselves."

While sports provide a natural environment for this, it can also be found elsewhere. Speech and debate clubs, theater companies, or artistic communities can all provide similar situations. A mixture of individual and group self and performance. Of seeing the full spectrum of emotions. These environments get the right balance. When accompanied by the right approach of belonging, instead of fitting in, it often leads to healthy, long-lasting bonds. There's a reason why, in such groups, we often use descriptors like brothers, sisters, or family to describe each other. I like to think of it as a real, not idealistic, family. We will occasionally fight, disagree, go our separate ways, and form our own identities, but ultimately, we have one another's backs.

In a world where loneliness is on the rise, is it any wonder we default toward surviving? Our brain thinks it's just us out there versus whatever challenge we face, that we don't have any support or backup. In many ways, protection or reaching for the superficial version, fitting in, to temporarily fill that void is a rational choice. But to thrive, we have to share the burden. To grow, we need the real thing, something that pushes us to be greater than the sum of its parts. Genuine belonging is expansive and growth-orientated. It balances distinctiveness and togetherness. And most important, it provides the security for us to take risks, fail, and get back up and keep exploring, because at the end of the day our family, friends, and those that truly support us will be there. It's what the best teams, organizations, relationships, and family's all provide.

Whoever we surround ourselves with, whatever groups we belong to—we essentially hand over a piece of ourselves to them. They can either help us grow and expand our perspectives or push us toward fear and constriction. The way out is to belong instead of fit in. To balance distinctiveness and others. To balance self and others. To not attach or fuse with any guru, group, or ideology. To have a scientific approach: a belief in a thing but with an eye toward disproving it. Feeling like we belong is more important than ever. In an increasingly isolated world, where we try to fill that void with superficiality, it's even more important to find meaningful connection without fusing.

PART FOUR

GETTING UNSTUCK

CHAPTER 9

REALIGNING WITH REALITY

I t was May 13, and summer break was on the horizon for the students and staff at Bay Harbor Elementary School. The cafetorium was filled with 170 kids participating in a music rehearsal. Sandy, a popular eleven-year-old, wasn't feeling well. She snuck out the back without many noticing, making her way to the clinic and collapsing on the couch when she got there. The clinic staff was on a break, but a nearby secretary noticed Sandy and quickly called the local emergency department.

As music rehearsal let out, the students were met with a frightening sight: firefighters carrying Sandy out of the school on a stretcher and taking her to the hospital. Shortly after, other kids started to get sick. At first a few, but then more reported feeling headaches, dizziness, chills, abdominal pain, shortness of breath, and hyperventilation. Within a few hours, seven kids followed Sandy to the hospital, twenty-five were sent home with family, and forty were being treated at school. The cafetorium had been transformed into a makeshift clinic. The local health authorities were contacted and told a pipe was leaking poisonous gas.

When physician Joel Nitzkin from the county's department

of health showed up with his colleagues, he was met with quite a scene. Ambulances, firefighters, police, news reporters, and parents had flooded the premises. It "was complete pandemonium. It had the look of a disaster." And when they entered the school, they noticed a strange odor. They didn't quite know what it was, except that it was very strong. The doctor and his team, including an epidemiologist and an occupational hygienist, went to work.

To Nitzkin, something didn't add up. There was a strong smell, but it was coming from the opposite side of the school from where Sandy got sick. The symptoms were a strange combination that didn't exactly point to poison. He called the hospital, and the kids there were improving quickly, and tests had returned normal. And that smell? Well, his team had determined it came from adhesive for new carpet that was put down. Gradually, Nitzkin came to realize what he was seeing. It wasn't poison. It was hysteria. Or as we now know it, mass psychogenic illness.

It might seem easy to brush off these experiences, but they occur regularly throughout the world, often with different manifestations. There was the 1962 laughing epidemic in Tanzania where people suffered from laughing fits that lasted from hours all the way up to sixteen days. It began with 3 girls in a school, spread to 95 out of 159 students, and over the next few months inflicted nearly 1,000 individuals in nearby villages. More recent examples include outbreaks of twitching, fainting, and even the mimicking of mental health disorders. Over the past few years, there's been an uptick in young patients with movement and verbal tics that resembled Tourette's syndrome. One medical report found an increase of 60 percent in movement disorder clinics in 2020. Except when clinicians investigated, a significant proportion wasn't Tourette's. The symptoms differed in key ways, and quickly resolved with therapy. When they went looking for an origin, they found a surprising culprit. In Germany, researchers traced the origin to a popular German YouTube star. In Canada, researchers linked the increase in tic-like symptoms to TikTok. This led to a new variation of the classic psychogenic illness, which researchers called a mass social media–induced illness.

These experiences have nothing to do with being weak-minded or crazy, as is often portrayed. The feelings, symptoms, and experiences are real. It's our brain doing its job: predicting. Think of it through the lens of what we've learned so far. Our predictions are a combination of expectations and experience, depending on how much significance and reliability we assign to each component. If we expect disaster, we often create the experience of it.

One of the oldest known forms was the dancing plagues that started in 1021 and continued off and on through the Middle Ages. It was a strange phenomenon of uncontrollable dancing, with people screaming in pain, claiming they could not stop. From the eleventh century until the seventeenth, there were reports of thousands of people taking to the streets. They danced for days, weeks, and months on end, and sometimes to death. Middle Age–era explanations often focused on the mysterious or occult. Modern explanations are more straightforward. Almost every dancing plague occurred while that city was going through strife, either from an actual plague, war, or famine.

When researchers studied the modern variations of these psychogenic illnesses, they found that the environment needs to be ripe for contagion. A feeling of fear, panic, unpredictability, and uncertainty. The environment primes individuals to have a "culture-bound stress reaction." The rise in Tourette-like symptoms largely coincided with the early days of the COVID pandemic. The Tanzanian laughing epidemic started in a British-run school shortly after that region gained independence from the

British. The takeaway is that our expectations (e.g., the world is uncertain) or our experiences (e.g., we see our friend on a stretcher) can cause our predictions to go haywire.

As we learned in chapter 2, to deal with this mismatch, we can either update or protect. In the cases described above, individuals didn't update. They protected by creating the symptoms that they expected. Kids start to experience headaches and dizziness. Adults start to experience nausea and hearing loss. We take action in an almost self-fulfilling way. Or, in the language we've used so far, we get stuck in a bad predictive rut. We think we're under threat. Our brain predicts how it should feel and act when we are, and it creates those perceptions, and we follow through with actions that match that expectation. In other words, when we think the world is scary and out to get us, we will create a world where we react as if it is scary and out to get us.

When we are in survival mode, our needs aren't met, and we become fixated or cemented, which distorts our predictive brain. We're more likely to take action to create an experience that matches our distorted prediction. As Andy Clark wrote in *The Experience Machine*, "attention is the brain adjusting its precision-weightings as we go about our daily tasks." If all our attention is attached to danger, threat, or survival, is it any wonder we get stuck in a doomed predictive rut? It's the same with choking.

LOSING OUR ABILITY TO ACT

"The greatest to ever do this event . . . there is not a question, no female gymnast in history has ever taken this event on like Simone Biles," veteran NBC announcer Tim Daggett gushed as Biles was standing at the end of the vault runway during the 2021 Olympic games. This wasn't hyperbole. By any measure, Biles had fundamentally altered the sport of gymnastics. As she ran down the runway to complete a vault, midway through the jump, in the air, she bailed. On air, Daggett gasped. A momentary silence filled the broadcast before Daggett let out a simple "Wow." His fellow commentator, former Olympic gold medalist Nastia Liukin, said with a mix of bewilderment and a genuine wish to understand what she'd just witnessed, "Very uncharacteristic vault for Simone. It looked like she . . . got almost lost in the air . . ." Moments later, Biles had withdrawn from the competition.

The twisties are gymnastics version of the yips. Instead of losing your ability to swing a golf club or throw a ball, you lose awareness of what your body is doing as you twist and turn in the air. Biles suffered from a perception-action disconnect, a prediction error where the sensory information coming from your body and the periphery doesn't align with your expectations or actions. Normally, gymnasts have a keen sense of where they are in the air. They start with an expectation of what's going to happen based on prior experience, and then get a mixture of sensory information from the eyes, the vestibular system providing insight on internal balance, and our proprioceptive system providing a sense of how our limbs are moving. An expert gymnast integrates this information. They know what to feel. And when it all goes well, you don't feel every twist and turn, it all flows together. You experience it as smooth action.

To get a sense of the twisties, go play the children's game pin the tail on the donkey. After twirling around, your perception of where your arm is going and where it actually goes misaligns. The body and brain are on different pages. Only with the twisties, it's like your brain gets stuck in this deep groove where that misalignment is the new norm. It's receiving so many signals from the muscles, nerves, feelings, emotions, and vision, and it can't make them add up. Our predictive software has gone haywire.

Embodiment is the connection between our inner and outer

world. It's feeling at home in our bodies. Connecting our perception and action, our cognition and experience, our body and self. When we choke, we lose this connection. As psychiatrist Julie Holland wrote in *Good Chemistry*, "When we are embodied, we are bonded with the self, feeling our feelings and trusting our body's signals. This allows us to hear our own quiet voices, and this connection is the basis of intuition and authenticity." When there's a disconnect, we are like the little kid who, for the life of him, can't pin the tail on the donkey. We fill the gap and latch on to something to eliminate the error, even if that means dancing in the streets or losing the ability to perform a simple task we've done for years.

When we are in survival mode, we often get stuck in a rut that connects bad information with poor action. Our predictive brain keeps telling us disaster is near, that we are in danger, and pushes us toward a maladaptive behavior. Usually, our perception aligns with an action. Our sensory information picks up an ever so slight gap in the defenders in front of us, and without consciously thinking about it, we've already pivoted and cut toward that nearly imperceptible hole. It's what makes great athletes great. They don't have to think about performing. Their brain perceives and does. Perception and action are aligned, acting as one, so that we don't even notice. But, as we saw with Biles, occasionally, anyone can get stuck in bad ruts.

We start giving importance to the wrong information. We latch on to threat or terror. We think it's the end of the world when it's just a game we are playing. We pay too much attention to the moment-by-moment movement, like a beginner learning to toss a ball, instead of the smooth flow of the expert we are. We stop being able to listen to our inner values. They've been replaced by the external. We get stuck. The cycle goes something like this:

1. We live in survival mode, believing we are under threat.
2. Our brain predicts doom: anxiety, fear, failure, protection.
3. We take actions to elicit or confirm the feeling and experience. Or we ignore anything that contradicts it, throwing our prior values or beliefs to the side.

This cycle applies to the big and small. We can look at prediction errors on a small scale (i.e., performing an athletic movement) and on a larger scale (i.e., Do my choices in the workplace reflect who I am and the values I espouse?). It's how we deal with the disconnect, the mismatch, the fragmentations in life. In chapter 3, we discussed a disconnect in motives: chasing external or internal. Chapter 4 discussed integration, compartmentalization, and avoidance in our self. Chapter 8 delved into belonging versus fitting in. All are errors. And too often, we act to conform or avoid instead of updating. It's easier to do so.

What's the solution? In the case of the elementary school sickness, Nitzkin recalled going over to a gathering of reporters, staff, medical personnel, and parents. "I had to believe I knew what I was doing. I took a deep breath and said that it wasn't an outbreak of gas poisoning or any other kind of poisoning. It was an outbreak of hysteria—mass hysteria. I said I didn't know just how it had started, but I knew how to stop it. I said the only way to bring it under control was to get things back to normal." Some parents were angry, believing that Nitzkin was calling their kids crazy. But he knew he had to give a reason to fill the gap, clear the grounds of firefighters that signaled emergency, decrease the commotion, and get the kids back into a routine: school. Lunch was set up, kids and teachers conversed, and classes resumed. He got the inner and outer to line up again—to have the environment, experience, and cognition start predicting reality instead of delusion. As outlined at the beginning of this book, we need to:

1. **Turn down the alarm.** Build up a robust inner game that
   shapes our expectations and experiences appropriately. Fill up
   with good stuff so we get out of threat mode. We feel secure,
   that we belong, that there is a path toward meaning, purpose,
   and significance. This decreases our overvaluing of the wrong
   information, the kind that nudges us toward survival.
2. **Disrupt and realign:** Nudge ourselves out of the rut and
   update your prediction and weighting of information.
   Realign your experience and expectations.

Throughout this book, we've focused on obtaining clarity in
our self, our pursuits, and our connections. This helps us turn
down the alarm and build a robust inner game. Clarity provides
firmer footing. When we are secure but flexible, when we belong
instead of fit in, when we ditch perfection for coherent messiness,
we are building a resilient self and story. It helps us stay out of
threat mode to make sure we aren't giving too much credence to
any signal that tries to tell us we are in danger. Having clarity
is the foundation. Now, it's time for the last part: How do we
knock ourselves out of a bad predictive rut and realign with reality? We've got to disrupt the pattern. Or, as I like to put it, every
once in a while, we need to see God.

FINDING GOD

A bald, middle-age white man with a hint of a Southern drawl stood
in front of a gangly bunch of teenagers, "Boys. Today, we are going
to go see God." The crowd stirred. Their eyes widened, trading glances at one another. A mixture of anxiety, excitement, and
wonder carried through the audience. Murmurs followed. Gerald
Stewart wasn't giving a sermon. They weren't in the pews at church.
They were sitting in the bleachers at the track.

Gerald Stewart was my high school cross-country and track coach. In a few short years, he took a bunch of misfits and turned us into one of the top teams in the country. While most of the hard workouts he prescribed were just on the right side of challenging but manageable, he'd pull out something special a few times a year. The "See God" workout meant it was time to go to the well. The goal was simple: Change your perspective by seeing how far into the depths of pain, fatigue, and discomfort you could go. By the end of the workout, you would be lying on the track, feeling like you were dying and maybe about to meet your maker.

Training in just about any endeavor is designed to gently embarrass your body so that it adapts. You lift a little more weight, run a touch faster or longer, and this gradual stimulus allows you to grow stronger or fitter. That holds true. But what Stewart realized was that every once in a while, you've got to do something that breaks you free from the rut of competence; that plateau we often settle into. Occasionally, we need something that will force a change in perspective and realign our expectations. By giving us permission to go for it in a workout, Stewart allowed us to take risks, to explore the bottom of the well. He wasn't the only coach who taught me the importance of altering one's perspective.

Tom Tellez is a legend in sport. When he talks, you listen. That's why I was thoroughly confused when he told me one day at the track, "I want you to run wrong. Reach out with your lower leg and slam your heel into the track." I did as directed, forcing my heel into the ground with every stride. My comfortable stride replaced with one that was clumsy and awkward. Once I completed the bizarre run down the track, he instructed, "This time run normally." Suddenly, the problem we had been working on for weeks, trying to get my foot to land closer underneath me, had been fixed. Tellez is as close to a magician as you can get for biomechanics, but what he did has scientific validation.

While repetition of the perfect movement has dominated our understanding of how to improve our skills in just about any task, recent work suggests a different path. It's the paradox of expertise. We get so good at something that we fall right into that deeply worn groove. Our brain has been here so many times before it stops listening to the actual experience. We don't feel what's occurring. Our predictive machinery works so well that it tunes out what our body is doing. We saw this in chapter 3 when researchers found that experts get stuck on exploiting their talents for too long; they become emotionally numb, losing the intrinsic joy that made them successful in the first place.

To experience again, we need to disrupt the pattern. When we knock ourselves out of the rut of competence, our brain wakes up. We feel again and commence a search for a solution to the problem. It's in this exploration where we become more adaptable and robust movers. Researchers call the tactic Tellez used "amplification of errors." Doing something wrong shifts our awareness and attention, knocking us out of our traditional way of doing something and allowing us to find other ways to accomplish the same task in a new manner. It changes our information weighting. Running wrong brought awareness to how I was landing, instead of ignoring how my foot struck the ground because it occurred thousands of times per day. And my body changed to another strategy in response to this new information. Going to the well in a workout reminds us that maybe the voices in our head telling us we were exhausted at rep number seven aren't that accurate, since we made it to rep ten. This is the essence of embodiment, reminding our brain that there are many signals we can pay attention to, that we need to make sense of, and sometimes we are listening to the wrong ones.

These are perspective changers. They open us to see and form new grooves. I like to call this collection of disruptors *doing crazy stuff.* If we want to get out of a rut, we have to shift our predictive weighting, to remind our body to feel and experience again, to sort through what is real and pertinent versus what we are blowing out of proportion or ignoring. We learn that there are other signals and pathways out there that we can pay attention to. We expand our potential paths.

Sometimes, to see things clearly, we have to change our viewpoint, and often that means going in the other direction. In my mental performance coaching, I've had athletes perform their sport in total darkness to disrupt their visual perception, forcing their brain to latch on to different signals and find a new pattern. Similarly, Michael Jordan used to practice with strobe lights on, while NBA star Steph Curry used occlusion glasses to block out some visual information while shooting. Psychologists have found some success with golfers who experience the yips practicing putting underwater. A radical shift in perception pushes the brain and body to reconfigure the relationship between perception and action, nudging them back on a positive track.

We're manipulating information sources to see where the catch is. We have to get the individual to let go and rewire the piece of information they are overweighting (e.g., parents in the stands putting pressure on their kid and triggering the threat response). When I surveyed sports psychologists on how they handle choking, one told me of a golfer who had his friends and family ridicule him while he putt. He had to train to let go of that information instead of valuing it. Or consider the work of former baseball player turned Navy Seal Jason Kuhn, who has brought an innovative approach to treating the yips. With major league pitcher Tyler Matzek, Kuhn played clips of pundits and announcers criticizing Matzek while asking him to pitch with a singular focus on his release. In this case, our brain latches on to the threat—external judgment or pressure—instead of what it needs to focus on: the ball's release. Disrupting and redirecting attention is one way to alter our predictions.

The same holds true outside of sport. Writers have their version of perception-action coupling. When they are stuck, everything mushes together. The words on the page look the same. The stories blend together and you can't separate yourself from the work. You become numb. Writers utilize a cacophony of perception disruptors to get back on track. Journalist Gay Talese put his work on the wall and looked at it through binoculars. "I want to look at it fresh, as if somebody *else* wrote it," he explained. Author Ashley Merryman told me she edits her books by reading them backward. Novelist Haruki Murakami uses the power of language to shift perspective, writing his first draft in English before translating it back into Japanese. A tactic J. R. R. Tolkien took to the extreme, inventing a new language and essentially pretending that he was translating and retelling the stories of an ancient text he discovered, called the *The Red Book of Westmarch*. Radical perspective shifting frees us up.

The same holds true for artists. Sculptor Emil Alzamora told me about a unique solution he uses when stuck, "I go outside my studio, which is right next to a steep hill, and I sprint up it." The adrenaline, fatigue, and exhaustion make Alzamora feel alive again, freeing him from his slump. Wilco singer Jeff Tweedy has a similar approach to Tellez. When he is stuck, he tries to write bad music. As he explained to Ezra Klein, "To avoid writer's block, I write songs I don't like. I get an idea for a song, and I just go ahead and do it, even though I don't think I'm going to like it. And that frees me up to go to the next song." While producer Brian Eno, best known for his work with David Bowie and Coldplay, introduces constraints to get out of a rut. He had a deck of one hundred cards with a simple command on each. They included such instructions as, "abandon normal instruments, tape your mouth, emphasize differences, reverse the tape." He called them *oblique strategies*. In a radio interview, Eno outlined their purpose: "If you're in a panic, you tend to take the head-on approach because it seems to be the one that's going to yield the best results. Of course, that often isn't the case . . . The function of the oblique strategies was, initially, to serve as a series of prompts that said, 'Don't forget that you could adopt this attitude.'" They are perspective changers, designed to knock you off the tried-and-true path and to remember that there are other routes.

The value of dislodging works for larger or more chronic situations. University of Utah cognitive psychologist David Strayer found that nature recalibrates our mind. While being out in nature for any time has cognitive and emotional benefits, in Strayer's research, he noted a "three-day effect," a parting of the clouds and clearing of the mind after a few days camping in the wilderness. As he told *National Geographic*, "On the third day my senses recalibrate—I smell things and hear things I didn't before. . . . If you can have the experience of being in the moment for two or three days, it seems to produce a difference in qualitative thinking." Strayer isn't just observing it. He found that after a three-day hike, people performed 50 percent better on a creative problem-solving task. Recent research found that nature replenishes our cognitive resources and improves our mood via modulating our brain activity and nervous system. For the modern, always-stimulated world, being in the woods without any beeping or buzzing is the ultimate crazy thing. We leave behind an environment where constant attention and task-switching are the norm, and our brain turns down its alarm. Or as Gina—the *Alone Australia* winner we met in chapter 7—put it, "Nature is the most incredible mirror and in that mirror, our stories can't hold up. Instead of seeing who we think we are or who we want to be, we meet ourselves."

Famed acting coach Jerzy Grotowski also used long hikes in the woods, as well as more eccentric activities, to help get actors out of their own way. There was the exploitation of errors exercise, where instead of stopping when actors messed up a line, they worked the error into their performance. If they mispronounced a word, they carried that mispronunciation through the rest of the play. There was the tiger exercise, where Grotowski chased the actors around like prey, goading them to roar like a tiger and get lost in the strange game of acting like an animal during rehearsal. Many of his techniques were absurd from the outside, but what he was after was simple: to get rid of the inhibitions, worries, fears, and insecurities that he believed blocked their potential. The shocks were "needed to get at those psychic layers behind the life-mask."

Grotowski realized the same thing that athletic coaches have known for years. Out on the track or field, when working hard with a team, you are exposed. You see one another's highest highs and lowest lows. People break down after a loss, grown men and women weeping uncontrollably. And they show unbridled joy and jubilation after a breakthrough. The vulnerability decreases our fears and creates bonds that often last a lifetime. Why? Because we stop hiding. We let go of the pretenses. We drop the facade. We see one another and ourselves for who we are.

DISRUPTING AND REALIGNING OURSELF

Now, we can put these pieces together. It's not a coincidence that many of these disruptors release a flood of feelings or change our attention or sensory experience. They force us to accept, connect, and integrate. Often through embodiment, reminding the brain there are other things worthy of our attention, and we don't have to get stuck on the same feedback loop. It jolts us away from hungry ghosts of information that we are tricked into thinking are important, and pushes us toward information that is actually important. We can now see how doing something hard, that makes us feel alive, can lead to connection and clarity. We need to take action, to connect our inner and outer worlds. We can't think our way out of choking. We have to connect what we're thinking and feeling through doing.

Philosopher Joseph Campbell pointed this out decades ago in an interview with Bill Moyers: "People say that what we're all seeking is meaning for life. I don't think that's what we're really seeking. I think that what we're seeking is an experience of being alive, so that our life experiences on the purely physical plane will have resonances with our own innermost being and reality, so that we actually feel the rapture of being alive." When Moyers asked Campbell about such experiences in his own life, he didn't describe his genre-defining work in mythology or his influence on the biggest movie of his lifetime, *Star Wars*. He replied by describing a relay race he ran in college at the Penn Relays. We need to connect the inner and outer worlds to make us feel alive.

CHANGE THE INPUTS

When we change the inputs, we can find a new predictive path. To do this, think of the various signals your brain uses to make sense of a situation or pursuit. If you are performing a skill, try turning the lights off to force you to rely on the feel of your muscles. Or, alter your environment: perform a skill in the water, throw a heavier ball, or wear large gloves instead of using your bare hands.

For less physical skills, this approach still works. Early in my speaking career, as a natural introvert, I started using a secret weapon: copying Superman. No, I am not adopting an alter ego, but taking off my glasses. Everything that is farther than a couple of feet in front of me is a blur. The clear faces of the audience turn into an indistinguishable amorphous blob. When I take my glasses off, my attention shifts, anxiety dissipates, and my brain is forced to change what it pays attention to and assigns value. It's as if my brain goes, "We are in a different, new place," and is forced to change its predictions. I no longer default to fear but am stuck with the knowledge in my head and the monitor right in front of me or the giant screen right behind that I can actually see. When we change our perception, we force our brain and body to reconnect. To find a new pathway or prediction.

INTERFERE WITH YOUR EXPERIENCE. GO IN THE OTHER DIRECTION.

If every signal around you is telling you to be afraid, to run away, do something that will send a different signal. Watch your mistakes while listening to calm music. Or, after a rough performance or experience, smile, tell a joke to a friend, or watch a comedy routine that makes you laugh. Laughing and smiling are powerful medicines because they don't just send a cognitive signal to reappraise but a deeply psychological and emotional one.

OVERLORD THE SYSTEM

We can dislodge our brain by overloading it with physiological stimuli. If you are on the brink of panic, holding your breath and dunking your head in a bucket of cold water will send a strong stimulus in the opposite direction. It activates the diving reflex, which will drop your heart rate as your brain overrides other signals to conserve oxygen. This is what I'd call a physiological disruptor—a short-term mood or body state shifter.

Although the mechanism is slightly different, we see a similar result with the example of artists sprinting up a hill or even in

"See God" workouts. A slew of feelings, emotions, and hormones takes you out of your current state and shifts your body and brain elsewhere. We can do the same with having moments of awe by experiencing natural beauty or doing novel, exciting, and interesting things, preferably with others. If you've seen a bunch of people taking ice plunges on social media, it's not because they help with recovery or rev our metabolic system. That's mostly oversold nonsense. What jumping into a freezing tub does is make us feel alive. It overloads us with feelings, sensations, and a touch of hormones. It helps tech bros feel again, to connect their inner and outer world, instead of being numb to it.

Remember the idea of embodiment. Taking action is often the catalyst that allows us to get on a new path. It connects our brain, body, and the many feelings and emotions we experience. It's the ultimate overload that brings us back into alignment. We often fail to get ourselves unstuck because our strategies are all cognitive. We try to think and reason our way out of choking. While cognitive strategies play an important role, to get out of a rut we need to shift our entire experience—our perception, feelings, emotions, movement, and thinking. The more of these we activate and invoke, the more likely we'll be able to shift onto a new path. To feel, sometimes you have to do.

USE FEAR TO REFRAME

When we get stuck on a disordered threat loop, we can use fear to disrupt us. When we go toward the fear, our body eventually realizes it isn't in danger and that it can turn down the alarm and exit survival mode. If you fear criticism, take a page out of Jason Kuhn's book and blare criticism while focusing on the task. Or, if you are a writer overly concerned with negative reviews, write out the worst things someone could say about you, then go back to writing your manuscript. Chances are your brain will learn that the thing you feared isn't a big deal.

We can use fear to reframe. You don't even have to be practicing your activity to let fear do its work. Sitting with fear or anxiety trains your mental muscle to turn down the threat signal. In his book *Anatomy of a Breakthrough*, Adam Alter details a unique experiment he assigns his students to help get them unstuck, "Their assignment was to face the rear of an elevator, rather than turning to face the doors as almost all elevator riders do. Try it sometime. It's incredibly awkward. The other passengers assume you're unhinged. I've tried this myself, and the urge to *do something* is almost irresistible."

There's not much more fearful than doing something that violates social norms and makes you look like an idiot. Get creative. Wear ridiculous clothes, stand up, and give a speech in the middle of a crowded coffee shop. Flexing your embarrassment muscle helps us reframe the experience of fear as something that kind of sucks but isn't life-threatening.

UNFREEZING

Parkinson's is an insidious progressive brain disease without a current cure. As the disease progresses, shaking, stiffness, and uncontrollable movements occur. Another symptom is called freezing. People stop being able to move. They are walking along and feel stuck in place, as if their feet are glued to the ground. It often occurs when moving to a new room, walking on a different surface, multitasking, or experiencing a lot of stress. But, according to the Parkinson's Foundation, the exact cause of freezing is unknown.

Gavin Mogan is a personal trainer who specializes in working with Parkinson's warriors. He has a theory for why freezing occurs.

Not just from his work with patients but from experience: He has Parkinson's. He showed me a video of a freezing experience. In the video, he's making laps through his house. It starts out relatively normal, but as the laps continue, the steps become smaller, balance becomes an issue, and he leans and sways with each step becoming a bit more rigid. While this is going on, Mogan reports, he gets "more foggy cognitively." Until he's stuck in his tracks. He stops being able to take steps. He freezes.

Mogan showed me another video. He's standing in front of a basketball hoop with a friend holding a ball. But Mogan is frozen. His body is rigid, slightly hunched. His friend passes him the ball. In a ballistic movement, Mogan catches the ball, lowers his shoulder, dribbles with his right hand before switching to his left midstride, and drives hard to the hoop, laying the ball up and through. He raises his hands in celebration, then gives a quick pump of the fist.

Mogan has figured out how to momentarily escape the freeze. Tossing a ball while walking, using a walker, "riding" his walker as one would a scooter, dribbling a basketball, walking on the grass, listening to music, pretending to step over a line, and even riding a bike down the street. He can even jump up and down on the bed normally. All can help get him unstuck. And Mogan isn't alone. The Parkinson's Foundation recommends several strategies, from music to stepping over a line to a strategy called Stop, Sigh, Shift, Step. This incorporates pausing, letting out a loud audible sigh, shifting your weight back and forth, and then taking exaggerated steps.

How does one go from freezing to jumping up and down on a bed like a child? Mogan has a theory. His brain is being protective. As he narrates himself moving from walking to freezing, he explains, "My brain is making predictions. [At first,] it's still allowing me to walk. It trusts me. But I sense it's becoming more skeptical. Until finally you'll see a freeze up starts to occur, where the brain says, 'Nope, I'm going to shut you down.'

"It's a physiological fear state that my body is in. It becomes very, very hard to escape it. It's almost like a survival mode," Mogan explains. The tools described above temporarily get him out of it. "Jumping on the bed . . . I feel free. I feel safe. So I can move pretty freely. I jump off the bed, and I'm stuck again. I bounce on the bed again, somehow, my brain knows I'm safe, and I can unfreeze and walk fine." It's why he can walk slightly better with a cane, much better with a walker, stroll around on grass but slow down on concrete, and crawl freely. The subtle shifts get him out of protective mode.

While I'm not insinuating that Parkinson's and experiencing the yips are the same, Mogan's experience provides a glimpse into how the brain works when it lives in survival mode. In this case, the danger is walking, and it puts a stop to that, even though he can walk backward or ride a bike just fine. It's a predictive response gone haywire. The underlying contributors and causes are different. One is from a disorder attacking the brain, the other from a conscious or subconscious threat that feels real. But Mogan's incredible insight and grit to navigate a degenerative disorder should inspire us and provide clues to tackle much more straightforward problems.

—

I've massed choking, yips, underperformance, freakouts, and a lot of things all together. Some distinctions and differences are important. One is that some are caused by a conscious fear or threat state. Something we experience, intimately feel, and leads us to choose to protect and defend. Think: the nerves that come with public speaking and choosing to shy away or end your talk early. Other times that threat is subconscious. A deeply ingrained protective mechanism that gets triggered by something we might understand afterward but aren't entirely sure of. Think: something more akin to trauma, or in the case of the yips, a kind of blip in the brain that we weren't aware of why it occurred at the time, but it got stuck. We may become aware of the thing through our actions, but it started largely subconsciously.

But underlying underperformance in life and choking in sport is a predictive doom loop we get in that shuts us down in a different way. We avoid, hesitate, shy away, or maybe even lose the ability to do what we've trained to do. We get stuck in survival mode, seeing threats everywhere, and our brain learns to overindex on them.

Mogan's experience teaches us something vital: the brain wins, but we can convince it that we are okay, even if it's just temporary. That might mean changing our environment, our intentions, or our actions. In sport and life, that might look a little different, but the underlying principle remains. Sometimes, we've got to convince our brain that it's okay. That we aren't going to experience some real or existential threat. Or, as we outlined in this chapter, we need to turn the alarm down, then dislodge and realign.

There's one final step to getting out of your own way and performing up to our potential. We need to embrace the doom and disaster. It might very well teach us how to get the best out of ourselves.

CHAPTER 10

MOVING FROM SURVIVING TO THRIVING

"We'll be fine. It's just another hurricane," my dad said before ending the call on the night of August 25, 2017. As a native Houstonian, I'd been through my share of hurricanes. My dad had seen even more. It's not that we discounted the impact. Some areas would flood, get major damage, and need repair. We knew where that would likely occur and how to help in the aftermath. But where both of us lived, outside of the five-hundred-year flood zones, we knew what to expect. We'd been here before.

After a night of torrential rain and wind, I stepped outside to see water up to my driveway. The street I lived on was flooded, with only the tops of cars peeking out over the water. Thankfully, my home had been spared. As I headed out the door to survey the aftermath, I was left in disbelief. Much of the city was underwater, including parts that hadn't flooded during any of the dozens of hurricanes and tropical storms I'd experienced in my nearly forty years of life on the Gulf Coast. The parks I regularly ran through were lakes. Highways turned into rivers. Cars rested on the side of grass embankments, presumably in a last-ditch effort by their owners to get them to higher ground before abandoning them. Parts of the city were a dozen feet under water. It was as if I'd woken up in the disaster movie *The Day After Tomorrow*.

After the initial shock, news stations warned of chaos. It wasn't bad enough that homes were underwater, hundreds of thousands of individuals were without power, and thousands needed rescue. Warnings of looters swarming the streets, armed robberies, and even people shooting at rescue workers began to circulate. Violence was surely coming. The mayor implemented a city-wide lockdown, setting a 10 p.m. curfew in an effort to protect against "potential criminal acts."

Whenever disasters strike, the assumption is that communities devolve into chaos, akin to the latest postapocalyptic movie where anarchy reigns. We become selfish, lawless, and unruly. It's written in our history. Following the 2005 Katrina hurricane, New Orleans was often portrayed as a war zone, full of looting and violence, with one former Navy Seal claiming he had to sit atop the Superdome and act as a sniper against looters. Go back a century to the great earthquake and fire that wiped out much of San Francisco in 1906, and the response was the same—fear of chaos and lawlessness. The military was even sent in to restore order. In just about every hurricane, earthquake, war, or similar disaster, the same story prevails: People will turn into selfish, lawless hooligans. Except, in just about every case, the opposite occurs.

In Houston, as reports of chaos escalated, the experience was different on the ground. As I walked around in the initial aftermath, relationships changed. The neighbors you only knew from watching them go to work or walk the dog suddenly became important. I talked to more neighbors in the days following the disaster than the previous year. In an age of isolation and disconnection, you saw people, instead of seeing through them. If you had power or water, you opened up your home. There was a pull to help others, not to greedily hoard. Every day people grabbed their boats and set up a makeshift rescue community, navigating through flooded streets to pick up people trapped in their homes. In the days and weeks that followed, the urge to volunteer, to donate, to do something positive skyrocketed. There's a sense of community, not despair but gratitude.

In New Orleans, it took time, but eventually, everyone from the news to the military admitted that the lawless chaos was mostly exaggerated nonsense. Sure, it occurred in pockets. But the vast majority of people were more selfless and orderly than selfish and lawless. The same held true for the San Francisco fires. The founder of American psychology William James told us as much over a century ago in his essay "On Some Mental Effects of the Earthquake." He noted two critical observations: "The rapidity of the improvisation of order out of chaos" and "the universal equanimity . . . I have always believed, that the pathetic way of feeling great disasters belongs rather to the point of view of people at a distance than to the immediate actions." James described a cheerful or at least steadfast tone that took over most of the city, and posited that while suffering was present, it was shared. And sharing the suffering decreased the insidious loneliness that often leads to despair.

It was the same during World War II. The prevailing thought in Western militaries was that bombing a city would demoralize citizens, pushing them toward depression and despair. As the British prepared for London to be bombed by the German Luftwaffe, they were afraid of the psychological impact. Panic was the expectation. One military planner reported, "London for several days will be one vast raving bedlam. The hospitals will be stormed, traffic will cease, the homeless will shriek for help, the city will be a pandemonium."

Yet, as London suffered months of devastating bombing, panic and despair didn't take over. Hospitalizations for mental health problems didn't increase. Instead, morale, resolve, and a sense of community grew. Modern research backs this up. In a study of over thirty-three thousand individuals, psychologists found that those who had experienced heavy wartime bombing were less likely to display neurotic traits and scored higher on levels of resilience. As Edgar Jones and colleagues concluded in a review, "civilians proved more resilient than planners had predicted, largely because they had underestimated their adaptability and resourcefulness, and because the lengthy conflict had involved so many in constructive participant roles." One of the pioneering disaster researchers, Charles Fritz, who got his start in answering the question on whether bombing causes listlessness or despair, summarized: "Disasters provide a temporary liberation from the worries, inhibitions and anxieties associated with the past and future because they force people to concentrate their full attention on immediate moment-to-moment, day-to-day needs within the context of the present reality."

There's a paradox in the research on disasters. While they bring enormous stress and can push some to the brink, for a brief period, they bring clarity and purpose. They detach us from superficial worries, amplifying actual concerns. The petty squabbles and differences fade away. This paradox is hard to understand, and it doesn't always last. (Think: COVID, where we moved from support to isolation to division.) But this trend shows up consistently throughout history, from hurricanes to wars to famines. We expect *Lord of the Flies*, without realizing that when a real-life version of the plot occurred a few years after the book's release, when six boys were stranded on the island of Ata for fifteen months, they didn't descend into chaos. Instead, cooperation and teamwork reigned supreme. In her book *A Paradise Built in Hell*, Rebecca Solnit traced more than a century of disasters. Contrary to popular belief, she concluded that the normal response to disaster isn't selfish chaos but selflessness, generosity, purposefulness, solidarity, connection, and almost a sense of joy.

Disasters are the ultimate disruptor. They knock our expectations and experience for a loop. They can free us up, temporarily causing us to let go of what we thought mattered and open us up to seeing the world through a different light. We realign on what is truly important. In a way, disasters free us from a superficial paradigm and allow us to turn to our deep inner needs.

PLAYING THE WRONG GAME

Almost every religion or ancient wisdom conveys a strikingly similar message: clinging leads to suffering, and we should practice some version of nonattachment. They warn us that we need to stop tying our identity to objects, things, groups, and ideologies. Jesus encouraged us to let go of the chase of worldly items: "None of you can become my disciple if you do not give up all your possessions." Or as catholic theologian Meister Eckhart summarized: "No one hears my word or my teaching unless they have first abandoned their self. For if we are to hear God's word, we must be wholly detached." The Hindu text, the Bhagavad Gita, says, "One who performs his duty without attachment, surrendering the results unto the Supreme Lord, is unaffected by sinful action, as the lotus is untouched by muddy water." Or as written in the Taoist text, *Tao Te Ching*, "Fame or Self: Which matters more? Self or Wealth: Which is more precious? Gain or Loss: Which is more painful? He who is attached to things will suffer much. He who saves will suffer heavy loss. A contented man is rarely disappointed."

In Buddhism, nonattachment plays a central role, as outlined by the Dalai Lama, "There are three stages or steps. The initial stage is to reduce attachment toward life. The second stage is the elimination of desire and attachment to this samsara. Then, in the third stage, self-cherishing is eliminated." Buddhism teaches that nonattachment leads to seeing the inherent value in every person and thing. While each belief system focuses on a slightly different aspect, from idols to objects to fame; the basic gist is the same: watch out for clinging. It distorts, distracts, and sends us down the wrong path.

In psychology, nonattachment is the absence of fixation on an idea, outcome, object, group, or thing. It's the "absence of internal pressure to obtain, hold, avoid, or change circumstances or experiences." When we attach and tie our sense of self to something, we fall into a state of protect and defend. It's the essence of living in survival mode. Clinging distorts our predictions, favoring the external.

Ancient wisdom and modern science tell us the same thing: We tend to attach or cling to wrong ideals as a way to cope with uncertainty, stress, insignificance, or loneliness. It's been part of our nature for millennia. We compensate for the insecurity of our inside game by narrowing and attaching to the external. And our values and morals fade away, hidden behind our desire to feel like we fit in and have achieved some sort of significance. Our understanding of the brain's predictive processing adds a new wrinkle. When we cling, we overweigh that information. Our predictions get stuck, seeing that label, group, job, or thing as the be-all end-all. We've turned the dial of importance on these to eleven.

And in turn, we choke. We start forcing things instead of letting them come. We get wrapped up in making everything public and personal. As we've seen throughout this book, survival mode narrows and deludes. It turns off our prefrontal cortex and focuses us on the wrong ideals: external success, our "tribe" instead of commonalities, winning over our values, and proving our status with meaningless measures. It's the scourge of modern society.

It's what occurred to me and others when working for Nike. The overidentification with a job, the pull toward accolades and achievements, living in an environment that pushed "win at all costs" as the way forward, and normalized sketchy behaviors all turned up the importance on the external while slowly pushing our inner values and ethics to the wayside. I was stuck valuing the wrong information, all while being afraid of losing my job and status. And, in turn, I became deluded. Survival mode makes us start playing games that we didn't sign up for. We chase clout instead of meaning, status instead of competency, fitting in instead of belonging.

Disasters make us realize we need to play a different game. They give us the opportunity to see clearly, to reweigh our experience, and to focus on what matters. We stop seeing our neighbors as others who are different from us but as people who are connected at a basic level. We stop comparing and focus on helping. We stop overly worrying about the past or future and get to work on what we can do right now to help our family and community. For at least a moment, our internal and external values and actions align. Disasters free us up because they loosen our attachments to the inconsequential and make us hold on tighter to our true needs and motives. In essence, we detach from the delusion of chasing that which doesn't really matter.

We don't need a catastrophe to get to this place. Perspective shifters help, but they are just a tool when we have gone astray, a reminder that we don't have to be in this rut we've found ourselves in. We have to shift our focus to realign with a more sustainable path. That's the secret of world-class performers. Think back to marathoner Roberta Groner, astronaut Chris Cassidy, and coach Olav Bu, who told us that it's about love, connection, and joy. Or Tony Hawk and Sara Hall, who performed best when they stopped trying to force things and let go. Believe Olympic champion Katie

Moon, who told us that a champion's mindset can mean sharing your triumph instead of winning at all costs. Remind yourself of Doug Bopst, who had to shift his story and fill the void left by his deep insecurities. Trust Tom House, whose legendary pupils aren't addicted to the outcomes but in love with the process. Those elite performers are playing a different game. It's not an easy one. It comes with setbacks and failure. But it's one that keeps joy, exploration, mastery, and connection front and center. It makes you secure in yourself.

Let's put it all together. When we get dragged to survival mode, we start overindexing on fear and uncertainty. Our predictive software gets stuck anticipating danger. Whether it's because of societal norms, holding on to the wrong narrative, not fulfilling our basic needs of self and identity, or attaching and overweighing parts of our experience that convince us that this game or speech is life or death, it's getting stuck overvaluing the external game.

It's what Simone Biles told the press two years after her Olympic twisties experience. She got caught up looking outward. "And then there were all those outside noises. And then everybody's telling me, like, you're a gold-medal token. And that's from our inside team. That was really tough. And then I would have a practice, and I would be concentrating and I would have fun. And then they would come up to me afterwards and be like, 'Simone, you need to be more cheery, the girls are struggling a little bit.'" Like so many, she let those external voices influence the internal. She wasn't having fun. During her 2023 comeback, Biles reflected on her new outlook, "I'm more mature. At this point it's like, nobody's forcing me out here. This is truly me." Even her definition of success had changed. "What success means to me is a little bit different than before because before everyone defined success for me, even if I had my own narrative that I wanted. So, now, it's just showing up, being in a good head place, having fun out there, and whatever happens,

happens." Days later, she nailed the much more difficult Yurchenko vault in competition, winning her eighth national title.

In many ways, Biles's new approach is a more mature version of how she started. During her comeback, she advised her younger teammates: "It's just gymnastics." When Biles won her first world championship in 2013, she was asked how that win would change things. She replied, "It's just gymnastics, so it can't really affect anything." We often start out with the right ideals, motivations, and perspectives. The external pulls on the internal, and before you know it, we're playing the wrong game with the wrong motivation and, ultimately, the wrong self. Often, all we need is to realign with the joy and experience we had when we started.

Throughout this book, I've offered a number of tactics and techniques, all centered around finding clarity. Getting unstuck is about making our world and self add up. It's making better predictions, ones that align our values and actions, our expectations and our experiences. We can broadly name these four key phases or tactics that help get us out of survival mode and free us up to perform:

1. **Reveal and fill:** Fill your basic needs with quality, genuine ingredients. Do something real. You can't fake your way through it. You can't put on a facade. You can't substitute synthetic junk food for the real thing.
2. **Decenter:** Let go of the protective mechanisms: ego, chasing external validation, attaching to groups, hiding behind labels or ideologies.
3. **Dislodge:** Update your predictive system. If you feel stuck, change your perspective to get back to exploring, to find a new path.
4. **Realign:** Focus on what matters. You have to align your expectations and experience, your values and actions.

We default toward survival mode when our brain predicts the world is scary and our place in it is insecure. We need to convince it otherwise—to let go of the pull toward fragmentation by doing real things in the real world, with real people, that occasionally push us out of our comfort zones—all while holding our groups, labels, and so-called identities loosely. When we do so, our values and morals rise to the surface, acting as waypoints to guide us as we find a new path to explore. That's how we realign with reality, how we move from choking to its opposite: coming through in the clutch.

SETTING OURSELVES FREE

Choking is real. According to an analysis of ten years of data on NBA players, there are hundreds of situations where a player's shooting percentage significantly drops in the waning minutes of a close game. And, most important, there is consistency across seasons in how often a player shows up on that "choke" list. Athletes who shot worse in high-pressure situations showed up for multiple seasons. On the flipside, the opposite of choking, coming through in the clutch, doesn't occur as consistently.

In the same analysis, the number of players who regularly rose to the occasion across multiple seasons was minimal, meaning that just because someone came through in the clutch one moment didn't predict whether they were likely to do so in the future. There is no clutch gene. Despite our propensity to label players as "clutch," the data largely isn't there. The same holds true when we look at clutch performers in the workplace. A study of more than twenty thousand salespeople found little meaningful impact on those who performed better under pressure. They concluded, "Star salespeople are consistently stars, while average employees are consistently average." Does this mean we give up on the idea of coming through in the clutch?

When studying clutch performances, we make a few assumptions. First, that pressure is objective. We define it by a scenario: the last minutes of a game that is within one or two scores. But, as we've come to realize, that's not how pressure works. Pressure, like all states, is dependent on our predictions. What elicits pressure for one, will not for another. And how we respond to that perceived pressure can go down one of many paths. The game can be on the line, and we can experience pressure, but our predictive machinery can send us toward approaching or avoiding, to feeling dread or excitement. Second, we assume that coming through in the clutch raises our game, becoming Superman. It's not. It's doing what we are capable of. Clutch is about being consistently good enough. It's getting out of our own way so that we can perform up to our potential, to function in a way that our body knows what to do, to be good enough when pressure is high.

Clutch is a state. Not a trait. Some people might get in that state more consistently, but we can all come through in the clutch or fail spectacularly. To get into that state, it's about finding clarity and security. It's filling your needs with quality instead of the superficial, creating an environment that supports instead of thwarts, and making sure your brain's predictions are tuned to the reality of the task instead of to a distorted expectation. When we get out of survival mode and have clarity on our inner world and where we stand, shooting that free throw or pitching our idea seems a little less threatening. We move from existential dread and anxiety to a sense of inner peace and confidence, with a touch of excitement.

—

My hands started to sweat, my heart pounded, and all the moisture in my mouth seemingly evaporated. I was nauseous, hands-shaking, and a bit delirious. It was two days before the first round of the NCAA championships in 2017. The team I was coaching was ranked second in the nation, about to make a run at a team title. But I wasn't there. I was standing outside a large office building in the middle of Los Angeles. I was experiencing my first panic attack.

I ducked into a bathroom, splashed water on my face, took a few deep breaths, and utilized every trick I'd learned from two decades of competing and coaching at a high level. I gathered myself just enough before taking the elevator and sitting down in front of a room full of lawyers to be grilled for the next six hours. It was five years after I'd blown the whistle, and I was finally testifying as a witness in the anti-doping case. I'd gathered myself enough to talk, but my brain was a mess. My sharp mind turned to mush. I'd reach for words and memories, and my brain wouldn't comply. I walked out a wreck. I was doing the best I could, but I felt like I barely survived.

While I'd made the so-called courageous decision to blow the whistle, the more challenging part was what followed. Uncertainty abounded. My career was on the line. I could be banned from the sport I loved. My future goals had disintegrated as I felt trapped with the label of whistleblower that limited my prospects in the sport. All the while, I had to wrestle with what occurred, where I messed up, and how, at least for a moment years ago, there was a discrepancy between my values and ideals and my actions.

Up until that first arbitration, I had been surviving. Sure, I knew I'd done the right thing in blowing the whistle, but even on my good days to handle the unknowns and stress, I avoided and compartmentalized. I tried to separate myself. There was the Steve who had to spend hours talking to investigators and the Steve who had to show up with a smile at practice as if I didn't just get interrogated by the FBI. It was spending hours going through scenarios, working through potentially career-altering consequences as threats were dangled before me for years while trying to go to work and act like I knew where I'd be in three or five years. The compartmentalization bled over into my relationships with friends and family. Even for those who knew it all and supported me, I shut down, refusing to talk about the experience. I didn't want to acknowledge the stress or the toll it took.

It wasn't until after going through that panic attack that things started to change. It started when my then-girlfriend, now-wife, pulled me aside one evening and said, "You get upset and shut down when any part of this investigation comes up. You are good for a while, then miserable when the next step in the process surfaces. You're carrying a burden you don't need to." She was right. After all, friends, family, and even some in the sport would tell me how "courageous" I was for taking on Goliath and doing the right thing. But deep down, I was struggling. I was stuck in a loop, surviving. And it wasn't just the stress of the situation. It was that I was clinging, attaching, and avoiding to deal with it. Instead, I had to reorient, accept, integrate, and let go.

It was staring me in the face. Here I was, hoping that success would fulfill me. If the athletes I coached would win a championship or make the Olympics, it would validate my work, and, to a degree, my identity. If I wrote a bestseller, achieved something notable, "whistleblower" wouldn't define me. I was so afraid that I'd lose it all. For a long time, running had become self-defining. It gave me my first sense of freedom and significance as a teenager. As I achieved success, it cemented. It was what I was known as. I was the fastest miler in the country my senior year of high school, with Olympic dreams swirling in my head. I became a prodigy who was a bust on the next level. As that success became harder to find, I struggled with the place running held. I loved the sport. It's what I did. But it left a void. And my coaching career was, in large part, a journey to make up for the lack of fulfilling my own potential. I didn't realize it at first, but my quest for success was one reason I choked.

Right before my eyes were the ills of that approach: finding validation through achievements. I'd lived through a "win at all costs" program. I saw individuals who had achieved at the highest level, becoming the best in the world at various points in their careers, but they were still chasing, clinging, and deeply unsatisfied. No amount of success was ever enough. I watched individuals push away their proclaimed ethics and values in search of some sought-after achievement. I saw people delude themselves, let go of friendships, look past the indefensible, and justify and rationalize it all the way around. I watched myself do many of the same things. As Adam Smith warned, we need tranquility to balance out unfettered pursuits. Or, as modern neuroscience shows, we need a robust contentment system to counteract our urge to drive and strive. Or else we live in survival mode.

When our identity is wrapped up in the external, when our motivation comes from chasing, when success is confused with status, it puts us on a track to never being or doing enough to let us be satisfied and content. It's a one-way ticket to never enough. That baggage weighs us down and, for most of us, leads to choking. We create a fragile, fragmented, and dependent self.

"But when it's time to step it up, they know how to separate and be *the guy*. They're secure in who they are. They're genuine. They know they're the baddest mother*****r on the field," explained former NFL coach Kliff Kingsbury when discussing how star quarterbacks come through when the game is on the line. What Kingsbury said is true. When we are who we are, when we are secure in our self and our ability to do the task in front of us, we feel free to perform. But that second part is key: being genuine. We often mistake what it means to be who we are. We are told to be ourselves, to be authentic. But when most of us hear the advice to "be who we are," we grasp onto the wrong interpretation. We simplify and narrow ourselves. We are experts at delusion. Our brains are meant to make sense of our inner and outer worlds and find coherence somehow.

Authenticity is about finding that coherence in an expansive way, where we realize that we are complex, nuanced, ever-evolving, and changing. It's not finding security and clarity through a static sense of self. It's security by recognizing the messiness, while holding on to the right motivation, expectations, and views underlying it. It's being able to weigh our expectations and experience correctly, by keeping what matters to us—our values, genuine relationships, goals—front and center. While recognizing that they may change, it must be for a worthwhile reason, not because we've let some external pursuit, person, or group delude our journey. Brené Brown wrote in her book *The Gifts of Imperfection*, "Authenticity is the daily practice of letting go of who we think we're supposed to be and embracing who we are. Choosing authenticity means cultivating the courage to be imperfect, to set boundaries, and to allow ourselves to be vulnerable." We can reach for clarity via avoidance and narrowing, or through approaching and expanding. To get to the latter, we often have to let go.

We can see the power of letting go in an unusual place: those who are cured of long-term disorders. When chronic epilepsy patients have successful surgery to eliminate seizures, one would expect mental health immediately improves. But researchers found that up to 60 percent of "cured" patients struggle mentally and emotionally years later. For much of their lives, that disorder has shaped expectations of what they are capable of, what they can do, and how their family sees them. But as a group of psychiatrists wrote, "the illness may serve both as a weapon and as a shield." Those who struggle after having their disease or disorder improve are suffering from what's been termed "the burden of normality."

It's the challenge of discarding part of their identity, of letting go and moving from seeing themselves as chronically sick to well. It can be tempting to want to return to "normal," even if that normal means pain and suffering. In epileptic patients, those who were able to embrace change and complete a process of meaning-making, fared better. Or as researchers summarized, "adjustment primarily depends on the patient's capacity to discard roles associated with chronic epilepsy and to learn to become well." Letting go, authentically, is part of that process.

After freezing at the 2017 hearings, I finally accepted things had to change. Until then, I was just trying to get through, to manage until the finish line. And it was making me miserable. It wasn't just the stress of whistleblowing; I had lost control of my story. I was so worried about losing myself because I'd wrapped up so much of my identity in the external. To truly free myself up, I had to stop resisting, fighting, avoiding, or worrying. And I needed, in the words of Brown, to "[let] go of who we think we're supposed to be." I took a page out of Tony Hawk's playbook. I stopped competing. I finally let go.

It started with me no longer trying to make up for my failures. I had to be okay with potentially losing my job, never coaching again, and perhaps never being involved in high-level running. It started with what you are doing right now: reading my work. My writing journey began as a way to understand and make sense of my experience. I had no delusions of being a writer; I just enjoyed it. It was play at a time when everything in my life felt out of my control. In many ways, every book I've written came from this need to understand. *Peak Performance* was written in 2015, before my case became public, and was about wrestling with the burnout I felt early on in trying to chase success while having this secret weight hanging over my head. *The Passion Paradox* was written in 2017 and explored whether you could be driven to achieve at the highest level without falling toward cheating and obsession. *Do Hard Things* was written in 2020 as I was going through the final stages of the case, trying to find ways to be resilient. And the book you are reading now began as my ten-year journey through whistleblowing was reaching its conclusion. It started as a way to make sense of the ordeal, a type of meaning-making.

Writing allowed me to let go of a career and self based solely on running. That freed me up to engage with other aspects of myself—to see that I enjoyed coaching people up, to help them see and reach their potential—but that could be done through a variety of avenues. Letting go allowed me to go back to dabbling and exploring, following my interests instead of my ego. It led me to working with athletes in other sports. To realize that a 300-pound lineman, a 130-pound distance runner, and a 7-foot basketball player have a lot more in common than we realize. More important, exploration pushed me outside of the comfort zone of athletics, freeing me up to work with a wide world of performers away from the athletic fields: physicians, educators, executives, entrepreneurs, artists, and much more. I stopped trying to force things, to tighten the instrument when it needed to be loosened.

It also took taking actions to dislodge and realign. Before the final arbitration had commenced, I decided to leave my job as a college coach. I loved working with the athletes and the coaching staff, but it felt like a part of my history, something that I enjoyed but needed to stretch beyond to continue to explore and grow. Stepping away from college coaching meant minimizing my involvement in a sport that had defined my life since the age of fourteen. At first, it was uncomfortable. It was a safe environment where I had success and stability. I had to venture onto unknown paths. While it was scary, it allowed me to put running in its rightful place: something that I enjoyed, that I cared about, that was always a part of me, but was not the sole defining thing that it had been for a large portion of my life. And that was okay. I could take the skills and lessons I learned and apply them elsewhere. I could be content jogging five miles a day instead of bashing out fifteen to try to eke out a second of improvement.

But it wasn't just my relationship with running that had to change. I had to discard the idea that single-minded focus was the path to greatness. To be able to strive but not obsess. I had to come to terms with and redefine success, that it wasn't measured in accomplishments and accolades. That success was a by-product of following my interests and fueling that journey with intrinsic motivation. Sure, my competitive streak wanted to win just as badly at competitions, but I could accept and be content that I did the work even if the result wasn't there. I had to use this experience to reframe and reorient around what truly mattered.

I had to accept the messiness of myself and others. In my own experience, I had both done something that I deeply regretted and followed up with actions that took the courage to stand up, when most stood down. I had to own my past. That dividing myself and others into good or bad, us or them, was a delusion. It flattened the world into a caricature of itself. And that started with me realizing that I wasn't good or bad; I was me. Someone who could strive to be a better version of himself, to live up to meaningful values, but who would also mess up along the way. And what mattered was how I moved forward after it. I had to act and be, make sense of and experience, feel alive and understand. Living with and accepting the messiness with clarity allows us to be courageous.

I was free to choose how to write my story. For the first time in a while, I had a clear view of who I was and who I wanted to be. I strove to act accordingly, knowing I wouldn't always live up to it. And that was okay. I now had an opportunity to act, and with that came a chance to match actions with values. Or as Olympic silver medalist rower Cath Bishop wrote, "Integrity isn't about never doing anything wrong. It's about owning up to it, being accountable, apologizing and learning from it, supported by those around you."

As I headed into that final arbitration to face hours of having every aspect of my life questioned, the panic attack of years ago had faded. There were still nerves and pressure, but they were a different kind. It was as if my brain was predicting that it needed to be alert and sharp, not overwhelmed and defensive. An incredible challenge was before me, but ultimately, I was on firm footing. I knew why I was there. I knew why it mattered. I stood by my values, and those values would still be there, in whatever pursuit I decided to apply them to in the future. I was at peace. They couldn't take anything from me. Win or lose, I was going to be okay. I had clarity.

FIND HARMONY, NOT BALANCE OR PERFECTION

According to self-discrepancy theory, we have three main selves: who we think we are, who we want to become, and who we think we ought to be. In other words, our current, ideal, and ought selves. Research shows when there's a discrepancy between who we think we are and who we ought to be or who we are striving to be, negative emotions abound. We feel a burden. We can't live up to our own ideals or those placed upon us by others or society. We default to what's-the-point or why-try mode. And we experience rumination, anxiety, guilt, shame, and anger. When there's a discrepancy that hits us hard, we self-protect. As clinical psychologist Kathryn Smith wrote, rumination and negative thoughts persist "until one resolves the discrepancy or abandons the goal." But one hits us harder than the rest.

In a meta-analysis, researchers out of the University of Southern

California found that the discrepancy between ourself and our ideals impacted mental health more than ourself and what we think we ought to be. As organizational psychologist Adam Grant summarized the research, "Mental health depends more on living up to your ideals than to others' expectations." It's winning the inside game.

Psychologist Kennon Sheldon developed the idea of self-concordance to define how our goals and values align. It occurs when individuals identify "with internally motivated values of personally meaningful activities and relationships rather than with extrinsically controlled values of social status and egoistic self-image." It's aligning our inner and outer self by continuously taking action on your goals that align with yourself. Or as Sheldon wrote, "owning one's actions." In research spanning different societies, they found that when we own our actions, seeing consistency between our values and behaviors, it predicts well-being.

When researchers studied the impact of dealing with change in our identities, they found that just about any degree of change in three aspects of our self is accompanied by a range of negative emotions. Those three selves are person, role, and group. There's a reason this book is organized around clarity in ourself, our pursuits, and others. Change or discrepancy in any area hurts, and as we've seen, we often try to fill that gap with the cheap stuff to deal with it. But not all change in our self is bad. Researchers found that the direction of change matters.

When we see it as developing out of an identity, fear and protection predominate. We are losing something. We get caught ruminating on what we're supposed to do or be. But when we focus on what we are developing into, the emotional impact changes. Our levels of authenticity, self-worth, and self-efficacy all increase when we feel we are developing into instead of out of that identity.

Whether we call it self-accordance, finding clarity and security, courage, or coming through in the clutch, the message is the same. We can perform up to our potential when we set the baggage aside. We stop looking to the external to fulfill our needs. We stop trying to write our story based on outside expectations. We own our actions. Sometimes we need a perspective changer to get us out of a rut, to dislodge us from a path where our actions, goals, and values don't align. But ultimately, we need to see things clearly, while minimizing the societal pull toward delusion. It's coming to terms with and owning the complex, messy, nuanced, sometimes contradictory people that we are.

It's clarity on all aspects of our self. As famed football coach Pete Carroll summarized, "The essence of being as good as you can be is you got to figure out who you are. . . . Relentless effort to get clear about what's important to you, what uncompromising principles do you stand by, what makes you who you are. . . . Maximize your authenticity and be connected to that true essence of who you are."

We get to determine our ideals and values, and that impacts us more than any that are placed upon us. Or as we learned from Hannah in chapter 1, we need to stop chasing what we think others want us to and "learn how to be me." Getting clarity, freeing ourselves up to perform, learning how to strive instead of survive, getting out of the predictive rut of choking is about finding a better alignment among yourself, your aspirations, and your relationships with others. It's not balance. It's dealing with the messiness, nuance, and nonduality of living and performing well. It's putting emphasis on what you are growing into, instead of what you are growing out of.

Courage comes from being okay, failing, messing up, or being embarrassed. It comes from aligning your values and beliefs with actions. It means holding genuine connections and values closely and identities a bit more loosely. It means ceasing to chase status because you realize that external validation is fleeting and that those who genuinely support you will do so, win or lose. All the while understanding that you will screw up. But what matters most is how you respond. When you stop acting like you are a middle schooler trying to fit in, you get the freedom to fulfill your potential. It's your story: own it, update it, sometimes disrupt it, and realize that you get to choose where you go from here. Choose wisely.

ACKNOWLEDGMENTS

This book is for those who stood up, found courage, and stuck to their values and ethics. It's a long road, and to anyone who has walked that path, you have my respect and thanks. I wouldn't have made it through my own journey and to this book without many who offered support and advice throughout. While other doors all around were closing, you opened them. Thank you, Andy Stover, Jon Marcus, Leroy Burrell, Will Blackburn, Nate Pineda, Drevan Anderson-Kaapa, Kyle Tellez, Tom Tellez, Shayla Houlihan, Paulo Sosa, Danny Mackey, Kara Goucher, and many others. A special thanks to my family, who provided endless support throughout: Elizabeth, Bill, Emily, and Phillip.

Next, I'd like to thank those who have paved the way to do the work. Thanks to my friends and colleagues at the Growth Equation. Brad Stulberg for always being there no matter what and insisting that our work is about quality, even if I want to just get it done. Chris Douglas for being the captain of the ship—without you, I'm sure we'd end up adrift somewhere. Clay Skipper and Nate Mechler for your insight and friendship. Thanks to our email group, who offered support, wit, and wisdom: Dave Epstein, Alex Hutchinson, Mike Joyner, Jonathan Wai, Amby Burfoot, and Christie Aschwanden. Thank you to the early readers who provided valuable feedback that made this book better.

No matter how many books I write, it never gets easier. Thank you to Laurie Abkemeier, who is the best agent one could ask for. Without your help, I'm sure this book never sees the light of day. To the entire team at HarperOne for believing in and crafting my little idea into the beautiful book that grew out of it. My publisher, Judith Curr, for understanding my vision for this work and giving me the opportunity to turn it into a reality. Anna Paustenbach for being a champion for the book, a friend with sage advice, and a wonderful editor who could take my ramblings and make them clear and concise. To Rakesh Satyal, thank you for picking up the baton and sprinting to the finish line with such care. To the marketing team, Aly Mostel, Louise Braverman, Ann Edwards, and the rest of the team for helping spread the word far and wide. And a special thanks to the countless people behind the scenes who do the tireless and thankless work to make sure every T is crossed.

To my family for all of the love and support: Bill, Elizabeth, Emily, Phillip, Todd, Sheryl, Serena, Mikaela, and Olivia. To my daughter Haizley. As I write this, you are only one, but I can already see the courageous, independent, and curious woman you'll grow into. And finally, to my wife, Hillary. This book wouldn't exist without your love, care, and support. You helped me navigate many of the more difficult stories told in this book with kindness, care, and wisdom. I couldn't imagine going through it without having such a strong, courageous, and loving wife. I love you.

NOTES

CHAPTER 1 | WE ARE ALL IN SURVIVAL MODE

7 *"He'll live on in Notre Dame":* C. Killoren, "Notre Dame Football: Manti Te'o Will Live on in Fighting Irish Lore," Bleacher Report, September 21, 2017.

7 *"Every day was [about]":* Tony Vainuku and Ryan Duffy, directors, *Untold: The Girlfriend Who Didn't Exist,* 2022.

9 *mental sketch pad":* L. Bonnet, A. Comte, L. Tatu, J. L. Millot, T. Moulin, and E. Medeiros de Bustos, "The Role of the Amygdala in the Perception of Positive Emotions: An 'Intensity Detector,'" *Frontiers in Behavioral Neuroscience* 9, no. 178 (2015).

10 *A twenty-nine-year-old builder:* Rachel Zoffness, "A Tale of Two Nails," *Psychology Today,* November 21, 2019, https://www.psychologytoday.com/us/blog/pain-explained/201911/tale-two-nails.

11 *ER physician Ryan Marino reported:* B. Mann, "Cops Say They're Being Poisoned by Fentanyl. Experts Say the Risk Is 'Extremely Low,'" *NPR,* May 16, 2023.

12 *Research has found that:* I. Ramos-Grille et al., "Predictive Processing in Depression: Increased Prediction Error Following Negative Valence Contexts and Influence of Recent Mood-Congruent yet Irrelevant Experiences," *Journal of Affective Disorders* 311 (2022): 8–16.

12 *"A depressed brain":* L. F. Barrett, *How Emotions Are Made: The Secret Life of the Brain* (Boston: Mariner Books, 2017).

12 *Prediction errors are a hallmark:* M. DeGuzman et al., "Association of Elevated Reward Prediction Error Response with Weight Gain in Adolescent Anorexia Nervosa," *American Journal of Psychiatry* 174, no. 6 (2017): 557–65.

12 *Getting stuck responding:* A. Ehlers et al., "The Nature of Intrusive Memories after Trauma: The Warning Signal Hypothesis," *Behaviour Research and Therapy* 40, no. 9 (2002): 995–1002.

15 *Research has found that depersonalization:* J. T. Vullinghs, A. H. De Hoogh, D. N. Den Hartog, and C. Boon, "Ethical and Passive Leadership and Their Joint Relationships with Burnout via Role Clarity and Role Overload," *Journal of Business Ethics* 165 (2020): 719–33.

16 *In the meaning maintenance model:* S. J. Heine, T. Proulx, and K. D. Vohs, "The Meaning Maintenance Model: On the Coherence of Social Motivations," *Personality and Social Psychology Review* 10, no. 2 (2006): 88–110, https://doi.org/10.1207 /s15327957pspr1002_1.

16 *We have a self-preservation system:* R. K. Henderson and S. Schnall, "Social Threat Indirectly Increases Moral Condemnation via Thwarting Fundamental Social Needs," *Scientific Reports* 11, no. 1 (2021): 2170.

18 *Increasingly, research shows that kids:* "Children Today Far Less Likely to Play Outside than Their Grandparents," *Save the Children*, August 5, 2022, https://www .savethechildren.org.uk/news/media-centre/press-releases/children-today-62-percent -less-likely-to-play-outside-than-their.

18 *Yes, phones and devices:* H. Lee et al., "A Meta-Study of Qualitative Research Examining Determinants of Children's Independent Active Free Play," *International Journal of Behavioral Nutrition and Physical Activity* 12, no. 1 (2015): 1–12.

18 *During the 2021 school year:* B. Dodson, "Study: 40% of School Administrators Threatened by Parents Last Year," WBTW News 13, March 22, 2022.

20 *Golden State Warriors coach Steve Kerr:* J. Lynch, *The Competitive Buddha: How to Up Your Game in Sports, Leadership and Life* (Coral Gables. FL: Mango Media Inc., 2021), 156.

20 *In studying meaning in life:* T. Schnell, "An Existential Turn in Psychology. Meaning in Life Operationalized," *Habilitation Treatise*, University of Innsbruck.

22 *But the status and health connection:* L. D'Hooge, P. Achterberg, and T. Reeskens, "Mind over Matter: The Impact of Subjective Social Status on Health Outcomes and Health Behaviors," *PloS One* 13, no. 9 (2018): e0202489.

22 *"adherents to a cult of productivity":* D. Thompson, "This Is the Beginning of the Fourth Revolution of Work," *The Atlantic*, April 4, 2023.

27 *low self-concept clarity is linked:* V. Noguti and A. L. Bokeyar, "Who Am I? The Relationship Between Self-Concept Uncertainty and Materialism," *International Journal of Psychology* 49, no. 5 (2014): 323–33.

27 *We are more trusting:* L. F. Emery, W. L. Gardner, E. J. Finkel, and K. L. Carswell, "'You've changed': Low self-concept clarity predicts lack of support for partner change," *Personality and Social Psychology Bulletin* 44, no. 3 (2018): 318–31; L. F. Emery, W. L. Gardner, K. L. Carswell, and E. J. Finkel, "You Can't See the Real Me: Attachment Avoidance, Self-Verification, and Self-Concept Clarity," *Personality and Social Psychology Bulletin* 44, no. 8 (2018): 1133–46.

27 *We are more likely to feel:* S. B. Richman et al., "An Unclear Self Leads to Poor Mental Health: Self-Concept Confusion Mediates the Association of Loneliness with Depression," *Journal of Social and Clinical Psychology* 35, no. 7 (2016): 525–50.

CHAPTER 2 | THE AMERICAN DREAM IS TO BLAME

33 *Adams warned that the:* James Truslow Adams, *The Epic of America*, 2nd ed (Greenwood Press, 1931), 405.

33 *"The original 'American Dream'":* A. Diamond, "The Original Meanings of the 'American Dream' and 'America First' Were Starkly Different from How We Use Them Today," *Smithsonian Magazine*, September 21, 2018.

33 *On* Fortune's *global list:* E. H. Dyvik, "Number of Fortune 500 Companies in Selected Countries Worldwide from 2000 to 2023," Statista, November 7, 2023, https://www.statista.com/statistics/1204099/number-fortune-500-companies -worldwide-country/.

34 *It's why a 2022 survey by Deloitte:* R. Bradshaw, "Startling Remote Work Burnout Statistics," Apollo Technical, November 28, 2023.

34 *In the classroom:* D. Bethmann and R. Rudolf, "The Paradox of Wealthy Nations' Unhappy Adolescents," Discussion Paper Series no. 2101 (2021).

34 *As economist Ban Ga-Woon summarized:* "South Korea's Education Success Is Faltering in Evolving Economy: Report," *The Straits Times*, November 13, 2022.

35 *In an aptly titled study:* E. L. Bradshaw, J. H. Conigrave, B. A. Steward, K. A. Ferber, P. D. Parker, and R. M. Ryan, "A Meta-Analysis of the Dark Side of the American Dream: Evidence for the Universal Wellness Costs of Prioritizing Extrinsic over Intrinsic Goals," *Journal of Personality and Social Psychology* 124, no. 4 (2023): 873.

37 In 1905, German sociologist: M. Weber, *The Protestant Ethic and the Spirit of Capitalism*, trans. Talcott Parsons (New York: Dover, 2003).

37 *In 2013, economists:* A. Van Hoorn and R. Maseland, "Does a Protestant Work Ethic Exist? Evidence from the Well-Being Effect of Unemployment," *Journal of Economic Behavior & Organization* 91 (2013): 1–12.

38 *In humans, as the threat:* D. R. Bach, M. Guitart-Masip, P. A. Packard, J. Miró, M. Falip, L. Fuentemilla, and R. J. Dolan, "Human Hippocampus Arbitrates Approach-Avoidance Conflict," *Current Biology* 24, no. 5 (2014): 541–47.

39 *When both systems conflict:* A. Mouratidis, A., Michou, A. N. Demircioğlu, and M. Sayil, "Different Goals, Different Pathways to Success: Performance-Approach Goals as Direct and Mastery-Approach Goals as Indirect Predictors of Grades in Mathematics," *Learning and Individual Differences* 61 (2018): 127–35.

39 *In a 2017 study out of Portugal:* C. Darnon, M. Jury, and C. Aelenei, "Who Benefits from Mastery-Approach and Performance-Approach Goals in College? Students' Social Class as a Moderator of the Link Between Goals and Grade," *European Journal of Psychology of Education* 33, no. 4 (2018): 713–26.

39 *Follow-up research found that:* C. Darnon et al., "Performance-Approach and Performance-Avoidance Goals: When Uncertainty Makes a Difference," *Personality and Social Psychology Bulletin* 33, no. 6 (2007): 813–27.

39 *Research shows that acute low-level pressure:* C. Vaishnav, A. Khakifirooz, and M. Devos, "Punishing by Rewards: When the Performance Bell-Curve Stops Working for You," *Nijmegen: International Conference of System Dynamics*, 2006.

39 *Other research shows that bonuses:* S. Bowles and S. P. Reyes, "Economic Incentives and Social Preferences: A Preference-Based Lucas Critique of Public Policy," CESifo Working Paper, no. 2734, Center for Economic Studies and ifo Institute (CESifo), Munich (2009).

41 *As Tore Øvrebø:* Dan Wolken, "Norway Is Dominating These Winter Olympics with a Unique Approach to Sports," *USA Today,* February 19, 2018, https://www.usatoday.com/story/sports/winter-olympics-2018/2018/02/18/norway-dominating-2018-winter-olympics-medal-count/350369002/.

41 *But it wasn't the direct relationship:* A. Mouratidis et al., "Different Goals, Different Pathways to Success," 127–35.

41 *In another study, mastery goals:* J. M Harackiewicz, K. E. Barron, J. M. Tauer, and A. J. Elliot, "Predicting Success in College: A Longitudinal Study of Achievement Goals and Ability Measures as Predictors of Interest and Performance from Freshman Year Through Graduation," *Journal of Educational Psychology* 94, no. 3 (2002): 562.

41 *Outcome goals had little:* O. Williamson et al., "The Performance and Psychological Effects of Goal Setting in Sport: A Systematic Review and Meta-Analysis," *International Review of Sport and Exercise Psychology* (2022): 1–29.

43 *The late Kobe Bryant echoed:* V. Villanueva, "'It's Not Even the Championships'—Kobe Bryant on the Quality that All Great Ones Have," Basketball Network, November 27, 2022, https://www.basketballnetwork.net/off-the-court/kobe-bryant-on-the-quality-that-all-great-ones-have.

44 *"The pleasures of wealth":* A. Smith, *The Theory of Moral Sentiments* (1869), Part IV, chapter 1.

45 *Smith outlined:* A. Smith, *The Theory of Moral Sentiments* (1869), section III, chapter 3.

46 *Smith implores us:* A. Smith, *The Theory of Moral Sentiments* (1869), section III, chapter 3.

46 *Three of the key systems are:* P. Gilbert, "Introducing Compassion-Focused Therapy," *Advances in Psychiatric Treatment* 15, no. 3 (2009): 199–208.

47 *As neuroscientist Jaak Panksepp noted:* J. Panksepp and L. Biven, *The Archaeology of Mind: Neuroevolutionary Origins of Human Emotions* (New York: W. W. Norton, 2012).

47 *Or, as Adam Smith wrote:* A. Smith, *The Theory of Moral Sentiments* (1869), chapter 3.

49 *Music producer Rick Rubin:* R. Rubin, *The Creative Act: A Way of Being* (New York: Penguin Press, 2023).

51 *According to one study:* P. G. Van der Velden, M. Pecoraro, M. S. Houwerzijl, and E. Van der Meulen, "Mental Health Problems Among Whistleblowers: A Comparative Study," *Psychological Reports* 122, no. 2 (2019): 632–44; P. Patrick, "Be Prepared Before You Blow the Whistle," *Fraud Magazine,* October 1, 2010.

CHAPTER 3 | SPEND LESS TIME SEEKING AND CHASING, MORE TIME EXPLORING

61 *Williams was Woods's caddy:* S. Davis, "Tiger Woods' Former Caddy Said He Once Had to Pull Over on the Side of a Highway Because Woods Was Determined to Practice His Swing," *Business Insider,* January 8, 2021, https://www.businessinsider.com/tiger-woods-caddy-pull-over-highway-practice-swing-2021-1.

64 *When asked for advice:* B. Smallwood, *This Wasn't Supposed to Happen to Me: 10 Make-or-Break Choices When Life Steals Your Dreams and Rocks Your World* (Nashville: Thomas Nelson, 2009), 131.

65 *The lucky combination of obsessive:* E. Winner, *Gifted Children,* vol. 1 (New York: Basic Books, 2009), 3–4.

66 *In a 2018 study:* L. Liu, Y. Wang, R. Sinatra, C. L. Giles, C. Song, and D. Wang, "Hot Streaks in Artistic, Cultural, and Scientific Careers," *Nature* 559, no. 7714 (2018): 396–99.

67 *Having identified that hot streaks:* L. Liu, N. Dehmamy, J. Chown, C. L. Giles, and D. Wang, "Understanding the Onset of Hot Streaks Across Artistic, Cultural, and Scientific Careers," *Nature Communications* 12, no. 1 (2021): 5392.

67 *As Wang reported, "Our data":* D. Thompson, "Creativity: Why Career Hot Streaks Don't Happen by Accident," *Australian Financial Review,* November 10, 2021, https://www.afr.com/work-and-careers/careers/why-career-hot-streaks-don-t-happen-by-accident-20211109-p5978y.

67 *Take it from Tiger Woods:* Golf Galaxy, "Tiger Woods on His Love of Sports," YouTube, July 15, 2021, https://www.youtube.com/watch?v=NgHmmTwfwbQ.

69 *As one of her close friends:* H. Hoby, "Harper Lee: A Late Twist in the Tale of an Adored Writer," *The Guardian,* December 2, 2017.

70 *As Baer explained:* Washington University in St. Louis, "One-Hit Wonder: How Awards, Recognition Decrease Inventors' Creativity," ScienceDaily, July 14, 2022, https://www.sciencedaily.com/releases/2022/07/220714165825.htm.

70 *Intensive pursuit of a singular role:* J. Coakley, "Burnout Among Adolescent Athletes: A Personal Failure or Social Problem?" *Sociology of Sport Journal* 9, no. 3 (1992): 271–85.

71 *According to a recent study:* B. Vötter, "Crisis of Meaning and Subjective Well-Being: The Mediating Role of Resilience and Self-Control Among Gifted Adults," *Behavioral Sciences* 10, no. 1 (2019): 15.

72 *She went on to conclude:* Winner, *Gifted Children,* 166.

72 *Those who adopted a fear:* M. J. Schmid, B. Charbonnet, A. Conzelmann, and C. Zuber, "More Success with the Optimal Motivational Pattern? A Prospective Longitudinal Study of Young Athletes in Individual Sports," *Frontiers in Psychology* 11 (2021): 606272.

72 *In studying more:* M. D. Rocklage, D. D. Rucker, and L. F. Nordgren, "Emotionally Numb: Expertise Dulls Consumer Experience," *Journal of Consumer Research* 48, no. 3 (2021): 355–373.

74 *Sometimes it shows itself:* M. Epstein, *The Zen of Therapy: Uncovering a Hidden Kindness in Life* (New York: Penguin Books, 2023), 66.

78 *In a 2023 paper:* P. Gray, D. F. Lancy, and D. F. Bjorklund, "Decline in Independent Activity as a Cause of Decline in Children's Mental Well-Being: Summary of the Evidence," *The Journal of Pediatrics* 260 (2023): 113352.

78 *Research by Michael Norton and Gabriela Tonietto:* G. N. Tonietto, S. A. Malkoc, R. W. Reczek, and M. I. Norton, "Viewing Leisure as Wasteful Undermines Enjoyment," *Journal of Experimental Social Psychology* 97 (2021): 104198.

78 *Stuart Brown of the National Institute for Play:* S. Yenigun, "Play Doesn't End with Childhood: Why Adults Need Recess Too," *NPR*, August 6, 2014.

79 *Or take note of 3M's:* P. D. Kretkowski, "The 15 Percent Solution," *WIRED*, January 23, 1998, https://www.wired.com/1998/01/the-15-percent-solution/.

81 *The latter involves "individuals confronting":* K. Howells and D. Fletcher, "Sink or Swim: Adversity-and-Growth-Related Experiences in Olympic Swimming Champions," *Psychology of Sport and Exercise* 16 (2015): 37–48.

82 *One study concluded, "recovery is":* Alcoholicsguide, "Recovery as a Process of Social Identity Transition," Inside the Alcoholic Brain, September 14, 2015, https://insidethealcoholicbrain.com/2015/09/14/recovery-as-a-process-of-social-identity-transition/.

CHAPTER 4 | ACCEPT THE MESSINESS OF WHO YOU ARE

89 *Centuries before these men:* S. Tzu, *The Art of War*, chapter 11.

90 *According to a fifteen-year study:* J. Raffiee and J. Feng, "Should I Quit My Day Job?: A Hybrid Path to Entrepreneurship," *Academy of Management Journal* 57, no. 4 (2014): 936–63.

90 *A 2021 meta-analysis:* A. Güllich, B. N. Macnamara, and D. Z. Hambrick, "What Makes a Champion? Early Multidisciplinary Practice, Not Early Specialization, Predicts World-Class Performance," *Perspectives on Psychological Science* 17, no. 1 (2022): 6–29.

90 *According to research out of Michigan:* R. Root-Bernstein et al., "Arts Foster Scientific Success: Avocations of Nobel, National Academy, Royal Society, and Sigma Xi Members," *Journal of Psychology of Science and Technology* 1, no. 2 (2008): 51–63.

92 *As clinical psychologist Darby Saxbe wrote:* D. Saxbe, "This Is Not the Way to Help Depressed Teenagers," *New York Times*, November 18, 2023, https://www.nytimes.com/2023/11/18/opinion/teenagers-mental-health-treatment.html.

92 *We overidentify or resort:* S. Roccas and M. B. Brewer, "Social Identity Complexity," *Personality and Social Psychology Review* 6, no. 2 (2002): 88–106.

93 *When individuals score low on complexity:* J. Coakley, "Burnout Among Adolescent Athletes: A Personal Failure or Social Problem?" *Sociology of Sport Journal* 9, no. 3 (1992): 271–85.

93 *They are more likely to:* L. F. Emery, W. L. Gardner, K. L. Carswell, and E. J.Finkel, "You Can't See the Real Me: Attachment Avoidance, Self-Verification, and Self-Concept Clarity," *Personality and Social Psychology Bulletin* 44, no. 8 (2018): 1133–46.

93 *On the other end of the spectrum:* S. Roccas and M. B. Brewer, "Social Identity Complexity," *Personality and Social Psychology Review* 6, no. 2 (2002): 88–106.

95 *The authors gave the conclusion away:* C. M. Brown and A. R. McConnell, "Effort or Escape: Self-Concept Structure Determines Self-Regulatory Behavior," *Self and Identity* 8, no. 4 (2009): 365–77.

95 *As he told writer Sam Borden:* S. Borden, "After HR Record, Aaron Judge Wants More MLB Success for the Yankees—ESPN," *ESPN.com*, April 4, 2023, https://www.espn.com/mlb/story/_/id/35926062/can-yankees-aaron-judge-top-record-breaking-season.

95 *As Maradona's fitness coach:* Abrahams, Daniel (@DanAbrahams77). 2023. "Diego Maradona had a Game Face." X, January 23, 2023, 12:00 p.m.

96 *As actress Brit Marling reflected:* T. Seymour, "The East: From Goldman Sachs to Freeganism, Brit Marling Is a Hollywood Conundrum," *The Guardian*, December 29, 2017.

97 *Research out of the University of Waterloo:* R. M. Ryan, J. G. LaGuardia, and L. J. Rawsthorne, "Self-Complexity and the Authenticity of Self-Aspects: Effects on Well Being and Resilience to Stressful Events," *North American Journal of Psychology* 7, no. 3 (2005): 431–48.

98 *At the time, nearly 70 percent:* Wikipedia contributors, "Poverty in Ethiopia," Wikipedia, April 13, 2024, https://en.wikipedia.org/wiki/Poverty_in_Ethiopia#:~:text=According%20to%20the%20UNICEF%20Annual,citizens%2C%20leaders%20in%20development%20are.

101 *Research shows that those who integrate:* M. Downie, R. Koestner, S. ElGeledi, and K. Cree, "The Impact of Cultural Internalization and Integration on Well-Being Among Tricultural Individuals," *Personality and Social Psychology Bulletin* 30, no. 3 (2004): 305–14.

101 *Psychologists Magdalena Mosanya and Anna Kwiatkowski:* M. A. Yampolsky, C. E. Amiot, and R. de la Sablonnière, "Multicultural Identity Integration and Well-Being: A Qualitative Exploration of Variations in Narrative Coherence and Multicultural Identification," *Frontiers in Psychology* 4 (2013): 37896.

102 *"When you have a more well-rounded life":* SCOTT-SRAM MTB Racing Team, "Blueprint | Rising with Kate Courtney–S2E1," YouTube, April 8, 2021, https://www.youtube.com/watch?v=GweoIuwZ3eI.

103 *As Shannon Lee, the daughter:* S. Lee, *Be Water, My Friend: The Teachings of Bruce Lee* (New York: Flatiron Books, 2020).

109 *According to Clapton and Hiskey:* N. Clapton and S. Hiskey, "Radically Embodied Compassion: The Potential Role of Traditional Martial Arts in Compassion Cultivation," *Frontiers in Psychology* 11: 555156.

110 *When asked about the graffiti:* P. Lodhia, "'Be Someone' Artist Speaks About Famous Statement," ABC13 Houston, May 28, 2016, https://abc13.com/people-be-someone-viral-photo-houston/1360192/.

112 *our foundational needs are substitutable:* S. J. Heine, T. Proulx, and K. D. Vohs, "The Meaning Maintenance Model: On the Coherence of Social Motivations," *Personality and Social Psychology Review* 10, no. 2 (2006): 88–110; D. R. Van Tongeren and J. D. Green, "Combating Meaninglessness: On the Automatic Defense of Meaning," *Personality and Social Psychology Bulletin* 36, no. 10 (2010): 1372–84.

112 *Or, as famed neuroendocrinologist Robert Sapolsky:* Andrew Huberman, "Dr. Robert Sapolsky: Science of Stress, Testosterone & Free Will," YouTube, August 30, 2021, https://www.youtube.com/watch?v=DtmwtjOoSYU.

113 *Writing about our experiences:* O. Glass, "Expressive Writing to Improve Resilience to Trauma: A Clinical Feasibility Trial," *Complementary Therapies in Clinical Practice* 34 (2019): 240–46.

114 *Neuroscience research has found:* B. C. DiMenichi, A. O. Ceceli, J. P. Bhanji, and E. Tricomi, "Effects of Expressive Writing on Neural Processing During Learning," *Frontiers in Human Neuroscience* 13 (2019): 389.

114 *Expressive writing works via confronting:* D. M. Sloan and B. P. Marx, "Maximizing Outcomes Associated with Expressive Writing," *Clinical Psychology: Science and Practice* 25, no. 1 (2018): e12231.

114 *She continued, "There has to be growth":* B. Murray, "Writing to Heal," American Psychological Association 33, no. 6 (June 2002), https://www.apa.org. https://www.apa.org/monitor/jun02/writing.

116 *a happy life includes a mixture:* J. J. Bauer, *The Transformative Self: Personal Growth, Narrative Identity, and the Good Life* (New York: Oxford University Press, 2021).

117 *As Oishi and Westgate wrote:* S. Oishi and E. C. Westgate, "A Psychologically Rich Life: Beyond Happiness and Meaning," *Psychological Review* 129, no. 4 (2022): 790.

CHAPTER 5 | LEARN HOW TO LOSE

122 *"Bo Davis is a winner":* Pate, Josh (@JoshPateCFB). 2021. "Bo Davis is a winner. Winners can sniff out losers really quick." X, November 9, 2021, 6:25 p.m.

122 *College GameDay correspondent Kirk Herbstreit:* Herbstreit, Kirk (@KirkHerbstreit). 2021. "How is this filmed and shared?" X, November 10, 2021, 6:03 a.m.

124 *In rhesus monkeys, the change:* E. P. Monaghan and S. E. Glickman, "Hormones and Aggressive Behavior," *Behavioural Endocrinology*, J. B. Becker, S. M. Breedlove, and D. Crews, eds. (Cambridge, MA: MIT Press, 2001): 261–87.

124 *According to one of the authors:* H. Devlin, "Scientists Discover Brain's Neural Switch for Becoming an Alpha Male," *The Guardian*, February 14, 2018, https://www.theguardian.com/science/2017/jul/13/scientists-discover-brains-neural-switch-for-becoming-an-alpha-male.

124 *According to the researchers:* T. Zhou et al., "History of Winning Remodels Thalamo-PFC Circuit to Reinforce Social Dominance," *Science* 357, no. 6347 (2017): 162–68.

125 *"the winner and loser effect":* S. N. Geniole, B. M. Bird, E. L. Ruddick, and J. M. Carré, "Effects of Competition Outcome on Testosterone Concentrations in Humans: An Updated Meta-Analysis," *Hormones and Behavior* 92 (2017): 37–50.

125 *For instance, Simon Fraser University:* S. Zilioli and N. V. Watson, "Testosterone Across Successive Competitions: Evidence for a 'Winner Effect' in Humans?'" *Psychoneuroendocrinology* 47 (2014): 1–9.

125 *Similar to animals:* A. L. Vermeer et al., "Exogenous Testosterone Increases Status-Seeking Motivation in Men with Unstable Low Social Status," *Psychoneuroendocrinology* 113 (2020): 104552.

125 *And in terms of functional outcomes:* K. V. Casto, D. A. Edwards, M. Akinola,

C. Davis, and P. H. Mehta, "Testosterone Reactivity to Competition and Competitive Endurance in Men and Women," *Hormones and Behavior* 123 (2020): 104665.

125 *Higher cortisol levels were linked:* B. T. Crewther and C. J. Cook, "Effects of Different Post-Match Recovery Interventions on Subsequent Athlete Hormonal State and Game Performance," *Physiology & Behavior* 106, no. 4 (2012): 471–75.

125 *Similar effects have been found:* S. N. Geniole et al., "Effects of Competition Outcome on Testosterone," 37–50; P. H. Mehta and R. A. Josephs, "Testosterone Change After Losing Predicts the Decision to Compete Again," *Hormones and Behavior* 50, no. 5 (2006): 684–92.

126 *Olympic-level female field hockey team:* K. V. Casto, D. K. Hamilton, and D. A. Edwards, "Testosterone and Cortisol Interact to Predict Within-Team Social Status Hierarchy Among Olympic-Level Women Athletes," *Adaptive Human Behavior and Physiology* 5 (2019): 237–50.

128 *As Wharton School professors:* A. M. Grant and M. S. Shandell, "Social Motivation at Work: The Organizational Psychology of Effort for, Against, and with Others," *Annual Review of Psychology* 73 (2022): 301–26.

128 *As Storr writes:* W. Storr, *The Status Game: On Social Position and How We Use It* (London: William Collins, 2021), 67.

128 *Or, as professor James Gilligan noted:* Storr, *The Status Game*, 66.

128 *humiliation occurs when we make:* W. J. Torres and R. M. Bergner, "Humiliation: Its Nature and Consequences," *Journal of the American Academy of Psychiatry and the Law Online* 38, no. 2 (2010): 195–204.

129 *"I can't function as a human being":* M. Laughton, "He 'Can't Function as a Human' When He Loses. NFL's Worst Hire Is Even Worse Than We Thought," *Fox Sports*, December 13, 2021.

129 *He didn't lose much:* Associated Press, "Never Used to Losing, Urban Meyer Admits He's 'Awful' at It," *The Denver Post*, December 17, 2013, https://www.denverpost .com/2013/12/17/never-used-to-losing-urban-meyer-admits-hes-awful-at-it/.

130 *As one Jaguars staffer reported:* B. Pickman, "Cracks Between Meyer and Staff Showed After Jags' First Preseason Game," *Sports Illustrated*, December 20, 2021, https://www .si.com/nfl/2021/12/20/urban-meyer-internal-trouble-first-preseason-game.

130 *As actual losses in the regular season:* T. Pelissero, "Tension Boiling over Between Coach Urban Meyer, Jaguars Players, Staff Amid 2–10 Start," NFL.com, December 11, 2021, https://www.nfl.com/news/tension-boiling-over-between-coach-urban-meyer-jaguars -players-staff#:~:text=During%20a%20staff%20meeting%2C%20Meyer,them%20 to%20defend%20their%20r%C3%A9sum%C3%A9s.

130 *Kurt Warner—who famously: The Rich Eisen Show,* "'Hard to Fathom'—Kurt Warner on What Led to Urban Meyer's Jags Firing," YouTube, December 17, 2021, https://www.youtube.com/watch?v=dFWF3coWgoE.

131 *As former chess prodigy and writer:* J. Waitzkin, *The Art of Learning: An Inner Journey to Optimal Performance* (New York: Simon and Schuster, 2008), 38.

132 *In a study out of Bowling Green:* L. V. Riters and J. Panksepp, "Effects of Vasotocin on Aggressive Behavior in Male Japanese Quail," *Annals of the New York Academy of Sciences* 807, no. 1 (1997): 478–80.

132 *In soccer players, winners tended:* I. La Fratta, S. Franceschelli, L. Speranza, A. Patruno, C. Michetti, P. D'Ercole . . . and M. Pesce, "Salivary Oxytocin, Cognitive Anxiety and Self-Confidence in Pre-competition Athletes," *Scientific Reports* 11, no. 1 (2021): 16877.

132 *Researchers out of the University of Sydney:* G. A. Alvares, I. B. Hickie, and A. J. Guastella, "Acute Effects of Intranasal Oxytocin on Subjective and Behavioral Responses to Social Rejection," *Experimental and Clinical Psychopharmacology* 18, no. 4 (2010): 316.

133 *Researchers found that how we handle:* M. Fülöp and G. Orosz, "State of the Art in Competition Research," *Emerging Trends in the Social and Behavioral Sciences*, R. A. Scott and S. M. Kosslyn, eds. (2015).

133 *As Michael Jordan told:* A. Krishnamurthy, "Michael Jordan and Stephen Curry Agree They Hate Losing More Than Winning: 'I Hate Losing. But Losing Is Part of Winning,'" Fadeaway World, 2021.

134 *resilience is an active process:* A. Feder, E. J. Nestler, and D. S. Charney, "Psychobiology and Molecular Genetics of Resilience," *Nature Reviews Neuroscience* 10, no. 6 (2009): 446–57.

135 *Research on professional rugby players:* B. T. Crewther and C. J. Cook, "Effects of Different Post-Match Recovery Interventions on Subsequent Athlete Hormonal State and Game Performance," *Physiology and Behavior* 106, no. 4 (2012): 471–75.

136 *Research shows that those who:* N. A. Puccetti, S. M. Schaefer, C. M. Van Reekum, A. D. Ong, D. M. Almeida, C. D. Ryff . . . and A. S. Heller, "Linking Amygdala Persistence to Real-World Emotional Experience and Psychological Well-Being," *Journal of Neuroscience* 41, no. 16 (2021): 3721–30.

137 *A variety of research shows:* Y. Rassovsky, A. Harwood, O. Zagoory-Sharon, and R. Feldman, "Martial Arts Increase Oxytocin Production," *Scientific Reports* 9, no. 1 (2019): 12980.

137 *In a study on professional athletes:* C. J. Cook and B. T. Crewther, "The Social Environment During a Post-Match Video Presentation Affects the Hormonal Responses and Playing Performance in Professional Male Athletes," *Physiology and Behavior* 130 (2014): 170–75.

138 *on Adam Grant's* ReThinking *podcast:* Adam Grant, *Rethinking Your Beliefs with Tara Westover*, TED Talks, https://www.ted.com/podcasts/rethinking-with-adam-grant/rethinking-your-beliefs-with-tara-westover-transcript.

139 *"If you spend five minutes with":* D. Brown, "How One Man Convinced 200 Ku Klux Klan Members to Give up Their Robes," *NPR*, August 20, 2017.

141 *As cognitive psychologist William Hirst reported:* B. M. Law, "Seared in our Memories," *American Psychological Association* 42, no. 8 (September 2011), https://www.apa.org/monitor/2011/09/memories.

141 *Therapists use memory reconsolidation strategies:* S. Barak and K. Goltseker, "Targeting the Reconsolidation of Licit Drug Memories to Prevent Relapse: Focus on Alcohol and Nicotine," *International Journal of Molecular Sciences* 22, no. 8 (2021): 4090.

145 *In studying how people navigate:* D. McAdams, "American Identity: The Redemptive Self." *The General Psychologist* 43, no.1 (Spring 2008), https://www.sesp.northwestern.edu/docs/publications/2094657112490a0f25ec2b9.pdf.

145 *Those who tell redemption stories:* Bauer, *The Transformative Self.*

145 *Growth themes lead to:* Bauer, *The Transformative Self,* 137.

145 *Years after his initial research:* A. Mufarech, "Understanding Our Personal Narratives with Psychologist Dan McAdams," North by Northwestern, January 27, 2022, https://northbynorthwestern.com/the-stories-we-tell-about-ourselves/.

CHAPTER 6 | CARE DEEPLY BUT BE ABLE TO LET GO

147 *"I didn't want to give up":* A. Mathur and A. Mathur, "Michael Jordan Played the Legendary 'Flu Game' Because He Felt He Had an Obligation to His Bulls Teammates and the City of Chicago," Sportscasting Pure Sports, October 26, 2021, https://www.sportscasting.com/news/michael-jordan-played-legendary-flu-game -obligation-bulls-teammates-city-chicago/.

147 *Jordan stopped the camp:* B. Gollivr, "Jordan Dominates a Trash-Talking Mayo in High School: 'Better Scream for Mama,'" *Sports Illustrated,* 2013.

148 *His son, Marcus, relayed:* "Michael Jordan's Kids Talk About Documentary Series 'The Last Dance,'" *Today,* YouTube, May 1, 2020, https://www.youtube.com/watch ?v=JpRUuaKg7Bc.

148 *As Jordan recalled years later:* ESPN, "Why George Karl Ignored Michael Jordan at Dinner," YouTube, May 11, 2020, https://www.youtube.com/watch?v=FV0PtZoB4ug.

149 *Decades later, Jordan reserved:* T. Lake, "A Letter to Michael Jordan: Shame on You for Refusing to Help Pop," *Sports Illustrated,* November 11, 2019, https://www .si.com/more-sports/2012/08/14/letter-michael-jordan.

149 *The entire Hall of Fame speech:* "'The Last Dance' Winners and Losers: Michael Jordan Gets Rosy Reflection; Bulls Owner Goes Out on Sour Note," May 14, 2020, CBSSports.com.

149 *As the sportswriter Rick Reilly wrote:* R. Reilly, "Be Like Michael Jordan? No Thanks—Rick Reilly," ESPN.com, September 16, 2009, https://www.espn.com /espn/columns/story?columnist=reilly_rick&id=4477759.

150 *It's linked to more physical:* J. A. Patock-Peckham et al., "Winning at All Costs: The Etiology of Hypercompetitiveness Through the Indirect Influences of Parental Bonds on Anger and Verbal/Physical Aggression," *Personality and Individual Differences* 154 (2020): 109711.

150 *In their book* Top Dog: P. Bronson and A. Merryman, *Top Dog: The Science of Winning and Losing* (New York: Random House, 2013), 12.

150 *To protect their self-worth:* D. Šimek and D. K. Grum, "The Role of the Different Aspects of Academic Motivation and Competitiveness in Explaining Self-Handicapping," *Psihološka Obzorja/Horizons of Psychology* 9, no. 1 (2010): 25–41.

151 *As they explain, "Constructing, inflating":* J. Crocker, M. A. Olivier, and N. Nuer, "Self-Image Goals and Compassionate Goals: Costs and Benefits," *Self and Identity* 8, no. 2–3 (2009): 251–69.

151 *Researchers found that high-pressure workers:* T. G. Kundro, C. D. Belinda, S. J. Affinito, and M. S. Christian, "Performance Pressure Amplifies the Effect

of Evening Detachment on Next-Morning Shame: Downstream Consequences for Workday Cheating Behavior," *Journal of Applied Psychology* 108, no. 8 (2023): 1356.

152 *When she received pushback:* Moon, Katie (@ktnago13). 2023. "The pole vault is not an endurance event." X, August 25, 2023, 4:05 a.m.

153 *The researchers concluded that:* C. J. Bryan, A. Master, and G. M. Walton, "'Helping' Versus 'Being a Helper': Invoking the Self to Increase Helping in Young Children," *Child Development* 85, no. 5 (2014): 1836–42.

153 *Other research found that kids:* D. Oyserman and M. Destin, "Identity-Based Motivation: Implications for Intervention," *The Counseling Psychologist* 38, no. 7 (2010): 1001–43.

154 *Similar results have been found:* A. Guevremont, "Can Human Brands Help Consumers Eat Better? Influence of Emotional Brand Attachment, Self-Identification, and Brand Authenticity on Consumer Eating Habits," *Journal of Consumer Behaviour* 20, no. 3 (2021): 803–16; C. J. Bryan, G. M. Walton, T. Rogers, and C. S. Dweck, "Motivating Voter Turnout by Invoking the Self," *Proceedings of the National Academy of Sciences* 108, no. 31 (2011): 12653–56.

159 *Maybe they weren't Buddhist monks:* G. Mumford, *The Mindful Athlete* (Berkeley: Parallax Press, 2016).

160 *To illustrate what this means:* "Insight Timer—#1 Free Meditation App for Sleep, Relax and More," Insight Network, Inc., 2021, https://insighttimer.com/blissfulpancake /guided-meditations/the-buddha-and-the-sitar-player-a-lesson-in-balance.

163 *"It was pure panic":* N. Squires, "Jonny Wilkinson Exclusive: England Rugby Hero Opens Up on Mental Health Problems," Express.co.uk, March 24, 2018, https:// www.express.co.uk/sport/rugby-union/935231/Jonny-Wilkinson-Toulon-Dave -Alfred-rugby-union-anxiety-coach-captain.

164 *"There's guys who made":* A. Bull, "Jonny Wilkinson: 'It Took a Few Years for the Pressure to Really Build. And Then It Exploded,'" *The Guardian*, October 19, 2022, https://www.theguardian.com/sport/2019/sep/08/jonny-wilkinson-mental-illness -rugby-union.

164 *Or, as Wilkinson put it:* Bull, "Jonny Wilkinson: 'It Took a Few Years,'" *The Guardian*.

164 *Research by psychologist Robert Vallerand:* D. Lalande, R. J. Vallerand, M. A. K. Lafrenière, J. Verner-Filion, F. A. Laurent, J. Forest, and Y. Paquet, "Obsessive Passion: A Compensatory Response to Unsatisfied Needs," *Journal of Personality* 85, no. 2 (2017): 163–78.

167 *Research shows that doing interesting:* A. Aron and E. N. Aron, "Self-Expansion Motivation and Including Other in the Self," in S. Duck (ed.), *Handbook of Personal Relationships: Theory, Research and Interventions*, 2nd ed (New York: John Wiley & Sons, 1996), 251-70.

CHAPTER 7 | CRAFT YOUR ENVIRONMENT TO WORK WITH YOU, NOT AGAINST YOU

175 *It was so horrifying:* M. McPadden, "What You Need to Know About the Bizarre McMartin Preschool Satanic Sex Abuse Trials," Investigation Discovery (2019).

176 *The vast majority of those convicted:* "Texas Couple Wrongly Convicted in "Satanic Panic" Receive $3.4 Million," Prison Legal News (n.d.), https://www.prisonlegalnews .org/news/2018/aug/6/texas-couple-wrongly-convicted-satanic-panic-receive-34 -million/.

176 *There were police training videos:* A. Romano, "Satanic Panic's Long History—and Why It Never Really Ended—Explained," *Vox*, March 31, 2021, https://www.vox .com/culture/22358153/satanic-panic-ritual-abuse-history-conspiracy-theories -explained.

176 *According to historian Sarah Hughes:* S. Hughes, "American Monsters: Tabloid Media and the Satanic Panic, 1970–2000," *Journal of American Studies* 51, no. 3 (2017): 691–719.

177 *A 2008 study found:* T. N. Ridout, A. C. Grosse, and A. M. Appleton, "News Media Use and Americans' Perceptions of Global Threat," *British Journal of Political Science* 38, no. 4 (2008): 575–93.

177 *News consumption is related to:* M. Smolej and J. Kivivuori, "The Relation Between Crime News and Fear of Violence," *Journal of Scandinavian Studies in Criminology and Crime Prevention* 7, no. 2 (2006): 211–27.

177 *A recent analysis found that:* M. Näsi et al., "Crime News Consumption and Fear of Violence: The Role of Traditional Media, Social Media, and Alternative Information Sources," *Crime and Delinquency* 67, no. 4 (2021): 574–600.

177 *A study following the Boston Marathon bombing:* E. A. Holman, D. R. Garfin, and R. C. Silver, "Media's Role in Broadcasting Acute Stress Following the Boston Marathon Bombings," *Proceedings of the National Academy of Sciences* 111, no. 1 (2014): 93–98.

178 *In a series of studies out of Princeton:* D. Graeupner and A. Coman, "The Dark Side of Meaning-Making: How Social Exclusion Leads to Superstitious Thinking," *Journal of Experimental Social Psychology* 69 (2017): 218–22.

178 *Other research points to:* J. W. Van Prooijen, "Psychological Benefits of Believing Conspiracy Theories," *Current Opinion in Psychology* 47 (2022): 101352.

179 *researchers put women through:* J. A. Coan et al., "Relationship Status and Perceived Support in the Social Regulation of Neural Responses to Threat," *Social Cognitive and Affective Neuroscience* 12, no. 10 (2017): 1574–83.

179 *Psychologists at UCLA found:* N. I. Eisenberger et al., "Attachment Figures Activate a Safety Signal-Related Neural Region and Reduce Pain Experience," *Proceedings of the National Academy of Sciences* 108, no. 28 (2011): 11721–26.

180 *Social baseline theory posits:* L. Beckes and D. A. Sbarra, "Social Baseline Theory: State of the Science and New Directions," *Current Opinion in Psychology* 43 (2022): 36–41.

180 *For instance, when standing:* S. Schnall, K. D. Harber, J. K. Stefanucci, and D. R. Proffitt, "Social Support and the Perception of Geographical Slant," *Journal of Experimental Social Psychology* 44, no. 5 (2008): 1246–55.

180 *The same effect was found:* A. Doerrfeld, N. Sebanz, and M. Shiffrar, "Expecting to Lift a Box Together Makes the Load Look Lighter," *Psychological Research* 76: 467–75.

180 *Other research has found that:* X. Zheng et al., "The Unburdening Effects of Forgiveness: Effects on Slant Perception and Jumping Height," *Social Psychological and Personality Science* 6, no. 4 (2015): 431–38.

180 *Shigehiro Oishi, Jamie Schiller, and:* S. Oishi, J. Schiller, and E. B. Gross, "Felt Understanding and Misunderstanding Affect the Perception of Pain, Slant, and distance," *Social Psychological and Personality Science* 4, no. 3 (2013): 259–66.

182 *When Jaak Panksepp and colleagues:* J. Panksepp et al., "Opiates and Play Dominance in Juvenile Rats," *Behavioral Neuroscience* 99, no. 3 (1985): 441.

183 *A small boost in opiate:* J. Panksepp, "An Archaeology of Mind: The Ancestral Sources of Human Feelings," *Soundings: An Interdisciplinary Journal* 86, nos. ½ (2003): 41–69.

185 *That distinction was important:* C. Bastow, "Alone Australia Winner Takes Home $250,000 After 67 Days: 'I Was Like, No! I'm Just Getting Started!'" *The Guardian*, May 25, 2023, https://www.theguardian.com/tv-and-radio/2023/may/25/alone-australia-winner-takes-home-250000-after-67-days-i-was-like-no-im-just-getting-started.

186 *Some research on soccer players:* N. Neave and S. Wolfson, "Testosterone, Territoriality, and the 'Home Advantage,'" *Physiology and Behavior* 78, no. 2 (2003): 269–75.

186 *While another study found that:* P. Furley et al., "Thin Slices of Athletes' Nonverbal Behavior Give Away Game Location: Testing the Territoriality Hypothesis of the Home Game Advantage," *Evolutionary Psychology* 16, no. 2 (2018): 1474704918776456.

187 *In a series of studies:* P. Barrett et al., "A Holistic, Multi-Level Analysis Identifying the Impact of Classroom Design on Pupils' Learning," *Building and Environment* 59 (2013): 678–89; P. Barrett, F. Davies, Y. Zhang, and L. Barrett, "The Impact of Classroom Design on Pupils' Learning: Final Results of a Holistic, Multi-Level Analysis," *Building and Environment* 89 (2015): 118–33.

187 *They spent all of twenty minutes:* G. Brown and M. Baer, "Location in Negotiation: Is There a Home Field Advantage?" *Organizational Behavior and Human Decision Processes* 114, no. 2 (2011): 190–200.

187 *In research by Craig Knight:* C. Knight and S. A. Haslam, "The Relative Merits of Lean, Enriched, and Empowered Offices: An Experimental Examination of the Impact of Workspace Management Strategies on Well-Being and Productivity," *Journal of Experimental Psychology: Applied* 16, no. 2 (2010): 158.

187 *Feeling ownership of your workspace:* G. Brown and H. Zhu, "'My Workspace, Not Yours': The Impact of Psychological Ownership and Territoriality in Organizations," *Journal of Environmental Psychology* 48 (2016): 54–64.

187 *Psychologists have tied the benefits:* J. L. Pierce, T. Kostova, and K. T. Dirks, "The State of Psychological Ownership: Integrating and Extending a Century of Research," *Review of General Psychology* 7, no. 1 (2003): 84–107.

188 *Research suggests there is:* J. L. Nasar and A. S. Devlin, "Impressions of Psychotherapists' Offices," *Journal of Counseling Psychology* 58, no. 3 (2011): 310–20, https://doi.org/10.1037/a00238.

188 *If you feel a sense:* J. Peck, C. P. Kirk, A. W. Luangrath, and S. B. Shu, "Caring for the Commons: Using Psychological Ownership to Enhance Stewardship Behavior for Public Goods," *Journal of Marketing* 85, no. 2 (2021): 33–49.

188 *Experiencing awe out in nature:* L. Wang, G. Zhang, P. Shi, X. Lu, and F. Song, "Influence of Awe on Green Consumption: The Mediating Effect of Psychological Ownership," *Frontiers in Psychology* 10 (2019): 2484.

189 *Our space or objects have:* C. P. Kirk, J. Peck, and S. D. Swain, "Property Lines in the Mind: Consumers' Psychological Ownership and Their Territorial Responses," *Journal of Consumer Research* 45, no. 1 (2018): 148–68.

189 *As neuroscientist Douglas Fields explains:* R. D. Fields, *Why We Snap: Understanding the Rage Circuit in Your Brain* (New York: Dutton Books, 2015).

189 *When we adopt such a mindset:* Brown and Zhu, "'My Workspace, Not Yours,'" *Journal of Environmental Psychology,* 54–64; G. Brown and M. Baer, "Protecting the Turf: The Effect of Territorial Marking on Others' Creativity," *Journal of Applied Psychology* 100, no. 6 (2015): 1785.

191 *In other words, King Arthur:* Magness, Steve (@stevemagness). 2023. "5. Make meetings & work better." X, January 27, 2023, 6:41 a.m.

191 *A recent study found that simply:* K. Sailer, P. Koutsolampros, and R. Pachilova, "Differential Perceptions of Teamwork, Focused Work and Perceived Productivity as an Effect of Desk Characteristics Within a Workplace Layout," *PloS One* 16, no. 4 (2021): e0250058.

193 *They drive more aggressively:* D. Hemenway, M. Vriniotis, and M. Miller, "Is an Armed Society a Polite Society? Guns and Road Rage," *Accident Analysis and Prevention* 38, no. 4 (2006): 687–95; B. J. Bushman, T. Kerwin, T. Whitlock, and J. M. Weisenberger, "The Weapons Effect on Wheels: Motorists Drive More Aggressively When a Gun Is in the Vehicle," *Journal of Experimental Social Psychology* 73 (2017): 82–85.

193 *A 2018 meta-analysis looking at:* A. J. Benjamin Jr., S. Kepes, B. J. Bushman, "Effects of Weapons on Aggressive Thoughts, Angry Feelings, Hostile Appraisals, and Aggressive Behavior: A Meta-Analytic Review of the Weapons Effect Literature," *Personality and Social Psychology Review* 22, no. 4 (2018), 347–77.

193 *As Jessica Whitt, the author:* "Expert: Holding a Gun Changes the Way People Perceive Others, Objects" (n.d.), Purdue University, https://www.purdue.edu/newsroom/research/2012/120326WittPerception.html.

193 *A study by psychologists Jaeyeon Chung:* J. Chung and G. V. Johar, "The Seesaw Self: Possessions, Identity (De)activation, and Task Performance," *Journal of Marketing Research* 55, no. 5 (2018), 752–65.

195 *If they were primed with:* Y. Chen, S. X. Li, T. X. Liu, and M. Shih, "Which Hat to Wear? Impact of Natural Identities on Coordination and Cooperation," *Games and Economic Behavior* 84 (2014): 58–86.

195 *In other research, reminding college students:* D. J. Yopyk and D. A. Prentice, "Am I an Athlete or a Student? Identity Salience and Stereotype Threat in Student–Athletes," *Basic and Applied Social Psychology* 27, no. 4 (2005): 329–36.

195 *Reminding a group of Asian:* M. Shih, T. L. Pittinsky, and A. Trahan, "Domain-Specific Effects of Stereotypes on Performance," *Self and Identity* 5, no. 1 (2006): 1–14.

196 *For instance, in an analysis:* S. Ahébée, "'They See Me as a Role Model': Black Teachers Improve Education Outcomes for Black Students," *WHYY,* February 19,

2021; S. Gershenson, C. M. Hart, J. Hyman, C. A. Lindsay, and N. W. Papageorge, "The Long-Run Impacts of Same-Race Teachers," *American Economic Journal: Economic Policy* 14, no. 4 (2022): 300–42.

196 *In a review of over:* J. R. Gladstone and A. Cimpian, "Which Role Models Are Effective for Which Students? A Systematic Review and Four Recommendations for Maximizing the Effectiveness of Role Models in STEM," *International Journal of STEM Education* 8 (2021): 1–20.

197 *As organizational psychologist Adam Grant:* Grant, Adam (@AdamMGrant). 2023. "The best way to find yourself isn't looking inward to see who you are." X, May 7, 2023, 10:45 a.m.

197 *In 2016, Masako Tamaki:* M. Tamaki, J. W. Bang, T. Watanabe, and Y. Sasaki, "Night Watch in One Brain Hemisphere During Sleep Associated with the First-Night Effect in Humans," *Current Biology* 26, no. 9 (2016): 1190–94.

CHAPTER 8 | FIND CONNECTION AND BELONGING WITHOUT FUSING

202 *In 1970, a poll commissioned:* "How Southern Baptists Became Pro-Life" (n.d.), Baptist Press, https://www.baptistpress.com/resource-library/news/how-southern-baptists-became-pro-life/.

203 *In 1974, the Southern Baptist:* "Resolution on Abortion and Sanctity of Human Life" (n.d.), SBC.net, https://www.sbc.net/resource-library/resolutions/resolution-on-abortion-and-sanctity-of-human-life/.

203 *According to one poll:* D. Masci, "American Religious Groups Vary Widely in Their Views of Abortion," *Pew Research Center*, 2018.

203 *The Pew Research Center categorized:* D. Masci, "Where Major Religious Groups Stand on Abortion," *Pew Research Center*, 2016.

204 *The researchers summarized their findings:* P. K. Hatemi, C. Crabtree, and K. B. Smith, "Ideology Justifies Morality: Political Beliefs Predict Moral Foundations," *American Journal of Political Science* 63, no. 4 (2019): 788–806.

204 *So much so that psychologist:* "How Political Parties Influence our Beliefs, and What We Can Do About It," ScienceDaily, February 18, 2018, https://www.sciencedaily.com/releases/2018/02/180220123127.htm.

205 *There were allegations from:* N. Fenno, "Olympic Swimmer Klete Keller's Journey to Capitol Riot," *Los Angeles Times*, January 21, 2022.

207 *So did boxing legend:* CommonLit (n.d.), "Life After Sport by Emma Vickers," https://www.commonlit.org/en/texts/life-after-sport.

207 *And research shows those with:* J. R. Grove, D. Lavallee, and S. Gordon, "Coping with Retirement from Sport: The Influence of Athletic Identity," *Journal of Applied Sport Psychology* 9, no. 2 (1997): 191–203.

208 *As Olympian Gary Hall Jr. reflected:* N. Fenno, "Olympic Swimmer Klete Keller's Journey."

208 *Bestselling author and researcher Brené Brown:* Brené Brown, "Life Lessons We All Need to Learn," Oprah.com, June 14, 2012, https://www.oprah.com/inspiration/life-lessons-we-all-need-to-learn-brene-brown.

209 *Researchers found that our social identities:* S. Roccas and M. B. Brewer, "Social Identity Complexity," *Personality and Social Psychology Review* 6, no. 2 (2002): 88–106.

209 *The surge only occurs:* K. V. Casto, Z. L. Root, S. N. Geniole, J. M. Carré, and M. W. Bruner, "Exploratory Analysis of the Relationship Between Social Identification and Testosterone Reactivity to Vicarious Combat," *Human Nature* 32 (2021): 509–27.

210 *Or it can be dangerous:* J. Tanghe, B. Wisse, and H. Van Der Flier, "The Formation of Group Affect and Team Effectiveness: The Moderating Role of Identification," *British Journal of Management* 21, no. 2 (2010): 340–58.

210 *In a review on the subject:* J. Hardie-Bick, "Escaping the Self: Identity, Group Identification and Violence," *Oñati Socio-Legal Series* 6, no. 4 (2016).

210 *As psychologist Scott Barry Kaufman:* Kaufman, Dr. Scott Barry (@sbkaufman). 2023. "i'm fascinated with the phenomenon of some fans . . ." X, February 22, 2023, 6:50 p.m.

211 *The bad side of groups:* R. F. Baumeister, *The Self Explained: Why and How We Become Who We Are* (New York: Guilford Press, 2022), 94.

212 *As social psychologist Jonathan Haidt:* Haidt, Jonathan (@JonHaidt). 2021. "Does it seem to you that American politics is getting dumber?" X, December 3, 2021, 4:37 a.m.

212 *Or as humanistic philosopher:* E. Fromm, *Psychoanalysis and Religion* (UK: Yale University Press, 1967).

213 *Social cohesion erodes when:* R. I. M. Dunbar, "Managing the Stresses of Group-Living in the Transition to Village Life," *Evolutionary Human Sciences* 4 (2022): e40.

213 *For example, religions became:* R. I. Dunbar and R. Sosis, "Optimising Human Community Sizes," *Evolution and Human Behavior* 39, no. 1 (2018): 106–11.

214 *As Moffett concluded in studying:* M. W. Moffett, "Human Identity and the Evolution of Societies," *Human Nature* 24 (2013): 219–67.

216 *They learn not only:* É. Leblanc, F. Dégeilh, V. Daneault, M. H. Beauchamp, and A. Bernier, "Attachment Security in Infancy: A Preliminary Study of Prospective Links to Brain Morphometry in Late Childhood," *Frontiers in Psychology* 8 (2017): 296993.

217 *We approach instead of avoid:* A. J. Elliot and H. T. Reis, "Attachment and Exploration in Adulthood," *Journal of Personality and Social Psychology* 85, no. 2 (2003): 317.

217 *A large meta-analysis found:* V. M. Bridgland, P. J. Jones, and B. W. Bellet, "A Meta-Analysis of the Efficacy of Trigger Warnings, Content Warnings, and Content Notes," *Clinical Psychological Science* (2022): 21677026231186625.

217 *If a mom, dad, or teacher:* K. VanLehn, S. Siler, C. Murray, T. Yamauchi, and W. B. Baggett, "Why Do Only Some Events Cause Learning During Human Tutoring?" *Cognition and Instruction* 21, no. 3 (2003): 209–49.

218 *In one study, participants completed:* A. Sheridan et al., "Presence of Spotters Improves Bench Press Performance: A Deception Study," *The Journal of Strength and Conditioning Research* 33, no. 7 (2019): 1755–61.

220 *So much so that when:* J. A. Simpson and L. Campbell, eds., *The Oxford Handbook of Close Relationships* (New York: Oxford University Press, 2013), 106.

220 *People who score higher:* M. R. Leary, J. M. Tipsord, and E. B. Tate, "Allo-Inclusive Identity: Incorporating the Social and Natural Worlds into One's Sense of Self," in H. A. Wayment and J. J. Bauer, eds., *Transcending Self-Interest: Psychological Explorations of the Quiet Ego* (Washington, DC: American Psychological Association, 2008).

221 *while relationships high in self-expansion:* A. Aron, G. W. Lewandowski Jr., D. Mashek, and E. N. Aron, "The Self-Expansion Model of Motivation and Cognition in Close Relationships," *The Oxford Handbook of Close Relationships*, 90–115.

221 *In a 2013 study:* M. J. Carter, "Advancing Identity Theory: Examining the Relationship Between Activated Identities and Behavior in Different Social Contexts," *Social Psychology Quarterly* 76, no. 3 (2013): 203–23.

222 *Research led by Ashley Hardin:* A. E. Hardin et al., "Show Me the . . . Family: How Photos of Meaningful Relationships Reduce Unethical Behavior at Work," *Organizational Behavior and Human Decision Processes* 161 (2020): 93–108.

222 *In a 2018 review:* L. van Doeselaar, A. Becht, T. A. Klimstra, and W. H. J. Meeus, "A Review and Integration of Three Key Components of Identity Development: Distinctiveness, Coherence, and Continuity," *European Psychologist* 23, no. 4 (2018): 278–88.

224 *In summarizing the research:* Baumeister, *The Self Explained.*

CHAPTER 9 | REALIGNING WITH REALITY

229 *It was May 13:* B. Roueché, "The Mystery of Mass Hysteria," *The New Yorker,* August 14, 1978, https://www.newyorker.com/magazine/1978/08/21/sandy.

230 *One medical report found:* M. Hull, M. Parnes, and J. Jankovic, "Increased Incidence of Functional (Psychogenic) Movement Disorders in Children and Adults Amid the COVID-19 Pandemic: A Cross-Sectional Study," *Neurology: Clinical Practice* 11, no. 5 (2021): e686–e690.

231 *In Germany, researchers traced:* K. R. Müller-Vahl, A. Pisarenko, E. Jakubovski, and C. Fremer, "Stop That! It's Not Tourette's but a New Type of Mass Sociogenic Illness," *Brain: A Journal of Neurology* 145 no. 2 (2022): 476–80.

231 *In Canada, researchers linked:* G. Browne, "They Watched a YouTuber with Tourette's—Then Adopted His Tics," *WIRED,* September 2, 2021, https://www.wired.com/story/they-watched-youtuber-with-tourettes-then-adopted-his-tics/.

231 *The environment primes individuals:* Müller-Vahl et al., "Stop That! It's Not Tourette's . . ."

232 *As Andy Clark wrote:* A. Clark, *The Experience Machine: How Our Minds Predict and Shape Reality* (UK: Knopf Doubleday Publishing Group, 2023).

239 *Psychologists have found some:* A. M. Smith, S. A. Malo et al., "A Multidisciplinary Study of the 'Yips' Phenomenon in Golf: An Exploratory Analysis," *Sports Medicine* 30 (2000): 423–37.

240 *"I want to look at it fresh":* D. Epstein, "A Technique Championed by Russian Writers (and Fraggles) Can Give You a New Perspective," *Range Widely,* November 16, 2021, https://davidepstein.substack.com/p/a-technique-championed-by-russian-21 -11-16.

240 *As he explained to Ezra Klein:* E. Klein, "Wilco's Jeff Tweedy Wants You to Be Bad at Something. For Your Own Good," *New York Times*, July 2, 2021, https:// www .nytimes.com/2021/07/02/opinion/ezra-klein-podcast-jeff-tweedy.html.

241 *In a radio interview, Eno outlined:* B. Eno. Radio interview with Charles Amirkhanian, KPFA-FM Berkeley, February 1, 1980. A transcribed at: http://www .rtqe.net/ObliqueStrategies/OSintro.html.

241 *As he told National Geographic:* F. Williams and L. Foglia, "This Is Your Brain on Nature," *Magazine*, n.d., https://www.nationalgeographic.com/magazine/article/call-to-wild.

241 *Recent research found that nature:* C. A. Capaldi, H. A. Passmore, E. K. Nisbet, J. M. Zelenski, and R. L. Dopko, "Flourishing in Nature: A Review of the Benefits of Connecting with Nature and Its Application as a Wellbeing Intervention," *International Journal of Wellbeing* 5, no. 4 (2015).

241 *Or as Gina—the* Alone Australia: S. Cain, "'It Was Horrible. It Was Glorious': Alone—the Most Gruelling Show on TV—Comes to Australia," *The Guardian*, March 29, 2023, https://www.theguardian.com/tv-and-radio/2023/mar/29/alone -australia-tasmania-reality-tv.

242 *The shocks were "needed to":* J. Grotowski and T. K. Wiewiorowski, "Towards the Poor Theatre," *Tulane Drama Review* 11, no. 3 (1967): 60–65.

243 *Philosopher Joseph Campbell pointed this out:* J. Campbell and B. Moyers, *The Power of Myth* (New York: Anchor, 2011).

246 *I've tried this myself:* A. Alter, *Anatomy of a Breakthrough: How to Get Unstuck When It Matters Most* (New York: Simon and Schuster, 2024), 91.

CHAPTER 10 | MOVING FROM SURVIVING TO THRIVING

251 *Warnings of looters swarming:* M. Chandler, "Hurricane Harvey Sparks Houston Curfew as Looters Swarm Deserted Streets," Express.co.uk, August 30, 2017, https:// www.express.co.uk/news/world/847619/Hurricane-Harvey-Houston-looting-curfew -flooding.

251 *Following the 2005 Katrina hurricane:* M. Guarino, "Misleading Reports of Lawlessness After Katrina Worsened Crisis, Officials Say," *The Guardian*, August 16, 2015, https://www.theguardian.com/us-news/2015/aug/16/hurricane-katrina-new -orleans-looting-violence-misleading-reports.

252 *The founder of American psychology:* William James, *Writings 1902–1910* (New York: Library of America, 1987), 1215–22.

252 *One military planner reported:* D. Brooks, "The Virus and the Blitz," *The Atlantic*, March 29, 2020, https://www.theatlantic.com/ideas/archive/2020/03/virus-and -blitz/608965/.

253 *Hospitalizations for mental health problems:* D. Jones, R. Woolven, B. Durodié, and S. Wessely, "Civilian Morale During the Second World War: Responses to Air Raids Re-examined," *Social History of Medicine* 17, no. 3 (2004): 463–79.

253 *In a study of over thirty-three thousand:* "World War II Bombing Associated with Resilience, Not 'German Angst,'" University of Cambridge, June 23, 2017, https://

www.cam.ac.uk/research/news/world-war-ii-bombing-associated-with-resilience-not-german-angst.

253 *As Edgar Jones and colleagues:* Jones et al., "Civilian Morale During the Second World War," *Social History of Medicine*, 463–79.

253 *"Disasters provide a temporary":* C. E. Fritz, "Disasters and Mental Health: Therapeutic Principles Drawn from Disaster Studies," University of Delaware Disaster Research Center, Series 10 (1996).

253 *We expect* Lord of the Flies*:* R. Bregman, "The Real Lord of the Flies: What Happened When Six Boys Were Shipwrecked for 15 Months," *The Guardian*, May 9, 2020, https://www.theguardian.com/books/2020/may/09/the-real-lord-of-the-flies-what-happened-when-six-boys-were-shipwrecked-for-15-months.

254 *Jesus encouraged us to:* Luke 14:33, New American Standard Bible.

254 *Or as catholic theologian Meister Eckhart:* M. Walshe, *The Complete Mystical Works of Meister Eckhart* (New York: The Crossroad Publishing Company, 2009), 295.

254 *The Hindu text, the Bhagavad Gita:* Bhagavad Gita, chapter 5.

254 *written in the Taoist text:* L. Tzu, *Tao Te Ching*, chapter 44, https://www.wussu.com/laotzu/laotzu44.html.

254 *In Buddhism, nonattachment plays:* His Holiness the Dalai Lama, *Path to Tranquility*, (Penguin Books India, 1998), 39.

255 *It's the "absence of internal":* J. Soler, J. Montero-Marin, E. Domínguez-Clavé, S. González, J. C. Pascual, A. Cebolla . . . and J. García-Campayo, "Decentering, Acceptance, and Non-Attachment: Challenging the Question 'Is It Me?'" *Frontiers in Psychiatry* 12 (2021): 659835.

257 *"What success means to me":* S. Bregman, "Exclusive—Simone Biles on Letting Go, Twisting Again, and Having No Regrets: 'What Success Means to Me Is Different than Before,'" Olympics.com, September 27, 2023.

258 *During her comeback, she advised:* C. Correa, "Simone Biles Shows She's Not Just Easing Her Way Back," *The New York Times*, August 27, 2023, https://www.nytimes.com/2023/08/27/sports/simone-biles-gymnastics-championships.html.

259 *On the flipside, the opposite:* C. Sarioz, "The 'Clutch Gene' Myth: An Analysis of Late-Game Shooting Performance in the NBA" (undergraduate honors thesis, University of California, Berkeley, 2021).

259 *They concluded, "Star salespeople are":* S. Carnahan, L. Pierce, and X. Tang, "Clutch Performers," *Academy of Management Proceedings* 2023, no. 1: 14489.

263 *"But when it's time to":* C. Skipper and P. Dukovic, "How Patrick Mahomes Became the Superstar the NFL Needs Right Now," *GQ*, July 14, 2020, https://www.gq.com/story/patrick-mahomes-cover-profile-august-2020.

264 *Brené Brown wrote:* B. Brown, *The Gifts of Imperfection: Let Go of Who You Think You're Supposed to Be and Embrace Who You Are* (New York: Simon and Schuster, 2022).

264 *But researchers found that:* H. Coleman, A. McIntosh, G. Rayner, and S. J. Wilson, "Understanding Long-Term Changes in Patient Identity 15–20 Years After Surgery for Temporal Lobe Epilepsy," *Epilepsia* 62, no. 10 (2021): 2451–62.

264 *But as a group of psychiatrists wrote:* S. Wilson, P. Bladin, and M. Saling, "The 'Burden of Normality': Concepts of Adjustment After Surgery for Seizures," *Journal of Neurology Neurosurgery and Psychiatry* 70, no. 5 (2001): 649–56.

268 *Or as Olympic silver medalist:* C. Bishop, "Compassion Can Produce Better Performance—Just Look at the Lionesses," *The Guardian*, August 14, 2023, https://www.theguardian.com/sport/2023/aug/14/compassion-better-performance -lionesses-england-sarina-wiegman.

268 *As clinical psychologist Kathryn Smith:* K. E. Smith, T. B. Mason, and J. M. Lavender, "Rumination and Eating Disorder Psychopathology: A Meta-Analysis," *Clinical Psychology Review*, 61 (2018): 9–23.

268 *In a meta-analysis, researchers:* T. B. Mason, K. E. Smith, A. Engwall, A. Lass, M. Mead, M. Sorby . . . and S. Wonderlich, "Self-Discrepancy Theory as a Transdiagnostic Framework: A Meta-Analysis of Self-Discrepancy and Psychopathology," *Psychological Bulletin* 145, no. 4 (2019): 372.

269 *As organizational psychologist Adam Grant:* Grant, Adam. (@AdamMGrant). 2023. "The core question of identity is not who others think you should be. It's who you aspire to be." X, September 30, 2023, 8:19 a.m.

269 *Or as Sheldon wrote:* K. M. Sheldon, A. J. Elliot, R. M. Ryan, V. Chirkov, Y. Kim, C. Wu . . . and Z. Sun, "Self-Concordance and Subjective Well-Being in Four Cultures," *Journal of Cross-Cultural Psychology* 35, no. 2 (2004): 209–23.

269 *When researchers studied the impact:* M. J. Carter and J. Marony, "Examining Self-Perceptions of Identity Change in Person, Role, and Social Identities," *Current Psychology* 40, no. 1 (2021): 253–70.

270 *As famed football coach Pete Carroll:* Seattle Seahawks (@Seahawks). "'You gotta figure out who you are.'" X, January 10, 2024, 1:33 p.m.

INDEX

ABOUT THE AUTHOR

Steve Magness is a world-renowned expert on performance. He is the author of the international bestseller *Do Hard Things* and *The Science of Running*, and coauthor of *Peak Performance* and *The Passion Paradox*. As a performance coach, he's worked with individuals and teams in every major professional sport, as well as artists, entrepreneurs, and executives. His writing has appeared in the *Atlantic*, *Sports Illustrated*, and *Forbes*. He is the cofounder of the Growth Equation. He lives in Houston with his wife and child.